The Origins of the Modern World

*A Global and Environmental Narrative from the
Fifteenth to the Twenty-First Century*

FOURTH EDITION

Robert B. Marks
Whittier College

ROWMAN & LITTLEFIELD
Lanham • Boulder • New York • London

Executive Editor: Susan McEachern
Assistant Editor: Katelyn Turner
Senior Marketing Manager: Amy Whitaker

Credits and acknowledgments for material borrowed from other sources, and reproduced
with permission, appear on the appropriate page within the text.

Published by Rowman & Littlefield
An imprint of The Rowman & Littlefield Publishing Group, Inc.
4501 Forbes Boulevard, Suite 200, Lanham, Maryland 20706
www.rowman.com

6 Tinworth Street, London SE11 5AL, United Kingdom

British Library Cataloguing in Publication Information Available

Library of Congress Cataloging-in-Publication Data Available

ISBN 9781538127025 (cloth : alk. paper) | ISBN 9781538127032 (pbk : alk. paper) |
ISBN 9781538127049 (ebook)

♾ ™ The paper used in this publication meets the minimum requirements of American
National Standard for Information Sciences—Permanence of Paper for Printed Library
Materials, ANSI/NISO Z39.48–1992.

Brief Contents

Contents

Figures and Maps

Figures

Maps

Preface and Acknowledgments

Why a Fourth Edition?

The past may not change, but our history of it does. History—the narratives that historians write—is relevant to us because historians are influenced in their selection of what and how to write about the past by their engagement with issues and problems that confront us today.

As I was working on the first edition of this book in the year 2000, environmental historian J. R. McNeill published *Something New under the Sun: An Environmental History of the Twentieth Century*. In that book, McNeill observed that he thought that a hundred years hence, at the end of the twenty-first century, historians and others looking back at the twentieth century would be struck by the significance, not of the two massive world wars, the rise and fall of fascism and communism, the explosive growth of the human population, or the women's movement, but of the changed relationship of humans to Earth's natural environment. As an environmental historian myself, I found that observation compelling and incorporated an ecological theme in my narrative. The world holds many surprises, but one has to be how much faster McNeill's prediction has arrived. It hasn't taken a century, but just a few years, for the importance of the change in our relationship to the environment to thrust itself to the forefront of our understanding of the recent past, and to give the epoch in Earth history we are now in a new name—the Anthropocene.

When I first wrote this book, I did so because a new body of scholarship on Asia had made it possible to reconsider the usual answer to the question of the origins of the modern world: "The Rise of the West." The new scholarship on Asia—which Jack Goldstone dubbed "The California School" because so many of us lived, worked, or published in California—raised questions about how and why the modern world came to have its essential characteristics: politically organized into nation-states and economically centered around industrial capitalism. Our findings that Asian societies had many of the characteristics others had seen as exclusively European and thus "causes" of the "European miracle" led us to argue that similarities cannot cause differences and to look for alternative explanations for how and why the world came to be the way it is. Andre Gunder Frank and Kenneth Pomeranz pulled this scholarship into two important books that changed the way we now understand how the world works, decentering Eurocentric explanations of history. One of the contributions of the first two editions of this book (2002 and 2007) was to bring to students and teachers a fresh narrative of the origins of the modern world that incorporated this new body of scholarship.

That continued to be the case with the third edition (2015), which in addition placed the environmental storyline into an ever more prominent position in the book's narrative. It was only in the 1980s that climatologists had begun to understand El Niño events, and in the 1990s that rising levels of carbon dioxide coming from industry and tailpipes might cause the global climate to warm. From that initial realization that humans are forcing global climate change, we have now come to understand that humans are changing, overwhelming, or displacing other global processes of Nature as well, on scales never before seen in human history. Readers or instructors familiar with earlier editions will notice sections on environmental issues throughout the book, as well as others highlighting Africa and income inequality. Those additions, combined with the placement of all notes at the end of the book, necessitated new pagination and a new index in the third edition.

Once again, recent developments have prompted me to offer a revised, fourth edition of this book. The fallout from the financial crisis of 2008, known as "The Great Recession," has shaken the faith of many around the world in the workings of the post–World War II global economy. Especially affected were those whose jobs vanished as factories closed or relocated to countries with lower wages and environmental protections, or residents of rural areas where farm incomes dropped and employment opportunities for young people eroded and many migrated to urban areas, fueling a sense of unfairness and anger toward those who allowed those downward pressures to continue to build. In many places around the world, the globalized economy and its easy flows of capital and labor have destabilized people's lives, fueling opposition to the globalized world and the elites assumed to be running it. Often these resentments come together in particular individuals who come to power as strong nationalists (such as Donald J. Trump in the United States, and others in Brazil, Hungary, and Poland), and in movements such as Brexit in the United Kingdom, where a slim majority of citizens voted to leave the European Union.

What I have attempted in this edition is to put these challenges into the long-term perspective adopted for this book. Doing so, we can see that Mr. Trump and nationalist leaders in other countries can best be understood in the context of the history of globalization and the differential effects those forces have had within nations and globally. I have also added three new sections on migration patterns in past eras (in chapters 3, 5, and 6) to put the current politicization of migration into a broader historical context. And I have re-envisioned nationalism, the significance of the Great Depression of the 1930s and the world wars that preceded and grew out of it, as a way of contextualizing what I think are the latent dangers now of the rise of nationalism around the world. These revisions have added several pages and new sections to chapter 6. Rather than break that chapter into two or three smaller chapters, I have chosen to keep the chapter intact but have reorganized the sections into four main parts and provided readers with a detailed table of contents that shows the headings and subheadings in each chapter. This should help readers and instructors alike plan the best way to approach each chapter.

My reason for recounting this story of the changing circumstances of this book is not to provide a rationale for another edition. Rather, it is to point out that history is living and relevant to current concerns, not the "dead hand of the past," as some might see it. Both new scholarship and new issues and problems can prompt us to reexamine the past and to rewrite history to take account of the changes in both. That way the stories we tell about the past continue to be relevant and helpful to us in the present. For if they weren't, what would be the point? We need all the help we can get, and historical perspective is an essential aid to living in and through the present to a better future.

In addition to the intellectual debt I owe to Andre Gunder Frank, Kenneth Pomeranz, and John R. McNeill, I want to thank them for their personal involvement with the first edition of this book. Others who were instrumental in conceptualizing that project include Dennis O. Flynn and Arturo Giraldez, whose work following the silver trail around the world opened new vistas for me and other scholars and who organized the 1998

Pacific Centuries Conference at the University of the Pacific in Stockton, California, where we thrashed out ideas over lunches and dinners, and where the idea for this book originated. Others who read and commented on the first edition include my Whittier College colleagues José Orozco and Dick Archer; Steve Davidson, professor of history at Southwestern University; and the editor of the Rowman & Littlefield series World Social Change, Mark Selden. Erik Ching, Bradley Davis, Kathryn Davis, Peter Lavelle, Ray Patton, and David Pizzo provided helpful comments and offered important suggestions for adding clarity and helping students navigate through my argument in this fourth edition.

For their response to the ideas in the book and the book itself, I want to acknowledge the first- and second-year students who have taken History 101, Introduction to World History, and read and commented on the first, second, and third editions of *Origins*, and to thank my colleagues, Professors Elizabeth Sage and José Ortega, who team-taught the course with me and from whom I learned much about the history of Latin America, Europe, and the Atlantic world. Like their predecessors, the history majors in History 480, Capstone Seminar, read widely and deeply on topics that found their way into this book, exploring environmental history (Spring 2010), the early modern world (Spring 2012), Eric Hobsbawm (Spring 2013), "the seventeenth-century global crisis" (Spring 2014), the Columbian Exchange (Spring 2015), the twentieth century in global, ecological, and historical perspective (Spring 2016), the environmental history of the early modern world (Spring 2017), and empire and environment in the modern world (Spring 2018). I especially want to thank the members of the Capstone Seminar (Spring 2019). These students read and critiqued the third edition and many of the draft revisions for the fourth edition. I found their comments and critiques invaluable. I say "thank you" to these students: Michael Atwood, Trent Beauchamp-Sanchez, Koren Dalipe, Brianna Drakopulos, Carlos Gonzalez, Madeline Kirkwood, Mikaela Malsy, Alicia Pennypacker, Jonathan Ramirez, Kelsey Sherman, Carly Stevens, Daniela Vega, Astra Yatroussis, and Jourdan Zelaya. Special thanks also goes to Professor Kenneth Curtis, who invited me to meet with the members of his graduate seminar at California State University–Long Beach. They engaged me in a wonderful discussion of the ideas that draft revisions of this book sparked.

A grant from the National Endowment for the Humanities (FB-36592) supported composition of the first edition. Philippe Beaujard kindly (and promptly) gave me permission to use one of his maps (see map 2.2). At Rowman & Littlefield, Susan McEachern was instrumental in bringing the first three editions to print, kept me apprised of feedback from students and faculty who read and used *Origins*, and encouraged me to get working on this fourth edition. For their attention to detail, I want to thank Professor Robert Entenman and Yuhin Ng for pointing out errors in the second edition that needed correction. Any that remain in this edition are mine. Joyce Kaufman continues to offer companionship, love, and support, knowing what it means to be a publishing scholar at a college that values teaching effectiveness first and foremost. And as did our faithful and beloved dog companions Budd, Rembrandt, and Stanton, Seger now reminds me to look forward to each new day.

The Rise of the West?

1.5° Celsius. Or a little less than 3° Fahrenheit above preindustrial levels. That is the amount of global warming scientists tell us the world can accommodate without tipping into uncharted and very dangerous territory for the stability of human societies.[1] Over the past decade global temperatures have steadily increased (twenty of the hottest years on record are in the past twenty-two years),[2] with discernable effects on weather patterns—hotter and drier summers in some places, wetter and wilder ones in others. And sea level increases are already worrying the leaders and citizens of oceanic countries. Stronger hurricanes and typhoons as well as longer and more intensive droughts are increasingly likely, leading to the loss of food security for affected peoples and the social and political disruption that follows. We know that global warming is caused by human activities, mostly the burning of fossil fuels that release carbon dioxide (CO_2) into the atmosphere, but also by methane (CH_4) released from rice paddies and the guts of dairy and beef cattle. Already the amount of carbon dioxide in the atmosphere has surpassed the safety level of 350 parts per million (ppm), and is now over 400 ppm. Because carbon dioxide is a greenhouse gas, projections are that Earth is heading for warmer global temperatures and serious challenges faster than had been expected. In the view of James Hansen, until 2013 head of the NASA Goddard Institute for Space Studies, this is a matter of concern because most of what we have called human civilization has developed in a temperate global climate with atmospheric carbon dioxide around 280 ppm. More than that, though, Hansen and other climatologists have concluded that the cause of the increase in atmospheric carbon dioxide is human action arising from industrialization over the past two centuries, and especially in just the past sixty years since the middle of the twentieth century.[3] The 2018 climate report issued by the U.S. Global Change Research Program sounds dire warnings that impacts from global warming will arrive sooner and be greater than previously estimated.[4] A powerful tool to address the problem of capping and decreasing CO_2 emissions is the use of a carbon tax, an innovation that is being implemented in several European countries, parts of Canada, and soon China. Several U.S. states have such a tax, but the economist who recently received the 2018 Nobel Memorial Prize in Economic Sciences for his work on the carbon tax, William D. Nordhaus,[5] thinks that all countries, the United States included, need to adopt the carbon tax as soon as possible, but that there are serious political obstacles to doing so in the United States.[6] Young people around the world certainly "get it" about the challenges posed by global warming and to the safety and security of the world that they and their children will inhabit, and they have been demonstrating and pressing their elders to "take action now!"[7]

The story of how the world got to the point where human actions could affect global environmental processes is complex but not mysterious. The tools of history can help us understand how and why the world we live in—the modern world—got to be the way it is. That understanding can be helpful as we search for ways to make the world a better, safer, more sustainable, and more equitable place for all people. But we need to take a long-term view to fully understand the past and its relationship to the present, and to envision alternatives for the future.[8]

Mostly, the story of the modern world revolves around the historical unfolding of four interrelated themes. The first involves the question of when, how, and why some parts of the world first industrialized, and how those processes were then picked up and used by people in other parts of the world. That story line is still unfolding, and it gets intertwined with another, that of the emergence of nation-states as the principal way people over the past two centuries have organized themselves politically. Industry initially gave some states in western Europe and North America increasing wealth and power—so much so that a large and growing gap emerged between the wealthiest and poorest parts of the world. The story of that "gap" and its consequences is the third of the themes taken up in this book.

The fourth theme explores the interrelationship between the environmental context in which those elements of the modern world emerged and the ways people and their actions in turn changed and continue to change the environment. The imprint of humans on our Earth's ecosystems has become so great that some scholars argue that we are entering a new geologic era—the Anthropocene—in which "humankind . . . has become so large and active that it now rivals some of the great forces of Nature in its impact on the functioning of the Earth system."[9]

Just 250 years ago, the human population of the world was less than one billion people, and two Asian countries—India and China—accounted for two-thirds of the world's economic output. In the brief span of history since then, global population has grown to over seven billion people (on our way to nine billion plus by 2050), and the world saw a great reversal of fortune: where once Asians held most of the economic cards, today it is primarily Western countries and Japan, although China and India once again are rising rapidly. The question centers on how this happened. How did industry and European-style countries called nation-states—rather than highly developed agrarian empires like China and India—come to define our world? Are the last two centuries of European and American economic and political domination a relatively brief aberration? And is China's (or all of Asia's) recent rise a return to the previous world order?

Thus, to understand our world, we have to understand not just how nation-states and industry came to shape the modern world, but how and why those European ways of organizing the world came to dominate the globe. Explanations abound, but for most of the past two centuries, the predominant explanation in the West, the United States included, has been "the rise of the West." As we will see, recent research has shown that that explanation is no longer persuasive, but because it is probably the one most readers may be familiar with, I will take some time exploring it and providing the basis for constructing an alternative explanation.

The Rise of the West

The concept of the rise of the West provides both a rationale and a story line that purports to explain not just the modern world, but why it is defined by primarily European features. The idea behind it is fairly simple and began to emerge shortly after the Spanish conquest of the Americas, during the Italian Renaissance of the sixteenth century. Europeans were quite astounded to see hundreds of Spanish conquistadors vanquish huge and very wealthy American civilizations, in particular the Aztecs and the Incas. Being ignorant of the germ theory of disease and the cause of the "Great Dying" in Mexico, where nearly 90 percent of the central Mexican population of twenty-five million succumbed to European diseases such as smallpox and influenza, Europeans first attributed their superiority to their Christian religion. Later, during the Enlightenment of the seventeenth and eighteenth centuries, they attributed their superiority to a Greek heritage of secular, rationalistic, and scientific thought.

In the late 1700s, this story line continues. The French Revolution of 1789 reinforced the awareness in European minds not just that Europeans were different from the rest of the world, but also that Europeans were "progressing" rapidly while the rest of the world appeared to be stagnating, that Europeans were somehow exceptional—better, even—than the rest. Nineteenth-century European historians, impressed with what many considered to be the universal appeal of the ideals of the French Revolution—*egalité*, *liberté*, *fraternité* (equality, liberty, and brotherhood)—looked back to the ancient Greeks, their institutions of democracy and republics, and their rationalistic bent toward understanding the natural world in scientific, not religious, terms. In this early telling of the "rise of the West," the story is somewhat like a relay race, with the ideas of democracy that arose in Greece passed off to the Romans, who dropped the baton (the fall of the Roman empire followed by the so-called Dark Ages), but Christianity was then on the scene to pick it up and run with it, creating a distinctive European culture during feudal times. The ancient Greek heritage was rediscovered in the Renaissance ("renewal"), elaborated during the Enlightenment, and ultimately fulfilled in the French and American revolutions and "the rise of the West."

If the West was "rising" during the eighteenth century, during the nineteenth its ascent was completed. As the Industrial Revolution of the late eighteenth and early nineteenth centuries was just beginning, the classical British political economists—Adam Smith, Thomas Malthus, David Ricardo, and their followers—developed another strand to be woven into the story of the rise of the West: the ideas of capitalist industrial development as "progress," the West as "progressive," and Asia (and by implication, Africa and Latin America, too) as "backward" and "despotic." To be sure, contrasts between the virtues of the West and the flaws of the East—the Orient—may have dated back to the Greeks, but eighteenth-century Europeans had been impressed with the wealth and governance of Asian countries, especially China. As the pace of economic change accelerated in nineteenth-century Europe, while much of Asia was in internal decline, European social theorists came to view the West as dynamic, forward looking, progressive, and free, and Asia as stagnating, backward, and despotic.

Even Karl Marx and Friedrich Engels, the most powerful critics of the new capitalist world order, believed that nineteenth-century European expansionism was bringing "progress" to the rest of the world. As they wrote in *The Communist Manifesto*, published in 1848:

The [European] bourgeoisie, by the rapid improvement of all instruments of production, by the immensely facilitated means of communication, draws all, even the
most backward, nations into civilization. The cheap prices of its commodities are
the heavy artillery with which it batters down all Chinese walls, with which it
forces the underdeveloped nations' intensely obstinate hatred of foreigners to
capitulate. It compels all nations, on pain of extinction, to adopt the bourgeois
mode of production; it compels them to introduce what it calls civilization into
their midst, i.e., to become bourgeois themselves. In one word, it creates a world
in its own image.[10]

Of more importance for Western conceptualizations of their own history,
though, has been Max Weber, a German sociologist who wrote around the
turn of the twentieth century. Where Weber shared with Marx a fascination
with explaining how and why capitalism developed in Europe—and only
Europe—Weber parted with Marx in his explanation. Instead of focusing as
Marx had on "materialist" explanations, Weber looked to those aspects of
Western values and culture, in particular the rationalism and work ethic that
he associated with Protestantism, as being crucial to the rise of capitalism.
But rather than basing his ideas about the rise of the West solely on studies
of the West, Weber actually investigated Chinese and Indian societies, compared them with Europe, and concluded that those two societies at least, and
by implication all other non-European societies, lacked the cultural values
necessary for capitalism. Nonetheless, they too could "modernize," Weber
thought, but only by going through a painful process of cultural change, getting rid of their cultural "obstacles" to capitalist development.

"The Gap" and Its Explanations

Since the mid-nineteenth century, then, European social theorists have been
aware of a growing gap between the industrialized countries and the rest of
the world. Believing both that western Europeans—and they alone—had
unlocked the secret of modernization,[11] and that others too could learn,
twentieth-century followers of Smith, Marx, and Weber have propounded a
"diffusionist" theory of how world history has unfolded. Europeans found out
how to get rich first by industrializing. Japan and a few other places learned
from the Europeans and have caught up, and eventually every other place on
the globe will too (as the story of "China's rise" over the past thirty years
appears to show), as long as they identify and eliminate the local institutions
and cultural traits that prevent them from becoming modern.

Viewed now from the beginning of the twenty-first century, these ideas
appear to be quite unconvincing in light of the facts that the gap between

the wealthiest and poorest parts of the world continues to grow and the environmental consequences of industrialization are coming home to roost. However, the fact that these eighteenth- and nineteenth-century European theorists—Smith, Malthus, Ricardo, Marx, and Weber—all accepted the idea of European exceptionalism and sought, as one of their primary intellectual goals, to explain it, is important. These men were the founders of modern social science theory, and in the twentieth century virtually all of the social sciences, in particular sociology and economics, have incorporated the idea of European exceptionalism into their basic assumptions. As historians sought to become more "scientific" in the twentieth century by adopting and adapting the insights of this social science to historical inquiry, they too became captivated by the search for the origins and causes of European exceptionalism. But as we will see, Europeans were not exceptional, and one of the most important points about the history of the world until about 1800 is the broad comparability of Asia with Europe, showing more surprising similarities than meaningful differences. Nevertheless, the search for answers to *why* Europeans were perceived as exceptional and hence ultimately superior continues among historians today, even though many now think it is the wrong question to be asking.

In the post–World War II era, this new historical search has produced an impressive body of scholarship looking for the key to what one economic historian has called "the European miracle."[12] These scholars begin with what they see as the fact of the rise of the West but propose differing solutions to the questions of when and why the "rise" or the "miracle" began. The question of when will be discussed first, since in many ways it is relevant to considerations of why.

Adam Smith saw 1492 and 1498 (the voyages of Columbus to the Americas and of Vasco da Gama around Africa to India, respectively) as the most significant years in history. As Smith wrote in *The Wealth of Nations* (1776): "The discovery of America, and that of the passage to the East Indies by the Cape of Good Hope, are the two greatest events recorded in the history of mankind." Marx, too, saw these two years as crucial, as have several twentieth-century scholars working in a Marxist tradition who have pointed to the subsequent European colonialism, slavery, and exploitation of colonies in the Americas and Asia as the primary explanations for the rise of the West. Many non-Marxists have contested the idea that Europe's rise was a result of the exploitation of others,[13] an inconvenient and awkward fact if true, and instead have turned their attention to those aspects of European culture that predate European colonialism, beginning with the Spanish conquest of the New World.

To avoid the possible embarrassment of attributing the rise of the West to its colonial ventures, and not its inherent virtues, much post–World War II scholarship on the origins of the rise of the West has looked farther back in European history, in some cases as far back as the Middle Ages in the eleventh and twelfth centuries, or yet earlier to the ancient Greeks, for factors that could be attributed only to Europe's own exceptional development. Factors that have been identified, in addition to the cultural values discussed by Weber, include environmental ones (temperate climates promote hard work, or poor soils stimulate agricultural innovation), technological ones (plows, stirrups, or reading glasses), political-military ones (feudalism leading to absolute monarchs and then nation-states and the evolving technology of war), demographic ones (small families promote capital accumulation), and in the minds of several historians, combinations of all or some of these.[14]

The implication of this body of scholarship is that Europe possessed some unique characteristics that allowed it—and only it—to modernize first, and hence gave it the moral authority and the power to diffuse "modernity" around the globe where cultural, political, or economic "obstacles" prevented modern development from occurring indigenously. Hence, this story line purports to explain, justify, and defend the rise of the West to global dominance. Just how wrongheaded this theory is will become clearer as the industrial superiority of much of Asia to Europe, at least prior to about 1750, is revealed in the course of this book.

In addition to the recent scholarship on Asia that is changing our understanding of how and why the modern world developed, another perspective is changing our views of the consequences of that development—environmental history. Broadly conceived, environmental history looks at the mutual interactions of humans with our environment—the ways environments conditioned human societies, the ways humans in turn changed their environments to meet human needs, and then the ways those environmental impacts created new sets of problems for humans to confront. This new field emerged around 1970 as mounting environmental problems such as industrial pollution of the air, water, and soil in the United States and Europe prompted historians to ask how and why that had happened. More recently, as the impact of humans on global ecological processes such as the carbon and nitrogen cycles has become apparent, environmental historians have adopted increasingly global views.[15]

Before turning to the question of why all this matters, let me first say a few words about geographic units used in this book. Earlier I mentioned a comparison between "Asia" and "Europe," implying both that these units are comparable and that they have some kind of unity that distinguishes each one from the other. That assumption is problematic, mostly for Asia, because of the immense variety of societies it includes, ranging from China and Japan in East Asia, through the pastoral nomads of Central Asia, to India in the south and the Muslim-dominated West Asia (Middle East). Even Europe has little coherence if it is taken to include everything from Portugal to Russia. Moreover, until very late in our story (at least until 1850 or so), Asia contained about two-thirds of the world's population and was larger than Europe in virtually every respect. To that extent, Europe and Asia were not comparable. Furthermore, one of the most important points I make in this book is that understanding the origins of the modern world requires taking a global view, first of how the vast continent of Eurasia, coupled with Africa, interrelated, and then after 1500, how the New World fit into the story. Finally, even the geographic terms "China," "India," and "England" or "France" conceal much variation within their borders—different peoples, many languages or dialects, and vast differences in wealth and power. Nevertheless, I will use these geographic terms to begin locating the story, but readers should be aware that generalizations based on large geographic units will not be true at all times and places within the places named, and that in reality what was truly comparable occurred in *parts* of China, *parts* of England or the Netherlands, and *parts* of India.

Readers may be wondering why the issue of the rise of the West matters. Indeed, why even study history? The brief response is because our understandings of the past—who we are, where we came from, why we are here—inform our definitions of who we are in the present and have real implications and applicability for actions taken by us or in our name to shape the future. And for that, taking a long-term view of the past—what the late French historian Fernand Braudel called the *longue-durée*—will be helpful for placing into context and critiquing explanations about how the world got to be the way it is.[16] The ideas developed by the story of "the rise of the West" to explain the nature of the world we live in, especially the values of marketplace capitalism and democratic institutions, are thought to have originated uniquely within Western civilization, yet to have universal applicability—to be "good," not just for the West, but for everybody. Following that assumption, the solution to virtually all problems in the world today, at least according to some U.S. and European political leaders, is the adoption of private property and free markets.[17] Thus, to Russia after the collapse of the Soviet Union, to the communist leaders of China, to the leaders of Mexico, Nigeria, and Indonesia, Western leaders have said that the answer to any and all problems they face is "more democracy and free markets." The idea is that the institutions and values that supposedly propelled the rise of the West are universal and can—indeed, must—be adopted throughout the world. That is a political agenda.

But what if this way of looking at the making of the modern world—the rise of the West and the spread of its system on the basis of its supposed cultural superiority to the rest of the world—is wrong? That is the possibility raised by a new body of scholarship, especially over the past forty years.

No longer do all historians picture the world as merely a continuation of universal and necessary trends that began centuries ago in Europe. What many are seeing instead is a world in which population, industry, and agricultural productivity were centered in Asia until 1750 or 1800. The European world of industrial capitalism and nation-states is thus both quite recent and a reversal—for how long, though, remains a big question—of long-standing historical trends favoring Asia.[18] Europeans may have painted a picture of the rise of the West over this original one, but the patterns of Asian strength and economic vitality are beginning to show through once again. Artists call this concept of one painting showing through an original painting or parts of it *pentimento*. As this book intends to show, the more we look at the world and its past through a new light, the more the pictures painted in our minds by the rise of the West will reveal another, and rather different pattern, underlying. To see it, though, we will have to begin shedding our Eurocentric perspectives.[19]

Eurocentrism

One critic has said that the idea that "the West has some unique historical advantage, some special quality of race or culture or environment or mind or spirit, which gave this human community a permanent superiority over all other communities" is a myth—the myth of Eurocentrism.[20] Another has seen Eurocentrism as an ideology, or a distortion of the truth, used by the West to mask its global dominance,[21] and still another deems it a "theoretical model," one explanation among several for how the world works.[22] In this section, we will examine two aspects of what critics call Eurocentrism: first, what it is; and second, the extent to which it can be seen as wrong, a myth, an ideology, a theory, or a master narrative.

The essence of Eurocentrism, according to the critics, is not merely that it views history from a European point of view (the "centrism" part)—it is not just one of many ethnocentric views of the world. A merely ethnocentric perspective recognizes that there are many different peoples and cultures in the world, but that mine is better *because* it arises from my people and culture. They are mine, better, and not yours. Eurocentrism also emphasizes the superiority of Western culture—all that is good, progressive, and innovative starts only in Europe—but it also sees that package as having universal applicability: it is not peculiar and limited to Europe, but has spread to encompass much of the globe by the twentieth century.

Going a bit deeper, critics say, Eurocentric views of the world see Europe as being the only active shaper of world history, its "fountainhead," if you will. Europe acts; the rest of the world responds. Europe has "agency"; the rest of the world is passive. Europe makes history; the rest of the world has none until it is brought into contact with Europe. Europe is the center; the rest of the world is its periphery. Europeans alone are capable of initiating change or modernization; the rest of the world is not.

On a deeper level yet, according to critics, Eurocentrism is not just a belief in the past or present superiority of Europe, but is "a matter of . . . scholarship" (i.e., of established "fact").[23] It is not a "bias," but a way of establishing what is true and what is false. To that extent, Eurocentrism is a way of knowing that establishes the criteria for what its practitioners deem to be "the facts." It is thus a *paradigm*, a set of assumptions about how the world works, that generates questions that can then be answered by ferreting out "the facts."[24]

Finally, Eurocentric ideas about the world and how it came to be the way it is are deeply held by Americans. Indeed, American history is often presented as the pinnacle, the purest and best expression, of Western civilization. European and even world history are most often presented from a Eurocentric point of view, whether or not students or teachers recognize it. Mostly, it is assumed to be "true." Simply collecting more facts would not suffice to dispel the Eurocentric viewpoint, since all the facts on the inside tend to confirm the reality, the truth, of the matrix one is in. Some facts that are collected might not fit, but mostly those are simply discarded or ignored as being anomalous—accidents, if you will. The same is true of Eurocentrism. If Eurocentric ideas about the rise of the West are wrong, how would we know it? The way to know is by getting outside of that way of explaining how the world came to be the way it is and thinking about other ways of understanding the big changes that have shaped our world.

Readers may sense a paradox here. On the one hand, I started by pointing out that key features of the modern world are European in origin and that I think a historical approach can explain how and why industry, the nation-state, the gap between the wealthy and the poor, and mounting human impacts on the global environment came to define our world. On the other hand, I have just rejected the usual Eurocentric explanations of the origins of the modern world. How can there be a non-Eurocentric explanation of a world that has European features? In short, we can find that by broadening the story line to include parts of the world that have thus far been excluded or overlooked—we can begin and end the story elsewhere.[25] When we do that, we will see that only a new, global story line—one not centered on Europe—will suffice to explain the origins of the modern world.

Stories and Historical Narratives

For historians, constructing a narrative—a story with a beginning, a middle, and an end—is central to how we know what we know, how we determine what is true about the past.[26] The rise of the West is a story—to be sure, a story at the core of Eurocentrism—that provides the criteria for selecting what is and what is not relevant to that story. But because the rise of the West informs all the other historical scholarship mentioned above, it is more than just another story or narrative; it is a "master narrative," "a grand schema for organizing the interpretation and writing of history," "sweeping stories about origins," as historians Appleby, Hunt, and Jacob put it.[27]

So the only way to determine if the story of "the rise of the West" is wrong is to construct an alternative narrative of how the world came to be the way it is: we have to get outside of the rise-of-the-West matrix. Doing so will accomplish three things. First, it will provide an independent way to tell which parts, if any, of the rise-of-the-West paradigm can be kept and which need to be rejected. Second, it will help readers to examine critically their own assumptions about how the world works. And third, it will raise the more general issue of how we know what we know about the world and its history. That is the task of this brief history. In the remainder of this introduction, I want to sketch out the elements of that alternative narrative.

I need first to introduce three additional concepts: those of historical contingency, of accident, and of conjuncture. We start with the idea of *contingency*. One very powerful implication of the story line of the rise of the West, though it is seldom made explicit, is that the way the world turned out was the only way possible. Because of the historical advantages enjoyed by Europeans, possibly since the fall of the Roman empire or even as far back as the Greeks or to the source of European genetics, this interpretation implies that the rise of the West was *inevitable*. It might have taken some twists and turns, had some fits and starts, but sooner or later the West would rise above all other parts of the world.

Although we will also have to deal with the political, economic, and military dominance of Europe and its offshoots (e.g., the United States) for the past 200 years, there is no reason to think that that dominance was inevitable or, for that matter, that it will continue. Indeed, it appears inevitable only because that story line was centered on Europe. But once a broader, global perspective is adopted, the dominance of the West not only happens later in time, probably as late as 1750–1800 and perhaps not until the early nineteenth century, but it also becomes clearer that it was *contingent* on other developments that happened independently elsewhere in the world.

Most important, the economic engine driving global trade—and with it exchanges of ideas, new food crops, and manufactured goods—was in Asia. Probably as early as 1000 CE, China's economic and population growth stimulated the entire Eurasian continent; another surge came after about 1400 and lasted until 1800 or so. Asia was the source of a huge demand for silver to keep the economies of China and India growing and also the world's greatest source of manufactured goods (especially textiles and porcelain) and spices. Also very significant in our narrative will be the beginning of Islam and the expansion, from the seventh to the seventeenth centuries, of Islamic empires westward into the Mediterranean Sea and eastward into the Indian Ocean as far as Indonesia. Where Asia attracted the attention and interest of traders from all over Eurasia, Islamic empires blocked direct European access to the riches of Asia, stimulating a desire among Europeans to find new sea routes to the Indian Ocean and China.

Even Columbus's "discovery" of the Americas and Vasco da Gama's sailing around Africa to get to the Indian Ocean would not have done much for European fortunes had they not found both vast quantities of silver in the New World with which to buy Asian goods and a supply of African slaves to work New World plantations after European diseases killed off most of the Native American population. As we will see, the creation of the institutions and sources of wealth and power in a few advanced parts of Europe, enabling these areas to establish dominance over the rest of the world, was *contingent* upon these, and other, developments.

As late as 1750, as parts of Europe approached the levels of development reached in key areas of Asia, all of these most developed parts of Eurasia—parts of Europe as well as Asia—began butting up against environmental limits to further growth, except in England, where easily accessible coal deposits enabled the British to escape these constraints by industrialization based on the new source of steam power. In the early 1800s this new power source was put to military use, and then—and only then—did the scale tip against Asians, and Europeans, led first by the British, moved toward establishing clear global dominance. The point is that the rise of the West was not inevitable but was highly contingent. The world we live in might have been different; there is nothing in the past—unless you adopt the rise-of-the-West construct—that indicates that the world had to become one dominated by Western institutions.

Moreover, if the rise of the West were not inevitable but instead contingent, that would mean that the future too is contingent, and that is why it matters what our view of the past is. If nothing anybody could have done would have changed the outcome of history, then nothing we can do *now* can shape our future: we are trapped in a further elaboration and extension of that which exists in the present, unless some huge accident of history pushes us in a different direction. On the one hand, if history—and our view of it—is contingent, then the actions that we take in the here and now do indeed have the possibility of changing the world. We are not trapped, but rather we (and I take that to mean all the peoples in the world, not just Americans or those in the West) can have agency. If the past could have been different, then so too can the future. To understand that, though, we need to take a long-term view of the past—that is why this book constructs a narrative that spans six centuries. Being "contingent," on the other hand, does not mean that European dominance of the world for the past 200 years was an accident, for there were causes for that development, as this book will make clear.[28]

That does not mean that historical *accidents* do not happen, for they do. Let me give two examples that will be discussed later in the book. In agricultural societies, which is what most of the world was until very recently, climate changes could have a major impact on the size of the harvest, not just in one year but over decades. More favorable conditions could produce larger harvests, lowering the price of food for everyone and stimulating the growth of the economy. Poor climatic conditions, such as happened in large parts of the world during the seventeenth-century "Little Ice Age," put whole economies under severe pressure and led to serious, worldwide crises, as we will see in chapter 3. Although our current climate problems have human causes and thus, in principle, are amenable to amelioration by human action, past climate shifts were accidents in the dual sense of being unpredictable and beyond human control.

Another "accident" is important to the story of coal and its relationship to industrialization. Coal deposits were laid down hundreds of millions of years ago by geologic processes, and where they were in terms of where people lived is purely accidental, as is the case with the main fossil fuel used over the last hundred years, petroleum (and with all other minerals too). Some coal deposits turned out to be near to where people both needed and knew how to use them, and some were far away and hence unusable. The Dutch, for example, had peat, but not coal. This was one reason that their economic growth in the eighteenth century slowed while that of Britain, which just happened to be sitting on huge, close, easily worked coal deposits, accelerated. The distribution of coal deposits thus is accidental as far as human history is concerned, but it certainly had a dramatic impact on which countries industrialized and which did not.

Next is the idea of *conjuncture*. A conjuncture happens when several otherwise independent developments come together in ways that interact with one another, creating a unique historical moment. For our purposes, one way to think about this is to consider the world as having had several regions that were more or less independent of one another, thus having their own histories. In China, for example, the decision in the early 1400s by the government to use silver as the basis for their monetary system arose out of circumstances particular to Chinese history. But this Chinese decision had a global impact in the sixteenth and seventeenth centuries when Europeans discovered both huge supplies of silver in the New World and an even larger Chinese demand for it. As a result, silver flowed into China (and India), and Asian silks, spices, and porcelains flowed into Europe and the New World, inaugurating the first age of globalization.* That was a conjuncture: things happening in different parts of the world for reasons having to do with local circumstances that then became globally important.

Conjunctures can also occur within a given region when several otherwise independent developments reach critical points and interact with one

---

*The origin, history, and application of the term "globalization" is swathed in controversy. For the moment, suffice it to say that I find "globalization" to be a helpful concept to describe the history of the early modern to modern world. Readers will find that I do not conflate it with the heroic story of the rise of capitalism and the spread of democratic ideas or institutions.

another. For instance, the development of nation-states as the dominant form of political organization in Europe happened for reasons quite independent of those leading to industrialization. Nonetheless, when the two converged in the nineteenth century—came together to produce a conjuncture—a very powerful global force developed, particularly when the two provided the basis for European military preeminence.

The attention we give to contingency, accident, and conjuncture means that our explanation of major developments in the making of the modern world will involve several causes, not just one. Monocausal explanations are too simple to take account of the complexity of people, societies, and historical change. We should thus not look for "the" cause of the Industrial Revolution, for it will not be there. Instead, we will find a complex of factors that go a long way toward explaining the Industrial Revolution. I say "a long way" because we have to leave open the possibility that as we learn more or as our perspective changes, we might see the shortcomings of the explanation offered here.[29]

So the narrative in this book about how the modern world came to be— the world of industrial capitalism, a system of nation-states and interstate wars, a growing gap between the richest and the poorest in our world, and mounting human impacts on the environment—will be one that has contingency, accidents, and conjunctures. The world could have been a very different place. Until about 200 years ago, the most successful way people found to organize themselves and to promote the growth of their numbers was in large land-based empires in Asia, Africa, the Middle East, and the Americas. But if not for a series of contingencies, accidents, and conjunctures, we might still be living in a world of agrarian empires.

Besides a plot, or a story line, though, a narrative has a beginning, a middle, and an end, the choices of which significantly affect the story that is told. We have chosen to begin our story with how the modern world came to be around 1400. The reason for beginning around 1400 is that it predates the circumnavigation of the globe in the early 1500s and hence allows us to examine the world and its dynamics prior to the first time a truly globally connected world became possible. The middle of the story revolves around the beginning of the Industrial Revolution in 1750–1800 with an explanation of why the most decisive events happened first in Britain and not elsewhere in the world. In the first edition of this book, the story ended around 1900 because that is when industrial capitalism and nation-states became fully elaborated on a global scale. The third edition continued the story into the twenty-first century.

This narrative of world history also strives to be an environmentally grounded *non-Eurocentric narrative*, that is, to provide an alternative to the story line developed around the existing master narrative of the rise of the West. But does it matter? Why should we care about constructing a new, non-Eurocentric narrative of the making of the modern world? That question can be answered on a number of levels. First, the overall story of the rise of the West may be misleading or wrong in fundamental ways, even though parts of it may be correct. For example, one of the most powerful of recent answers to the question of what caused "the European miracle" concerns families and the number of children each family had. The argument goes something like this: After the Black Death of the mid-fourteenth century, various economic and environmental pressures prompted European families to marry late, thereby reducing family size. Fewer children meant farming families could begin to accumulate capital, thus sending Europe on its way to an "industrious revolution." "By delaying marriage," according to a recent history, "European peasants set a course that separated them from the rest of the world's inhabitants."[30]

Although it may be true that West European peasants did behave that way, thereby freeing themselves from "instinctive patterns of behavior" (i.e., unregulated childbearing) that supposedly condemned other peoples to over-population and poverty, it simply is not true that European peasants were unique in this behavior. Scholarship on China shows that rural families there too—and probably for a lot longer—limited family size, although the methods used differed.[31] In this instance alone, one prop has been removed from underneath the claim of the uniqueness of Europeans and the reasons for their "rise." Indeed, scholars have shown that virtually every factor that its proponents have identified with the "European miracle" can be found in other parts of the world;[32] that is, they were *not* unique to Europe, and hence cannot be invoked to explain the rise of the West.

This narrative also is non-Eurocentric because much of it will be devoted to showing the ways other parts of the world were either more advanced or at least equivalent to the most developed parts of Europe, over many centuries, at least until about 1800. This book could not have been written without the vast amount of scholarship published in English on Asia, Africa, and Latin America, which provides the basis for a non-Eurocentric narrative. We are thus fortunate to no longer be dependent for our understanding of the world on the accident that most of what has been written in the past 200 years has been by and about Europeans exploring their own history. As one critic put it, until recently historians have been like the drunk under the streetlight trying to find his lost car keys: when asked by a police officer why he was looking there, he said, "Because this is where the light is." Fortunately, scholars recently have begun to shine a lot of light on other parts of the world, so we do not have to fumble around in the dark. We now know enough about the rest of the world to question the master narrative of the rise of the West and to begin constructing another, non-Eurocentric narrative.

If the concept of the rise of the West cannot adequately explain why the West and its institutions became the dominant force in the world over the past 200 years, still less the sustained rise of East Asia over the past four decades,[33] then continued use of it does indeed perpetuate a mythology. Some mythologies may well be harmless, at least when they are recognized as such, as when we find Greek or Native American stories about the constellations charming. But when a mythology perpetuates the idea that one group of people is superior, has been for centuries if not millennia, and that all others are thus in various ways inferior, as the ideas inherent in the rise of the West do, then the mythology does violence to others and should be abandoned.

The Elements of an Environmentally Grounded Non-Eurocentric Narrative

First, we have to take the entire world as our unit of analysis, rather than particular countries or even regions (e.g., "Europe," "East Asia").[34] We will have the opportunity to discuss developments in particular nations and empires, but always in a global context. For instance, we will see that while the Industrial Revolution started in Britain (and even there, in just a part), it was not because of English pluck, inventiveness, or politics, but rather because of global developments that included India, China, and the New World colonies. Moreover, nearly all of the world's most advanced pre-industrial economies were reaching significant environmental constraints to further growth. In other words, the Industrial Revolution was historically contingent on global forces, and indeed might never have happened at all.

However, taking a global perspective does not imply that the world has always been interconnected with a single center from which development and progress spread to less-developed regions. Instead, it makes much more sense to think of the world in 1400 as having been composed of several regional systems, or in other words to have been "polycentric,"[35] each with densely populated and industrially advanced cores supplied from their own peripheries. Although trade and cultural exchanges did mean that most of the world regions interacted, or overlapped, on the margins (with the exception of the regional systems in the Americas, which interacted with one another, but not until 1492 with Eurasia-Africa), what happened in these regions was more a result of dynamics specific to that place.

The assumptions that the world in 1400 was polycentric and large parts of Eurasia were broadly comparable in terms of levels of development and environmental constraints help us understand how a much more integrated world came about, and how and why Westerners ultimately came to dominate it. The implication of the Eurocentric model is that development and progress originated in Europe and spread outward from there to encompass the rest of the world: Europeans acted, and the rest of the world was passive or stagnant (until having to react to Europe).[36]

In the narrative in this book, by contrast, we will see that China and India in particular play significant roles, and that we cannot understand how and why the world came to be the way it is without understanding developments in Asia. We will learn how and why China developed such a huge appetite for silver that it created a global demand, drawing silver from around the world to China and flooding the world market with Chinese manufactures. We will also investigate other commodities and their global supply and demand as well, especially for sugar, slaves (unfortunately, human beings were commodities), and cotton textiles, all of which were first produced (and produced more efficiently) in parts of the world other than Europe. Ecology mattered.

This book will emphasize historical contingencies and conjunctures; China and India; and silver, sugar, slaves, and cotton as we develop an environmentally grounded non-Eurocentric picture of how the world came to be the way it is.

CHAPTER ONE

The Material and Trading Worlds, circa 1400

We are born and raised under circumstances neither of our own choosing nor of our own making, and those include both the human and natural worlds. The human world we confront is composed of social, economic, political, and cultural *structures*. These large structures usually change very slowly, seldom as a result of conscious action on the part of a single person, and mostly only as a result of huge processes that are hardly detectable, by large and sustained social movements, or, as we will see, during historical conjunctures. Moreover, the world in 1400 consisted of a biosphere that contained life on Earth, humans included, extracting sufficient energy and nutrients from their environment not just to survive but if possible to increase their numbers, thereby changing and increasingly humanizing the environment.

To understand the vast changes that accompanied the origins of the modern world, we thus need to start with some of the natural and human structures into which people in 1400 were born, lived, and died. Of course, we cannot possibly examine every facet of human life at that time, so we must be quite selective. What I have chosen to emphasize are but two of the major structural aspects of the world in 1400: first, the material and natural conditions under which most people lived, an overwhelmingly agricultural world, or what can be called "the biological old regime," and second, the trading networks that connected most of the Old World together. This chapter thus introduces two kinds of worlds, the material and environmental one in which most people lived quite restricted lives, and the trading or commercial world, which brought the parts of the world into increasingly greater contact. To show how these are interrelated, the chapter concludes with an examination of the causes and consequences of the mid-fourteenth-century Black Death—one of the great catastrophes to befall human society—in western Europe and East Asia.

This chapter also introduces key concepts that will be used throughout the book. Most of this chapter focuses on the material world, in particular the size of the human population and the economic, social, and environmental conditions under which most people lived. The concepts that will be introduced in this chapter include the rise of *civilization* and the *agricultural revolution*, the relationships between towns or *cities* and the countryside, between *ruling elites* and *peasants*, also called *agriculturalists* or *villagers*, between civilizations and *nomadic pastoralists*, and between people and the *environment*. Taken together, these relationships constitute the *biological old regime*, the working out of which is examined in the Black Death of the mid-fourteenth century.

We will also examine the *world system* as it existed around 1400. Today, there is much talk about the benefits and dangers of *globalization*. In this context, many people apparently consider globalization to be a new phenomenon, whether or not they think its impact is on the whole beneficial or harmful. However, I hope readers will take away from reading this book the idea that "globalization" is hardly new: it has been unfolding for a very long time. Key concepts in this chapter will include *polycentric* (to describe a world system with many centers), and *core* and *periphery*, whether applied to a single or a polycentric world system.

Another major point about the fifteenth-century world is that most of its people—regardless of where they lived, their civilization, or even their various folk customs—shared a basically similar material world. The reason is that people had to eat, and after the transition to farming between 11,000 and 4,000 years ago, the way most people have obtained their living has been from agriculture. To be sure, whether the main crop was wheat, rye, or rice mattered, but all of the agriculturists faced similar challenges in dealing with nature, the ruling elites, and one another. For this reason, much of this chapter will deal with the social, economic, and political structures and environmental constraints essential to understanding the material world from about 1400 to 1800. The following chapters then take up the story of what happened after 1400; in this chapter we establish a baseline in terms of material life against which changes in the world can be assessed.

The Biological Old Regime

The number of people on Earth is an important indicator of the relative success humans have had in creating the material conditions under which the human population can either increase or decline. Of course, there are tremendous variations in time and place of population dynamics, and we will consider some of them here. As a first approximation, though, we can start with simple global totals.[1]

The Weight of Numbers
Here we look at the weight of numbers[2] to get an overall picture. Today, there are over 7 billion people on Earth. Six hundred years ago, in 1400, humankind was just 6 percent of that, or about 380 million people, slightly more than the 2010 population of the United States of 310 million. By 1800, the population had more than doubled, to 950 million.[3] Moreover, in that 400-year period from 1400 to 1800, as much as 80 percent of that population were farming peasants, people who lived on the land and were the direct producers of food for themselves and the non-farming population. The world was overwhelmingly rural, and the availability of land and nutrients to produce food was a constant constraint on the number of people alive at any given moment. For most of that period, the population rose and fell in great waves lasting for centuries, even if the very long-term trend was very slightly upward and the declines came sharply and swiftly. In very broad terms, we can see three great waves of population increase and decrease over the past one thousand years. Beginning about 900–1000 CE (probably simultaneously in China and Europe), the population rose until about 1300, crashing precipitously around 1350 as a result of the Black Death. Another period of increase began about 1400 and lasted until a mid-seventeenth-century decline. The third advance, beginning around 1700, has yet to halt, although population experts expect it to top out by about 2050 at 9 to 9.5 billion people.

Climate Change
It now appears that climate change was a general cause of the premodern population increases around the world. Given the interest in our current problem of global warming, historians and climatologists have reconstructed past climates and have indeed found significant variations in temperatures and rainfall.[4] The connections between climate change and human population dynamics are complex, but the major linkage, especially in a world where 80 to 90 percent of the population made their living from the land, had to do with food production. Variations in temperature, radiation, and rainfall affect all growing things, trees as well as wheat or rice. Warmer climatic conditions improved harvests, while cold- or drought-induced harvest failures could spell disaster. Long-term cooling trends could thus seriously

shrink the food supply and hence the ability of a society to sustain a given population, leading to population declines. On the other hand, generally warming conditions could mean larger harvests and a growing human population.[5] As we will see, though, climatic changes count less for population growth in the period since 1700, when New World resources and industrialization began to ease prior constraints on population growth.

Population Density and Civilization

The 380 million people living in 1400 were not uniformly distributed across the face of the Earth, but rather clustered in a very few pockets of much higher density. Indeed, of the sixty million square miles of dry land on Earth, most people lived on just 4.25 million square miles, or barely 7 percent of the dry land. The reason, of course, is that that land was the most suitable for agriculture, the rest being covered by wetlands, steppe, desert, or ice.

Moreover, those densely populated regions of Earth corresponded to just fifteen highly developed civilizations, the most notable being (from east to west) Japan, Korea, China, Indonesia, Indochina, India, Islamic West Asia, Europe (both Mediterranean and West), Aztec, and Inca. Surprisingly, nearly all of the 380 million people alive in 1400 lived in a handful of civilizations occupying a very small proportion of the Earth's surface. Even more surprising, that still holds true today: 70 percent of the world's seven billion people live on those same 4.25 million square miles.[6]

With the exception of the pre-Columbian Americas, which as we will see in chapter 3 had very large population centers before 1492, the densest concentrations of human population by 1600 were (and still are, for the most part) on the Eurasian continent: China in the east, Europe in the west, and India in the south, with the populations of China and Europe about equal over large periods of historical time. So large are those three populations relative to the rest of the world that China alone represented 25 to 40 percent of the world's population (the latter percentage attained in the 1700s), Europe was 25 percent, and India was perhaps 20 percent. In other words, those three centers alone accounted for about 70 percent of the population of the world in 1400, increasing to perhaps 80 percent by 1800. Those amazing figures go a long way toward explaining why what happened in China, India, and Europe plays such an important role in this book.

The fifteen densely populated and highly developed civilizations shared several features, the most important of which was the relationship between those who lived in the countryside producing the food supply and those living in the cities consuming surpluses from that food production, even though the elites in the cities may have devised different means by which to ensure that food produced in the countryside made its way to the cities. This extractive relationship between town and countryside has a long history, going back to the emergence of farming.

The Agricultural Revolution

About 11,000 years ago, first in the part of the world aptly called the "Fertile Crescent" (today's Iraq), people learned how to grow their own food and to raise their own animals, thereby increasing the amount of food available. This change, from a hunting-and-gathering society to a sedentary agricultural society, occurred over long periods and independently in at least seven parts of the world: about 11,000 years ago in the Fertile Crescent along the Tigris and Euphrates Rivers, in northern China about 9,500 years ago, around 5,500 years ago in what is now Mexico in Mesoamerica, and around 4,500 years ago in what is now the eastern United States. It may have happened independently in parts of Africa, Southeast Asia, and New Guinea as well, although it did not happen everywhere: grasslands suitable for animal pasture retained that character until well into the twentieth century.[7]

Although some have objected to the term "revolution" because the development of agriculture took such a long time even in the areas where it began,[8] it was nonetheless a revolutionary change in the way people lived, socialized, and died, for what agricultural advances made possible was ever-greater amounts of food than the direct producers could consume in any given year—in other words, an "agricultural surplus"—giving rise to social groups who did not have to produce their own food: priests, rulers, warriors, and outside raiders, usually nomadic people. The existence of this agricultural surplus meant that others could take it, either by force if necessary or more regularly as taxes. In either case, a major schism opened in society between the agriculturists and the non-producing ruling elite: the job of the agriculturists was to produce the food and the surplus, the role of the priests was to explain how and why the world had come to exist in the first place, and the role of the rulers was to protect the agricultural surplus from invading outsiders.

The agricultural revolution also gave rise to two additional defining characteristics of "civilization": cities and writing. Since priests and rulers did not have to produce their own food, they could live separate from the villagers, in their own compounds as it were. Rulers also gathered around themselves artisans to produce needed clothing, weapons, and buildings, giving rise to the larger concentrations of people we have come to call "cities." From there, the elite could rule their lands while keeping track of the number of agricul-turists, the amount of food they produced, and in particular the amount they owed the rulers in taxes, developing systems of accounting and writing. Besides keeping count of population and taxes, writing was also useful for priests to record their origin stories, to compute calendars for agricultural and ritual purposes, and to forecast the future.

A city and its surrounding agricultural area typically were not self-sufficient, so people traded with other cities or with nomads or other pasto-ralists for raw materials (e.g., metals such as copper and tin, the makings of bronze, or later iron ore) or animals (especially horses). If the required goods were also strategic—that is, related to military sources of power—ruling elites tended to distrust trade and wanted to secure the strategic materials by bringing the producing region under their control, through the use of force if necessary. This dynamic gave rise, over time, to *empires*: geographically large political units ruled and controlled by a single ruling elite in which the sub-ject population offered up their agricultural surplus to the ruler and the land-owning elite, usually in the form of taxes and rents.

Towns and Cities in 1400

Although most of the world's population lived in the countryside, towns and cities of various sizes and functions did exist, and we can use the number and sizes of towns and cities as a very rough indicator of the overall wealth of a society (or to put it differently, of the ability of the peasantry to produce a surplus large enough to support those who did not grow their own food). A list of the twenty-five largest cities in the world in 1400 produces few sur-prises, in that most remain large cities today, but the world's largest urban populations in 1400 amounted to little more than 1 percent of the world's population.[9] What may be surprising, however, is that nine of the world's largest cities, including the largest, Nanjing, were in China. The second-largest city was in south India (Vijayanagar), and the third was Cairo. Only when we get to the fourth-ranked city (Paris) do we get to Europe, which did have five cities in the top twenty-five. Other large cities included Constanti-nople on the Mediterranean; Samarkand, the Central Asia link in east-west trade routes across Eurasia; Baghdad, likewise an important trading city; and Fez in Morocco, which played an important role in African trade routes. We now also know that the capital city of the Aztec empire, Tenochtitlán, had perhaps 250,000 people in 1500 (see chapter 3).

Of course, these largest cities in 1400 (which ranged in size from 80,000 people to nearly 500,000 at the top) represented but 1-plus percent of the world population, while another 9 percent or so (or thirty million people) lived in towns and cities ranging in size from 5,000 to 75,000 people. Not surprisingly, most of these too were in Asia, with China, Japan, and India accounting for the most. In Europe, by contrast, the largest city in Germany was Cologne at just 20,000 people. The wealth of the world in 1400, as measured by the number and size of cities, was thus concentrated in Asia.

To villagers, these towns and cities were somewhat magical places where people with great wealth ate foods peasants could only dream of and wore clothing of such quality that it put their coarse cloth to shame, all without most of the elite doing any visible work. Of course, the taxes, tithes, and rents the peasants paid supported these towns and cities, and the peasants knew it. This transfer of food from producing farms to consuming cities also had an environmental aspect: the nutrients taken up in the growing of crops were removed from the soil and, if not replaced, could result in the depletion of soils, the collapse of farming, and crisis for the humans in those societies. Some scholars have called this a "metabolic rift" between town and country-side, between consuming cities and farming villages.[10]

Nomadic Pastoralists

The agriculturally based civilizations occupied the best land for agriculture throughout the Eurasian continent. The great grassland known as the steppe, stretching east to west across the continent, as well as the deserts and wet-lands, while not amenable to agriculture because of too little (or too much) water, were not uninhabited. On the steppe especially, groups of people obtained their living from the land by hunting and gathering and following their herds.[11] For these pastoral nomads, mobility on horses was a way of life, taking their herds of horses, sheep, cattle, and goats wherever the grass was green. Their way of life was not completely self-sufficient, for they needed things that cities had—salt, pots and pans, textiles, other manufactured goods—trading in return horses, meat, honey, or other products they could gather and that people in the cities prized. Civilizations and nomads across the Eurasian continent thus had a symbiotic relationship—they depended on each other.

The relations between the two groups were for the most part peaceful, but the nomads could constitute fearsome fighting forces. As hunters, they were expert horsemen and archers. And when climate changes desiccated their grazing lands and threatened their food supplies, they were not averse to raid-ing the food supplies stored by the civilizations, whether they were cities or empires. Of course, ruling elites of civilizations had armies—and a duty—to protect the food supplies from raiding nomads. To those within the centers of the civilization, these nomads appeared to be the opposite of civilized: they had no cities, were crude and illiterate, and were probably superstitious as well. In short, they were "barbarians." And when the civilizations themselves weakened, for various reasons, they became susceptible not just to nomadic raids but to invasion, destruction, or conquest, all of which happened. Notable examples include the fall of the Roman and Han Chinese empires (300–600 CE; not discussed in this book) and, as we will see shortly, the Mongol invasions of China and Europe in the thirteenth century. Of course, when the centers of "civilization" weakened, rulers sometimes incorporated nomadic warriors into their frontier armies, further weakening the civilization and opening it to conquest from within by partially acculturated nomads.[12]

Nomads were not the only ones to challenge the civilizations. In the forests, wetlands, brush, and mountains there were other groups, who, unlike the nomads, were often quite self-sufficient and could obtain everything they needed from their environment. They did come into contact with the forces of civilization though, especially during periods of population growth when peasant farmers or the empire sought new land to accommodate the larger population. The Chinese, for example, had a long history of contact with these kinds of peoples, and in fact had come to classify non-Chinese "barbarians" into two groups: the "cooked," or those willing to accept some of the trappings of Chinese civilization, and the "raw," or those who were not.[13]

Wildlife

Even though most of the weight of the world's population lived in just a few highly developed islands of civilization, the intervening expanses were inhabited by differently organized people to be sure, but people nonetheless. Indeed, by 1400 humans had migrated through or to virtually every place on the globe. Of course, the hunters and nomadic pastoralists who lived in the vast spaces outside the densely populated civilizations were very few and far between, leaving much room for wildlife of all kinds. Three examples will suffice.

Wolves roamed through most of Europe, as can be attested by *Grimm's Fairy Tales*. But even more grimly, when human populations declined or hard winters made food precious for both humans and wolves, packs of wolves could—and would—enter the cities, as they did in Paris in 1420 and 1438, and even as late as the 1700s, when the French went on a campaign to annihilate the species there "as they did in England six hundred years ago," according to a contemporary writing in about 1779.[14] In China, tigers at one time inhabited most of the region and periodically attacked Chinese villages and cities, carrying away piglets and babies alike when humans disrupted their ecosystem by cutting away the forests that provided them with their favored game, deer or wild boar. Tigers remained so plentiful in Manchuria that the emperor's hunting expedition could bag sixty in one day, in addition to a thousand stags, and reports of tiger attacks on south China villages continued until 1800.[15]

The two areas of Earth with the greatest diversity and density of animal species in the period we are now considering, from 1400 to 1800, were Africa and the Americas, albeit for very different reasons. In Africa, humans and animals had evolved together. Despite relatively nutrient-poor soils, Africa has more plant and animal species, and total biomass, per unit of area than anywhere else on Earth. Because large animals, from elephants to rhinos, giraffes, and lions, had evolved with humans, as humans became efficient hunters, these animals learned to be wary and keep their distance.[16] Large animals thus continued to exist in Africa into the modern world, where in many other parts of the world, especially those where large animals had no experience with humans, they were quickly killed off after humans migrated into these spaces, in what scholars call "megafaunal extinctions."[17]

In the Americas, the explanation for the large number of animals involves the story of what happened to the native human inhabitants in the century following Columbus's 1492 voyage. This story will be taken up in more detail in chapter 3, but briefly, Europeans brought numerous communicable diseases with them to the Americas, and the native peoples—who had no experience with these diseases—died off in staggering numbers. Where there may have been as many as seventy million people in the Americas in 1491, by 1600 there only about eight million left.[18] And when those people vanished, forests returned to overtake the abandoned farms, and animal populations of all kinds, from fish and fowl to wolves and deer, exploded in numbers in the reconstituted natural environment. Not knowing about any of this, the first English visitors to North America in particular described "unbelievable" numbers and sizes of fish, birds, deer, bear, and trees,[19] a condition of natural bounty that continued through the nineteenth century.

Thus from 1400 to 1800, when Earth's human population increased from 380 to 950 million, there was still plenty of room for wildlife of all kinds. Nonetheless, the relationship between the two populations clearly was inverse: the more people, the less wildlife, especially as those in the "civilizations" developed a desire for wearing furs (in China, Europe, and North

America) or eating exotic fish and fowl. Great hunting expeditions to kill whales, tigers, bison, beavers, homing pigeons, sharks, foxes—the list goes on—for their hides, their meat, and their various other body parts started then and continue to this day, except for those species already extinct or, in some parts of the world, protected.

The expansion of the human population on Earth thus meant less land and hence habitat available for other species. Although we depend on the environment for our survival, our species has been willing to sacrifice others for our *Lebensraum*.[20] Sometimes the end for other species has come like a rifle shot, with the species wiped out without altering the rest of the physical environment, as when wolves were eliminated from England, France, or Wisconsin, or bison from the Great Plains, leaving the forest or the plains intact—impoverished, but intact. At other times, the end of a species comes as a holocaust, where expanding human populations have burned and slashed entire ecosystems to turn them into agricultural fields, as happened to the south China tiger. However, with each of the great human population declines in the mid-fourteenth and then in the mid-seventeenth century, wildlife populations reestablished themselves and once again expanded. But since the mid-1700s, the human population of the world has steadily increased, putting pressure on all remaining wildlife. Of all the human impacts on the environment—and there are many, as we will see in chapters 5 and 6—perhaps the most significant is the extinction of species and the loss of biodiversity. Pollution of land, air, and water in principle can be abated and remediated, and even the challenges of global warming caused by emissions of greenhouse gases can be addressed, but once a species is gone, it is lost forever.

Population Growth and Land

Population growth and decline each brought certain benefits and difficulties to a society. On the one hand, and as with any living organism, an increase in human numbers is an indication of our species' success in obtaining greater food energy from the ecosystem. Higher populations and greater densities made possible civilizations, cities, education, and trade, as well as a growing awareness and understanding of the human and natural worlds. Population growth thus could accompany improving conditions and rising standards of living for most people, at least up to a certain point, where the limits of land and soil nutrients constrained the ability to feed the growing population. In those instances, the human population could overshoot the capacity of the land to feed them, leading to deteriorating living conditions and greater susceptibility to death from disease and famine. As the population fell back, a better balance between the numbers to be fed and the amount of land available to feed them was reestablished.

A growing human population requires additional food and energy supplies to support it, and given the agricultural technology available in 1400, those increases could come from but three sources: bringing more land under cultivation, increasing the labor inputs on a given plot of land (including selecting better seed), or increasing the amount of water or fertilizer. In China over the period from 1400 to 1800, for example, the population almost quadrupled, from 85 to 320–350 million, the increase being sustained almost equally by increases in the land under cultivation and by more intensive tilling and fertilizing of the land already under the plow.[21]

Of course, bringing new land under cultivation implied human migration to new lands, fighting and displacing the wildlife as necessary, and also battling the "uncivilized" people of the mountains, forests, and bush. Some migrations, though, were easier than others, especially if the new lands were sparsely populated and poorly defended or the migrating people had the military might of their empire backing them (as was the case in China). Some areas, though, were for all intents and purposes off limits; Europeans, for example, could not look too far east because the lands were already occupied by various strong nomadic peoples: Turks, Tartars, and Mongols all sent shivers of fear down the spines of most Europeans and Asians.

In summary, nearly all of the world's 380 million people living in 1400 were rural people producing food and raw materials for handicraft industries to sustain both themselves and a small ruling elite that took a portion of the harvest as taxes (to the state) and rent (to landowners). Peasant families often spun and wove textiles that they used both for themselves and traded in local markets for goods they themselves could not produce, and at times their textiles entered into some very long-distance trade circuits, as we will see shortly. With good climatic conditions and hence better harvests, peasant families might look to increase their size,[22] especially if additional land were available nearby, or if their government encouraged more distant migration and would protect them from the wolves or tigers and nomadic invaders. If the population grew too much or too fast, overshooting the ability of the land to support them, a couple of poor harvests could spell famine and increase susceptibility to epidemic disease, as happened in the early 1300s, and would happen once again in the late 1500s and early 1600s.

Diet and caloric intake, along with epidemic disease, famine, war, and other disasters, kept human life expectancy much shorter than it is today. In many of the richest and most advanced parts of the premodern world, from China and Japan in East Asia to England and Germany in Europe, life expectancies at birth were thirty to forty years,[23] or half of what they are today for most of the developed world. Of course, those life spans were short largely because infant and childhood mortality were high: women bore many children and were lucky if half survived to age fifteen. Once past the dangers of death from childhood disease, many people could expect to live into their sixties—under good agricultural conditions, that is.

Famine

Food shortages, dearth, and famine were an all-too-real part of life (and death) for most of the people living in 1400. It is of course all too easy to blame such disasters on "natural causes" alone. But in that time period, 80 to 90 percent of the world was composed of one vast peasantry, rural people who produced the food and industrial raw materials for the society and who were obligated to give up a certain amount of their harvest each and every year to agents of the state in the form of taxes and, unless they were in the small minority lucky enough to own their land free and clear, in the form of rent and labor services to the landowner.[24] Throughout much of the most densely populated part of Eurasia (that is, in China, Europe, and India), peasant families gave up as much as half of their harvest to the state and landlords as taxes or rents.[25]

In good or improving times, peasant families might be able to make ends meet, providing for their own subsistence needs and also meeting their obligations to the tax man and rent collector, and to produce a surplus that might be sold in the market. But what about those times when the harvest fell short? A "good" government or a "good" landowner might recognize that to take their regular share would push the peasant family below *subsistence levels*, and thus would lower or cancel taxes and rents for that year. But if the government or landowners either could not or would not—if they had debts to pay others, for instance—then the squeeze would be on. Indeed, Japanese landowners said of peasants that they were like sesame seeds: the more you squeezed, the more you got. And as we will see more in chapter 3, across Eurasia during the "global crisis" of the seventeenth century, rulers of states insisted on collecting taxes to fund their wars even as harvests shrank because of unusual cold and peasants died off from the resulting famines.

So famine in rural societies was not so much a "natural" as a "social" phenomenon.[26] This is important to understand because it is in this context especially that peasants developed concepts of their own about what rights they had in society, and under what conditions they could press them. The agrarian world that we have been considering thus was not made by the ruling elites, but came about as a result of the interactions, understandings, and agreements (both explicit and implicit) among state agents, landowners, and rural peasant producers, and interactions between human societies and the natural environment.[27]

The Nitrogen Cycle and World History

The world in 1400 was one limited by the material constraints of the "biological old regime" that I have just described. Of those limitations, two of the most important were energy and nutrients, especially nitrogen and phosphorus. I will take up nitrogen here and discuss phosphorus in chapter 6. I have already touched on the fact that in the preindustrial world, energy for humans to do work came mostly from tapping into stores of biomass—trees and other vegetation—for fuel to heat, cook, and make things. People did most of the work themselves, although horses, donkeys, mules, and other animals in some parts of the world plowed or hauled things too.[28] Sails, water wheels, and windmills also did some work, but mostly work was done by human and animal muscle, especially in agriculture.[29] One historian thus called this world a "somatic energy regime" ("somatic" meaning "of the body").[30] And the two things essential for muscles to form and to move—to do work—were food energy (calories) and an essential chemical that forms the basis for the amino acids that are building blocks of muscle tissue—nitrogen.

Humans (and other animals) get their nitrogen by consuming plants or from animal protein (by eating animals that have consumed plants). Without getting too technical, plants use a substance called chlorophyll to tap solar energy to transform carbon dioxide and water into carbohydrates, a source of caloric energy when consumed by animals. One of the chemicals plants use to make chlorophyll is nitrogen. Without it, plants do not have chlorophyll and cannot convert solar energy into usable forms; life as we know it could not exist without nitrogen. So here is where the natural world places limits on what and how much plants can grow—the availability of nitrogen—and hence upon how much food humans can grow and consume.

Although 78 percent of the air we breathe is composed of nitrogen, and we might think that it is overly abundant and readily available, atmospheric nitrogen is in the form of a molecule of two tightly bound nitrogen atoms (N_2) that is mostly inert; we breathe it in and out, and nothing happens. In that molecule form, nitrogen does not react with other substances and cannot be used by plants to make chlorophyll or proteins. To be useful to plants and animals, nitrogen must be a single atom that can react (N_r) and combine with other atoms to form other substances, in particular chlorophyll and other amino acids in plants. The problem is that the supply in nature of this reactive nitrogen N_r is limited because it can be produced by natural processes in just a few ways. Lightning strikes provide sufficient energy to break the bonds of the N_2 molecule; plants that die and decompose put their N_r back into the soil; and some species of plants called legumes (e.g., beans, peas, clover) have evolved a symbiotic relationship with a form of bacteria attached to their roots that converts N_2 into N_r that those plants can then take up directly. In the process of living, humans and other animals metabolize energy and nutrients and excrete the waste, including nitrogen, in feces and urine, which also goes back into the environment. Biologists call this process of using, reusing, combining, and breaking up nitrogen the "nitrogen cycle," and we now understand that it is a global process.[31]

The limited supply of reactive nitrogen in the natural environment placed a serious limit on the amount of food that farmers could grow and created significant problems that farmers and their broader societies had to solve to remain viable. Farmers select certain favored plants to grow because they can be consumed by people, providing us with energy and nutrients, especially nitrogen in the form of preformed amino acids, which constitute building blocks for protein and muscle. Growing the crops, harvesting them, and removing them to other places to be consumed takes nitrogen from the soil with each crop. If that nitrogen is not replaced, the soil is depleted of it (and other nutrients) and eventually becomes degraded and incapable of being farmed.

To farm the same land year after year and not have to move to new virgin land, farmers had to figure out how to replace the nutrients in their soil. Prior to the development of soil science in the nineteenth and twentieth centuries, farmers did not specifically know what those nutrients were, but they discovered by trial-and-error techniques and substances that they understood would (mostly) maintain the fertility of their farmlands. European farmers used the "three field" system where they rotated use of their land in a three-year cycle, leaving a third fallow, allowing animals to graze (and defecate) on another third, and farming the other third. Asian farmers farmed their same plots year after year but learned how to add animal manure and human waste (often collected from cities) as well as "green manure" (chopped up legumes) to maintain the fertility of their fields. Aztec farmers in central

Mexico raked up nitrogen-rich muck from lake bottoms. In short, farmers in the biological old regime had to be attentive recyclers.

The point is that in the biological old regime, natural processes limited the availability of reactive nitrogen, and that fact limited the supplies of both energy and nutrients available to humans. During the period from 1400 to 1800, farmers and their rulers struggled very hard to increase the food supply available to humans, mostly by removing forest to make more farmland (and to a lesser extent by farming existing land more intensively).[32] Across the globe, but mostly in temperate regions, in the four hundred years from 1400 to 1800, humans almost tripled the amount of farmland, from 180 to 540 million hectares, and the world population grew by a nearly commensurate amount, from 380 to 950 million.[33] As we will see in chapter 6, the invention in the early twentieth century of a way to synthesize nitrogen fertilizer lifted the natural limit on the availability of reactive nitrogen to foster plant growth, and with a greater food supply, the human population on Earth soared from 1.6 to over 7 billion in just one century, and industrially produced reactive nitrogen (in bags of fertilizer you too can buy at your local home center) has come to exceed that created by natural processes.

Epidemic Disease

The 80 to 90 percent of the world that comprised the biological old regime peasantry—whether in China, India, the various parts of Europe, or Mesoamerica—supported the elites who governed, warred, ministered, and traded. The peasantry, in the words of one historian, thus made it possible for various forms of human "*macroparasites,*" such as landlords and the state, to live off them. Additionally, the entire human population was subject to epidemic disease carried by *microparasites* (e.g., the plague bacteria of the Black Death, the smallpox or influenza viruses, the bacteria causing dengue fever or dysentery, and all the other germs and pathogens that caused diseases we now cannot identify because they have since mutated or died away).[34]

To be sure, the wealthy in both town and countryside had more ways of avoiding death from epidemic disease than the peasants or the poor of the towns and villages, but epidemics could—and did—affect entire populations. Epidemic diseases also traveled the world, slowly at first because of the slowness of trade and contacts between the centers of civilization, as in the period just after the collapse of the Roman and Han Chinese empires, when smallpox and the measles spread from their point of origin in Europe to China. As the world became even more linked together in the thirteenth century by long-distance trade, a single epidemic disease could—and did—move much more rapidly from one end of the Eurasian continent to the other: the Black Death spread from eastern Asia to Europe in a matter of years, and once in Europe it engulfed nearly the entire region within three years, from late 1347 to 1350. To understand how and why the Black Death could move so rapidly across Eurasia, and then spread within Europe, we need to understand the trading networks that linked most parts of Eurasia and made it possible for goods, ideas, and germs to travel from one end of the continent to the other.

The World and Its Trading System circa 1400[35]

During the fourteenth century, the Old World—the Eurasian continent and Africa—was connected by eight interlinking trading zones within three great subsystems.[36] The East Asia subsystem linked China and the Spice Islands in equatorial Southeast Asia to India; the Middle East–Mongolian subsystem linked the Eurasian continent from the eastern Mediterranean to Central Asia and India; and the European subsystem, centered on the fairs at Champagne in France and the trading routes of the Italian city-states of Genoa and Venice, linked Europe to the Middle East and the Indian Ocean. Moreover, these subsystems overlapped, with North and West Africa connected with the European and Middle East subsystems, and East Africa with the Indian Ocean subsystem (see map 1.1).

Three primary trade routes linked the subsystems, enabling us to talk about an integrated trading system: all terminated in the eastern Mediterranean. The northern route went up through the Black Sea, and then overland through the Mongol empire, with Mongol blessing and protection, all the way to China. It was via this route, for instance, that Marco Polo ventured to China in the late 1200s. A central trade route went through Baghdad (controlled after 1258 by the Mongols) and then via the Persian Gulf into the Indian Ocean, thereby giving traders access to the spices and products of East and Southeast Asia. A southern route went from Cairo, controlled by the Mamluk empire, overland south to the Red Sea, and from there into the Indian Ocean as well.

This trading system that linked most of Afro-Eurasia in the thirteenth century is remarkable for a number of reasons. First, that it existed at all is surprising to historians who have focused their attention upon one or the other part of the world—China, India, or France, for example. Until quite recently historians have practiced their craft by taking current nation-states

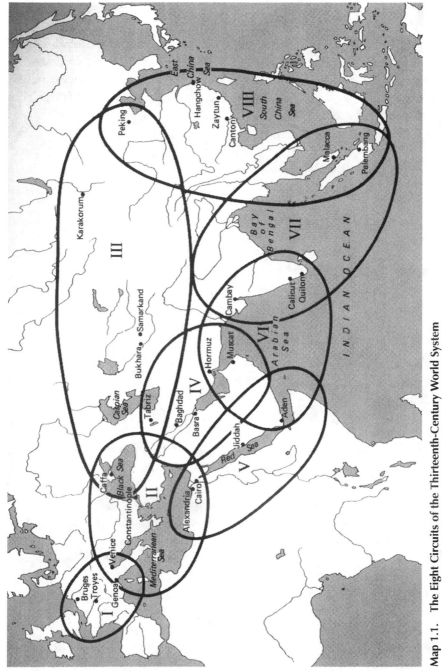

Map 1.1. The Eight Circuits of the Thirteenth-Century World System

Source: Janet L. Abu-Lughod, *Before European Hegemony: The World System A.D. 1250–1350* (New York: Oxford University Press, 1989), 34.

(and their historical development) as their unit of analysis, rather than adopting a more global approach. Even historians who pioneered a more global perspective on the period since 1500 and invented the term "world system" argued that the world system only came into being following the voyages of Columbus and da Gama; prior to that, empires tended to dominate the global landscape with little, if any, contact among them.[37] Even if there was trade among these empires, they argue, it tended to be only for precious goods destined for a small ruling elite. That many historians now recognize the existence of this previous world system thus raises questions about the connection between it and the one that developed after 1500: Was the post-1500 system a wholly new creation, or did it arise out of the elements of the preceding one? I tend toward the latter interpretation, as will become clearer in the next chapter.[38]

The other quite remarkable feature of the thirteenth-century world trading system is that it functioned without a central controlling or dominating force. To those who conceive of the modern world system as growing under the domination of a single state or group of states, the idea that a system could work without a controlling center is somewhat novel.[39] To be sure, each of the trade circuits did have a predominating group—the Italians in the European system, Arabs in the Middle Eastern circuit, and Chinese in the East Asian circuit—but no one of these controlled the whole system. Force thus was not used to keep goods flowing throughout the system, although rulers in various parts did offer protection to traders, caravans, or ships. Indeed, most of the rulers recognized that trade was valuable— especially when they could tax it—and hence encouraged and protected it, not wanting to kill the goose that was laying golden eggs by trying to seize by force the goods of traders from another part of the world.

The world in the fourteenth century thus was polycentric: it contained several regional systems, each with its own densely populated and wealthy "core," surrounded by a periphery that provided agricultural and industrial raw materials to the core, and most of which were loosely connected to one another through trade networks. Moreover, I will argue, the world remained polycentric until quite late in our story, around 1800, when Europeans put into place the elements necessary to colonize most of the globe, in the process creating a global system with a highly developed core and an underdeveloped periphery. Even then, some regions—especially parts of East Asia—remained highly resistant to being fully colonized. The importance of conceiving of the world as polycentric rather than dominated by a single center will become more evident as we proceed with this narrative. Suffice it to say here that a polycentric conception of the world will attune us to voices and actions coming from several parts of the world, and not just Europe. It is, in short, a crucial part of a non-Eurocentric narrative of world history.

Finally, the Afro-Eurasian system circa 1300 is called a "world system," not because it literally spanned the entire globe, but because it was greater than any one given part.[40] Indeed, for all practical purposes, it was a world system, for it involved all those parts of the world where people traded and thus did know something, no matter how little, about one another. Obviously not yet connected to the Afro-Eurasian trading system were the Americas and the empires arising independently there, or Australia and the Pacific Islands; some of what we know about those parts of the world will be taken up in chapters 2 and 3.

The method I have used to describe the world, focusing on the linkages among the various regional systems, emphasizes the role of trade and merchants in forging those links. To be sure, the role of merchants and trade in creating the world system was important, and as recent research has shown, so too was the culturally constructed consumer demand that pulled commodities like cacao and cotton from one part of the world to another.[41] As I will show in more detail in the next chapter, not only did trade allow different parts of the world to sell what they could best produce or gather, but merchants also served as conduits for cultural and technological exchange as well, with ideas, books, and ways of doing things carried in the minds of the merchants while their camels or ships carried their goods.[42] Additionally, epidemic disease and death, soldiers, and war also followed trade routes, as we can see by examining the world's experience with the Black Death in the mid-1300s, after which most Eurasians shared a common disease pool.

The Black Death:
A Mid-Fourteenth-Century Conjuncture

The mid- to late 1300s constituted a serious crisis in world history. The collapse around 1350 of the Mongol empire, which had served as the glue holding much of Eurasia together, was part of that crisis, and so were the ravages of the Black Death, a virulent epidemic disease also known as the bubonic plague, which killed tens of millions of people in the mid-1300s. The reasons why the Black Death occurred when and how it did are complex and debatable, but its consequences are not: "The Black Death killed an estimated 40% to 60% of all people in Europe, the Middle East, and North Africa when it first struck there in the mid-fourteenth century."[43] We can begin to understand better how and why this happened by applying the conceptual tool of "conjuncture" discussed in the introduction.

The bubonic plague is a result of a bacillus—that is, a disease-producing bacterium (*Yersinia pestis*)—that a 2013 study shows exploded, from its point of origin on the Tibetan-Qinghai plateau, in a "big bang" (a "polytomy"), into four strains that Mongol armies then spread into various parts of China and Mongolia.[44] The plague bacillus is hosted by various kinds of rodents, and while it does not necessarily kill them, it can be deadly when passed to humans by direct contact with the rodent, its feces, or fleas that have bitten infected rodents. Prior to spreading to Europe, North Africa, and the Middle East, the plague probably had ravaged various parts of China earlier in the thirteenth century, being brought to cities in northern, southern, and southwestern China in the supplies or bodies of conquering Mongol troops. Whether the plague bacillus spread west toward Europe via Mongol troops who had spread it to China, via trade routes connecting Central Asia with the Mediterranean, or over shipping routes through the Indian Ocean, is not certain.[45] However it spread westward, Mongols or their allies were involved in the trade routes that linked the eastern, central, and western parts of Eurasia.

Regardless of how it was transmitted to Europe in 1347, the conditions had been set for it to spread rapidly and virulently. First, a rodent host population in Europe established itself in town and countryside alike—for whatever reasons, the black rat (*Mus rattus*) took up residence in the attics and rafters of people's houses. Second, the European population had increased substantially from about 1000 CE on, with shortages of land and forest for fuel being notable by 1300. Then the climate worsened, with winters becoming longer and harder and the growing season shorter, putting the population under severe stress. Circumstances were ripe in Europe for some kind of disaster: if it wasn't the plague, it might have been something else, maybe not at the same time or place, but surely the kindling had been laid and all that was needed to set it afire was a single spark. That it was the plague, and that it spread rapidly, was likely occasioned by Mongol military actions in and around the Black Sea.

Europeans had developed a regional trading network linked by the activities of Italian merchants from the city-states of Genoa and Venice. Still, the plague might not have spread to Europe had it not been for another circumstance. The trading city of Caffa (Kaffa), located on the Black Sea, was the link between the trans-Eurasian trade routes: it was the western terminus for caravan trade from China and the eastern terminus for trade carried on Venetian and Genoese ships, both of which apparently docked at Caffa in December 1346. At the time, Caffa was being besieged by the forces of a Mongol prince, and the city might have fallen had not the plague broken out among the Mongol troops, killing most and forcing the prince's withdrawal. The plague might have stopped there had not fleas, rodents, or infected Italians climbed aboard their ships bound for home. When they reached there in December 1346, the plague was let loose in Europe, and it spread rapidly to other towns via the trade routes that had been established, especially the shipping routes. Not only did the black rats now living in European houses spread the plague to people; infected humans too could spread it directly to others by coughing. The plague raged across Europe, the Middle East, and North Africa, where it arrived first in Egypt in 1347 with a ship full of corpses drifting into the port city of Alexandria. From there it spread among farming communities up the Nile River and on to Cairo, along the way depopulating Egypt's rural areas and crippling its irrigation systems.[46] By 1350 it had spread all the way to Sweden and then that winter on to Moscow before killing its hosts and burning itself out.

Like famine, the plague was not a purely "natural" phenomenon but instead required a host of circumstances—a *conjuncture*—to come together for it to have such a major impact on the world and its history. The population of Europe plummeted from 80 to 60 million in just a few years, while in China, the plague coupled with civil war in the 1350s and 1360s saw the population tumble from 120 million in 1200 to 85 million by 1400. Plague ravaged the Mediterranean world as well. Although few records exist to confirm it, the plague probably decimated the Islamic world, India, and the nomadic Mongol peoples of the steppe as well.[47]

The death toll was high, and it etched a powerful memory in the minds of the living. But despite the horror of corpses piled high in village lanes, carted off for burial, or set afire on rafts pushed out to sea, those living fifty years later in 1400 did have more and better land, more fuel, and more resources of all kinds, even if the tempo of trade among the various regions of the global trading system had slowed considerably and more limited plague outbreaks periodically recurred for a few centuries more. The story of the fourteenth-century Black Death thus not only illustrates the impact of epidemic disease on human populations and the course of world history; it also demonstrates the very early connectedness of world regions. Not only did commodities, people, and ideas ride the trade routes—so did horrifying disease.

Conclusion: The Biological Old Regime

This balancing act of people fending off or dying from both macro- and microparasites—elites living off peasants, civilizations fighting off or losing to nomadic invaders, and germs multiplying inside of and then killing nomads and city dwellers alike, all in the context of environmental circumstances that limited the nutrients and food humans could gather or raise for themselves—has been called our "biological ancien regime," or biological "old regime."[48] In this world—the world not just of 1400 but the world for millennia before and then afterward until well into the nineteenth century (as we will see in chapter 5)—the human population lived very much in the environment and had to be very mindful of the opportunities and limits it placed on human activity. As a result, the human population did not increase so much or so fast as to threaten the environmental basis of society, except in a few cases,[49] or until later developments shattered the biological old regime and opened up new possibilities, but that is a story for later in this book.

Agriculture provided not only food for the entire society, but most of the raw materials for whatever industry there was, especially textiles for clothing. In China, silk and cotton reigned supreme; in India, cotton and silk; and in northwestern Europe, wool—the raw materials all coming from farms. Fuel for processing these materials, as well as for keeping warm, came from forests. To this extent, the biological ancien regime was organic; that is, it depended on solar energy to grow crops for food and trees for fuel.[50] The biological old regime thus was one that limited the range of possibilities for people and their history because virtually all human activity drew upon *renewable* sources of energy supplied on an annual basis by the sun.

All living things need food for energy and nutrients to live, and increasing amounts of both to sustain larger populations. What agriculture allowed people to do, in effect, was to capture natural processes and to channel that energy into the human population. In the biological old regime, agriculture was the primary means by which humans altered their environment, transforming one kind of ecosystem (say, forest or prairie) into another (say, rye or wheat farms, rice paddies, fish ponds, or eel weirs) that more efficiently channeled food energy to people. The size of human populations was thus limited by the amount of land available and the ability of people to use the energy and nutrients such as nitrogen harvested from that land for their purposes.

Regardless of whether the Eurasian world population was pushing environmental limits by about 1300, as some historians think, the Black Death drastically reduced the global population, in particular in China and Europe. Then, from about 1400 onward, the human population of the world began increasing again, and, as we will see, 400 years later once again was reaching some of the limits imposed by the biological old regime. To be sure, by 1800 the population of the world had reached some 950 million people, two and a half times that of the medieval maximum of 360 million in the year 1300. To support more than twice as many people as before, something had to change in terms of the relationship of people to the availability of land and their efficiency in working it. On the one hand, Europeans were to encounter a whole new world, the Americas, with vast new resources. Although this New World was already quite populated in 1400 and the land already used by Native Americans, a massive biological exchange would radically alter those relationships, making the Americas a relatively depopulated world by the year 1600. We will examine that story in chapter 3. On the other hand, global trading relationships became reestablished, allowing a considerable increase in overall production and productivity as specialization allowed people in one part of a regional trading network to produce goods that their environment was especially suited to, and to trade via markets with countless others who were doing the same thing. Market specialization spread, thereby allowing economies throughout the world to produce more than they ever had in the past, yet without escaping the limits of the biological old regime. How those global networks became reestablished is in part the story of the next chapter.

CHAPTER TWO

Starting with China

Most historians agree with Adam Smith (see the introduction) that the voyages of Christopher Columbus across the Atlantic in 1492 and of Vasco da Gama around Africa's Cape of Good Hope into the Indian Ocean in 1498 constitute key moments in the emergence of the modern world. Indeed they were. Where historians disagree is *how* important they were: Did they represent a new era? Did they really change all that much? Eurocentric interpretations tend to see them as major steps taken toward the inevitable rise of the West. Some, on the other hand (myself included), think it is important to place those voyages of discovery in a broader global context of the real structure of wealth and power in the world around 1500. From that perspective, the Indian Ocean can be seen as the most important crossroads for global exchanges of goods, ideas, and culture, with China, India, and the Islamic Near and Middle East meeting there as the major players. The map on this book's cover by the European Gerardus Mercator makes that point forcefully by placing the Indian Ocean at the center of his map.[1] From the perspective of the Indian Ocean world, Europe was a peripheral, marginal player trying desperately to gain access to the sources of wealth generated in Asia.[2] How Europeans ultimately did so, and accumulated wealth through the Asian trade, is a story that is contingent upon what happened in China. Our story in this chapter thus starts there.

China

When the founding emperor of China's Ming dynasty (1368–1644) died in 1398, succeeding him to the throne was not one of his sons, but his grandson. The emperor had wanted his eldest son to succeed him, to establish a firm principle of primogeniture to be followed for the rest of the dynasty, but when that son died, the emperor anointed his eldest son's eldest son as heir to the throne. This decision did not sit well with the emperor's fourth son, the Prince of Yan, a man with impressive military credentials, who waited only eighteen months after his father's death to begin unseating his nephew, now the emperor. In a civil war that lasted from late 1399 to mid-1402, the Prince of Yan destroyed his nephew's forces and captured the throne, but not without some ambiguity, for rumors abounded that the nephew had escaped the inferno that had burned down his palace.

As the new emperor Yongle, the Prince of Yan sought to extend China's power and influence in all directions. He campaigned to the north and northwest against the Mongols, trying to push China's previous rulers so far into the steppe that they would never again threaten China. As part of this policy, he moved the capital from Nanjing ("Southern Capital") on the Yangzi River farther north to Beijing ("Northern Capital"), less than one hundred miles from the Great Wall and the last defense against Mongol invasions. He sent embassies far into Central Asia to secure the acknowledgment by those rulers of China's preeminence. He also intervened in affairs in Vietnam, hoping to put rulers favored by China on the throne and to incorporate Annam, as northern Vietnam was then called, into the Chinese empire. And in one of the greatest adventures in world history, he launched massive maritime expeditions into the Indian Ocean.

The Voyages of Zheng He, 1405–33

In the autumn of 1405, the largest fleet of ships the world had ever seen— or would see for another 500 years—began assembling in the mouth of the Yangzi River on China's eastern coast.[3] Over 300 ships manned by 27,000 sailors waited for the reliable winter monsoon winds to begin blowing from the northwest to take them south toward Indonesia and then west through the Strait of Melaka into the Indian Ocean, where they had set Calicut, a major trading city on India's west coast, as their destination.

Under the command of Admiral Zheng He, this armada had three primary objectives. First, the emperor ordered it to track down his nephew, the emperor he had deposed, who was rumored to have escaped. Second, the emperor was outward looking and wanted to "show the flag," impressing all of the foreign countries in that part of the world. Confident that China was the wealthiest, most powerful civilization in the world, he wanted to prove it. And finally, the emperor wanted to encourage overseas trade.

In this regard, the emperor was like the emperors of earlier dynasties, especially the Tang (618–907) and Song (960–1279), and even the hated Mongols who had ruled China under the Yuan (1279–1368), who had encouraged overseas trade, well aware of the wealth that could be generated both for society and the state. His father and nephew, though, had wanted a China that returned to and celebrated its agrarian roots, with a staunchly conservative and inward-looking Confucian philosophy.[4]

But when the Prince of Yan took the throne (literally) as the Yongle emperor, China was experiencing some economic difficulties. To be sure, his father's policy of "agriculture is the foundation" had some success as farmers reclaimed land and set about growing food for themselves and to support the empire. But China's monetary system, based on paper money, had collapsed along with the Mongols. Initially, the Ming (as the new dynasty was called) government simply printed large amounts of paper money, resulting both in inflation and loss of public confidence in the currency. Soon the government decided to abandon paper money altogether, leaving a huge unmet need for currency.

At first, copper coins from previous dynasties were used, but eventually the regime reopened silver mines and allowed silver bullion to be used to settle private commercial transactions. China's domestic production of silver was insufficient for its uses, so it imported more from Japan. Eventually, sufficient amounts of silver were circulating in some parts of the empire that the government commuted taxes there from payment in kind (grain, silk, etc.) to silver, creating a huge demand within China for silver.[5] We will return to this part of the story in the next chapter. Here, suffice it to say that the collapse of the Mongol empire in the mid-1300s led to the severing of overland trade routes linking east and west Eurasia and a recognition by the emperor that an aggressive foreign policy might bring some rewards to China, pushing back the Mongols in the north and exploring opportunities in what the Chinese called the "Western Ocean," that is, the Indian Ocean.

To prepare for these voyages, China had undergone "a frenzy of shipbuilding." Between 1404 and 1407, some 1,681 ships were built; the largest—the gigantic nine-masted "Treasure Ships" of Admiral Zheng He—were about 400 feet long and 160 feet wide, longer than an American football field. Other ships of the fleet, ranging in size and function, carried horses, goods for trade, supplies, water tankers, and marines; some were warships bristling with cannons and rockets. So much wood was required to construct the fleet that much of China's southeast coast was deforested, and timbers had to be floated a thousand miles down the Yangzi River to the shipyards.

When the first armada assembled under Admiral Zheng He that fall day in 1405, it must have been an impressive sight: hundreds of colorfully painted, watertight ships unfurling bright red silk sails. Altogether, the Chinese mounted seven two-year voyages (they had to await favorable winds to return to China) between 1405 and 1433. During that period, Chinese ships sailed as far as Mozambique on the east coast of Africa, into the Persian Gulf, all around the Indian Ocean, and throughout the Spice Islands of Southeast Asia. They navigated their huge ships through unknown waters and into unfamiliar harbors, traded with local rulers, collected curiosities such as rare gems and even a giraffe, and in a few instances intervened in local affairs to install rulers more friendly to China (see map 2.1).

For the fourth voyage (1413–15), planned for the Arabian port city of Hormuz and the Persian Gulf, the admiral took on board Ma Huan, a Chinese Muslim well versed in both Arabic and classical Chinese. Being Chinese and Muslim was not unusual: Admiral Zheng He himself was Muslim, and his father's given name, Hajji, suggested that he had made the pilgrimage to Mecca. Pilots speaking Arabic had been on all the previous voyages, since the language of commerce and shipping in the Indian Ocean from eastern Africa to the Spice Islands was Arabic, and the Chinese needed Arabic-speaking guides to get around. For the fourth voyage, which apparently had the express aim of establishing diplomatic relations with the Islamic world, Admiral Zheng He and his emperor brought their own interpreter, Ma Huan.[6] Indeed, as a result of the fourth voyage, ambassadors from a large number of Muslim lands, including those in East Africa, returned with the fleet to the Chinese capital, and on the seventh voyage (1431–33), while in the Red Sea, Admiral Zheng He contacted the sultan of Egypt, who allowed him to call at the port of Jedda, just a few days from Mecca on the Arabian peninsula. On the return trip, China established formal relations with twenty more realms.

By 1435, it appeared that a powerful Chinese presence in the waters of the Indian Ocean was secure, opening a sea route linking the eastern and western parts of the Eurasian continent with trade circuits in India and Africa, and placing much of the oceangoing trade in the world under Chinese eyes, if not control. Surprisingly, though, the seventh voyage was the last, and Chinese seaborne power declined so rapidly and thoroughly that by 1500 not only were there no Chinese warships in the Indian Ocean, but the Chinese navy had even ceased to exist in the waters off China's own shores.[7] Fortunately for Chinese merchants, the Indian Ocean was a mostly peaceful place to conduct trade, and they continued doing so, even after the withdrawal of the Chinese navy.

As we will see, China's withdrawal of the most powerful navy on Earth from periodic patrols on and around the Indian Ocean turned out to be of immense importance for the course of world history. For now, though, we have to ask why the Chinese court abandoned the Indian Ocean. The short answer is that political struggles within China, struggles that had been going on for some time at the imperial court between those who wanted the voyages to continue and those who wanted China to apply its resources to the greater threat of the Mongols to the north, finally resolved themselves in favor of the latter when the emperor died in 1435. From that point forward, the Chinese state abandoned the seas, paid attention to how an agrarian economy could feed a growing population, and saw its main enemy as the nomads roaming the steppe to the north. Rebuilding and lengthening the Great Wall became of greater importance to China's rulers than continuing the expensive voyages of the Treasure Ships.[8] The abandonment of a navy, though, did not mean that Chinese commercial voyages ended as well; quite the contrary, for the Indian Ocean was the world's most important crossroads of trade. That European ships were even able to enter the Indian Ocean and proceed from there to China and Japan was contingent on the prior withdrawal of the Chinese fleet from the Indian Ocean for reasons internal to Chinese political decision-making. Without that happening, it is doubtful that Europeans would have had much role in linking the wealth generated in Asia to European development.

India and the Indian Ocean

The Mongols' overland trade route linking east and west on the Eurasian continent had not been the only, or even the most important, trade route. Where the collapse of the Mongol empire and the ravages of the Black Death may have been part of a wider mid-fourteenth-century crisis that affected much of Eurasia, there is little evidence of much of a slowdown in trading on the Indian Ocean. Indeed, the Indian Ocean had been, and would remain, not just a crucially important link in the global trading system, but a source of great wealth and access to luxuries, spices, and manufactured goods to any and all who could get their merchants, goods, or ships to the major trading cities on the Indian Ocean. The Chinese thus had not been wrong in seeing the importance of the Indian Ocean and wanting to send their ships there.

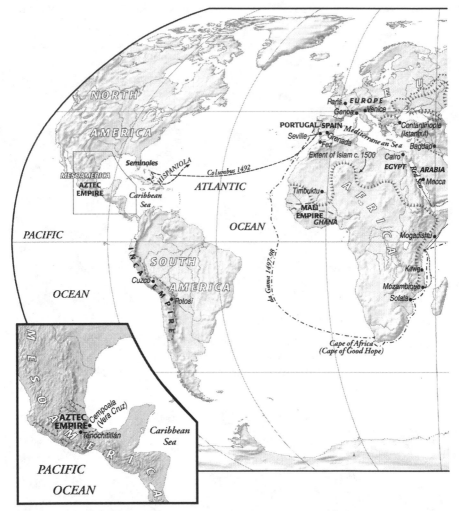

Map 2.1.   The World circa 1400–1500

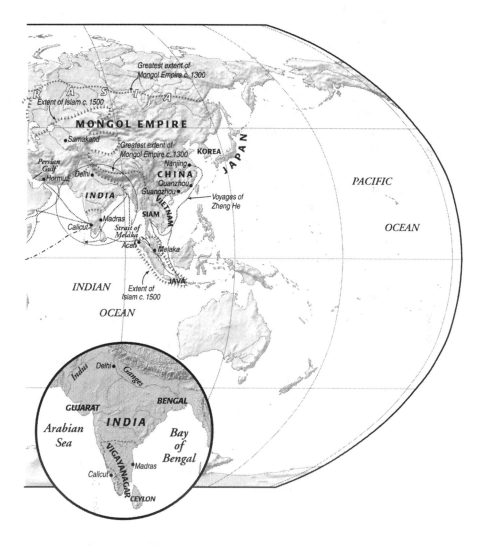

In fact, the Chinese excursion was but one episode in a longer history of the Indian Ocean, starting in about 650 with the expansion of the Islamic world and the establishment of the Tang dynasty in China and ending around 1750 with the British colonization of India on the eve of the Industrial Revolution.[9] During those 1,100 years, the Indian Ocean arguably was the single most important crossroads of trade and generator of merchant wealth in the world, and for our purposes its history can be usefully subdivided into three periods.

From 650 to 1000, Arab traders and mariners carried goods and ideas all the way from the Islamic Near East to Southeast Asia and China, and back again. Arab traders spread their language and the Islamic religion throughout the region, from East Africa to Indonesia, providing a common language and culture for those who traveled there. In the ninth century, for instance, over 100,000 Arabs, Persians, and Jews had taken up residence in the south China city of Guangzhou, and the Islamic mosque built there served as a beacon for ships sailing into its port. In the second period, beginning around 1000 and lasting until 1500, Chinese merchants saw the profits to be made in the trade and, with or without the support of their government, sailed into the Indian Ocean to compete with the Arabs.

The Chinese entrance into the Indian Ocean divided trade into three overlapping circuits, determined largely by the pattern of monsoon winds and hence the opportunities for sailing. Arab traders were still important throughout the region, but they were not the only ones plying the waters of the Indian Ocean. In the western zone, from East Africa to the Red Sea, the Persian Gulf, and the west coast of India, Arab traders were most active, although Indian merchants also participated in that trade. The central circuit from Ceylon to the Bay of Bengal and to Southeast Asia was dominated by Indian merchants, although Arabs and other Muslims were very active there too. The Chinese dominated the South China Sea trade circuit from China to Indonesia and the Strait of Melaka.

Within and among these three zones, great trading cities arose to handle the trade. In the western circuit, the ports of Aden, Hormuz, Cambay, Calicut, Mogadishu (Mogadiscio), and Kilwa (the latter two on the east coast of Africa) were the most important. Linking the eastern and middle circuits was Melaka (Malacca), a trading port that arose in a strategic strait where the monsoon winds shifted, thereby making a convenient layover place for traders waiting for the next leg of their journey.[10] Nothing else accounts for the rise of this city, but the economic and strategic importance of Melaka was not lost on either the Chinese in the early 1400s or, a century later, the Portuguese (see map 2.2).

During the first two periods (spanning 650 to 1500), trade in the Indian Ocean seems to have been self-regulating. No one political power dominated, or tried to dominate, the trade linking those three zones; this was true even during the voyages of the Chinese admiral Zheng He, for Arab and Indian merchants continued on with their activities unobstructed by the Chinese or shut out in favor of Chinese merchants. Another notable feature of the trade was that it was conducted largely without resort to force of arms. African dhows (traditional boats), Chinese junks, and Indian and Arab merchant ships all sailed without naval convoys from their native lands. None of the great ports of trade—Aden, Hormuz, Calicut, Puri, Aceh, or Melaka— were walled or fortified. The assumption in this wide-ranging trade seems to have been that force of arms was not needed to protect shipping or to enforce deals.

During the third period, from 1500 to 1750, all of this changed when first the Portuguese and then the Dutch, English, and French introduced "armed trading" into the Indian Ocean, forcing others already there to arm themselves in defense or to pay the intruders for protection (this topic will be taken up in more detail later in this chapter). Europeans literally tried to muscle in on the huge and profitable trade in the Indian Ocean, to control shipping lanes and port cities by force, and to monopolize, if they could, trade in commodities valued in Europe.[11] Despite the fact that Europeans introduced a new element into Indian Ocean trade, the trade there was so great that they did not dominate it until the advent of steamships in the late 1800s enabled them to undercut trade carried by Arab, Indian, or Chinese ships.

Four great centers of civilization and economic power provided the impetus for the Indian Ocean trade: the Islamic Near and Middle East, Hindu India, China, and Indonesia, or the Spice Islands. To Melaka, the Chinese brought manufactured goods, in particular silk, porcelain, and iron- and copperwares, and in return took to China spices, other edibles, pearls, cotton goods, and silver. Indians brought cotton textiles and returned with spices. To the Middle East and East Africa, India exported cotton textiles, some of which found their way to West Africa, and other manufactured goods. From Africa and the Arabs, Indians received palm oil, cocoa, groundnuts, and precious metals. In general, agricultural and other raw or primary products of the ocean, forest, or mines, including silver and gold, flowed to China and

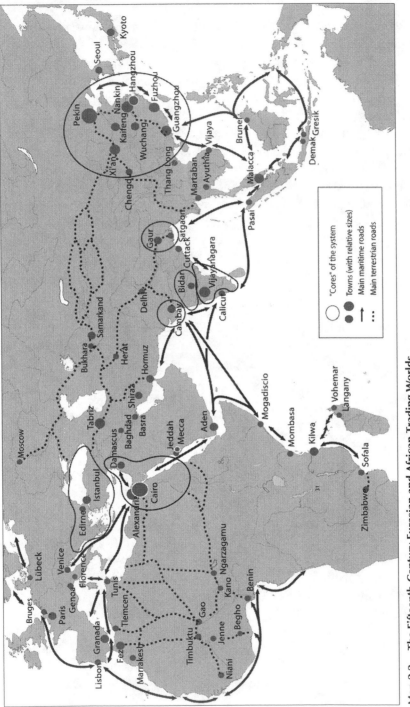

Map 2.2. The Fifteenth-Century Eurasian and African Trading Worlds

Source: Philippe Beaujard, "The Indian Ocean in Eurasian and African World Systems before the Sixteenth Century," *Journal of World History* 16, no. 4 (December 2005): 429, map 5.

India, while those two areas exported manufactured goods, especially textiles (cotton in India and silk in China).

The engines of this immense global trade were primarily China and India. In the fifteenth century, in the words of one historian:

China was still the greatest economic power on earth. It had a population probably in excess of 100 million, a prodigiously productive agricultural sector, a vast and sophisticated trading network, and handicraft industries superior in just about every way to anything known in other parts of Eurasia. After a visit to the great Central Asia political and commercial center of Samarkand early in the fifteenth century, for example, a European diplomat described the Chinese goods he found there as "the richest and most precious of all [imported into the city] . . . , for the craftsmen of [China] are reputed to be the most skillful by far beyond those of any other nation."[12]

As a great agrarian empire, China produced much of what it needed, although it did have to trade for horses, some raw materials, preciosities, and silver. Its rulers mostly saw foreign trade as useful if it could bring additional wealth to the state or satisfy consumer demand for black pepper (which had become an integral part of Chinese cuisine) or other exotic foods like edible bird's nests or sea slugs. The rulers of the Chinese empire found most of these imports to be useful, but saw the potential troubles caused by Chinese and foreign merchants to be large, so for most of the time China controlled foreign trade through its tribute trade system of official monopolies, in addition obtaining substantial revenues for the imperial treasury as a result. However, beginning in the early 1400s, China's new and growing demand for silver to keep the wheels of its domestic economy going could not be satisfied by domestic mines alone. Thus, to obtain its silver, China had to engage in foreign trade, at first getting most of its silver from Japan, but then increasingly in the 1500s from Europeans, a story we will explore in the next chapter.

India had three great textile manufacturing centers: Gujarat on the west coast, Madras in the south, and Bengal on the east. Cotton was spun and woven in artisan homes with material advanced to them by merchants, who then collected the thread and cloth for dyeing and printing before being brought to market to sell. Most of this cotton cloth met internal Indian demand, but a considerable amount was produced for export. Some, as we have seen, was bound for Africa or China, but Indian textiles traded as far as Poland and the Mediterranean. Silver, gold, and other commodities flowed to India to pay for its wonderfully wearable and brightly colored cotton textiles.[13] To meet both domestic and foreign demand for their cotton textiles, Indians had created a whole manufacturing system, from growing the cotton to finishing it. In turn, those Indians who participated in the textile industry had to look to the market to supply their food needs, further commercializing the Indian economy and increasing both production and productivity. Much like the Chinese economy, the Indian economy was highly developed and was the source of select but important manufactured goods for much of the Old World.

Unlike China, though, India at this time was not a unified empire and indeed had a history of both political disunity and unity imposed by outside conquerors. Although India looks like a "place" on a map because of its distinctive geography, it was never really politically unified until the mid-1500s, and then only tentatively because it broke apart again by the mid-1700s. The center of Indian civilization was in the north, in particular the Indus River valley, an agriculturally rich area open to conquest by invaders coming through the Khyber Pass. The Huns did so first in the sixth century, leaving in their wake numerous weak, warring states.

In the eighth century, Arabs spreading the Islamic faith invaded north India and did so again at the end of the tenth century. At the end of the twelfth century, north India was invaded yet again, this time by Turkish Muslims who established a new kingdom, which lasted for two hundred years, the Delhi sultanate. Islam thus gained a stronghold in northwest India where Pakistan now sits, and mosques were built wherever the sultan's power extended. The Delhi sultanate lasted until 1398 when Timur the Lame invaded, ravaged northern India, and sacked Delhi. South India was never easily conquered; it had its own language (Tamil) and political history. Despite the political disunity, Hindu religious ideas spread south in the seventh and eighth centuries, and political leaders soon found Hinduism useful in ruling there too. Thus, not only was India politically divided, but a major religious divide between Muslims and Hindus had opened as well.

Because the rulers of most Indian states supported trade, political and religious disunity did not hinder economic activity, for as we have seen, there was much to be traded when the Chinese admiral Zheng He began visiting Indian ports in the early 1400s. Muslim merchants, speaking Arabic, could trade easily within a linguistic sphere that spread from East Africa to the Red Sea and the Persian Gulf, all the way to Aceh and Melaka, both of which had rulers who had converted to Islam in the thirteenth century. Muslims have played an important part in our story so far, and it is now time to explore the question of how Islam originated and spread so far from its point of origin on the Arabian peninsula.

Dar al-Islam, "The Abode of Islam"

In 1325 at the age of twenty-one, a young Muslim man by the name of Ibn Battuta left his home in Tangiers on the North African coast for his pilgrimage (*hajj*) to the holy city of Mecca. Traveling overland to Cairo, he visited Damascus and Medina before reaching Mecca in October 1326. But rather than returning home, Ibn Battuta decided to see more of the world, setting out on a twenty-nine-year journey of 73,000 miles (almost three times the distance around the world). He traveled to Iraq, Persia, down the east coast of Africa, across Anatolia (Turkey) and Central Asia, across the Indian Ocean with stops at the islands of Ceylon and the Maldives, to northern and southern India, probably to south China, back to North Africa and across the Strait of Gibraltar to the city of Granada, and then back across the Saharan desert to the West African kingdom of Mali.[14]

Amazing by any standard, what makes Ibn Battuta's travels significant for us is that almost everywhere he traveled in the mid-1300s was *dar al-Islam*, "the abode of Islam," or places in the world where Islam was practiced and educated people spoke (or wrote) Arabic, the language of the Quran (Koran). Everywhere he went, Ibn Battuta encountered familiar cultural and linguistic signposts, much like a North American traveling to western Europe today. Although that part of dar al-Islam that he visited was vast, it was not all of it, for Islam had spread to parts of Indonesia and Southeast Asia as well. A fundamental fact of the fifteenth century, then, was the extent of the Islamic world and what that meant for how the world worked (see map 2.1).

Islam had burst upon the world in the early seventh century, and in the century following the death of the Prophet Mohammed (in 632 CE), Muslim (meaning "believer") armies had unified the Arabian peninsula, captured much of Persia, and took Mesopotamia, Palestine (including Jerusalem), and Egypt and North Africa. Although virtually all other political forces on the Eurasian continent had become seriously weakened prior to the arrival of the Muslims, Byzantium in the west (Eastern Orthodox Christianity, with its capital at Constantinople) and China in the east still had sufficient force to check the Muslim advance. Nonetheless, Muslim cavalry consolidated control of North Africa and then took most of the Iberian peninsula within seven years before being turned back by the French, while simultaneously pushing into north India. By 750, a huge new Islamic empire (a "caliphate") had arisen in the middle of the Eurasian continent.

The significance of the spread of Islam for the course of world history was profound. First and foremost it created a realm of common language and custom covering much of the Eurasian world within which trade, ideas, and culture could develop. Fortunately for the rest of the world, the Islamic world loved books and libraries; indeed, the largest libraries in the world from the eighth to the fifteenth century were in Islamic lands, the most famous perhaps being the library at Alexandria in Egypt. In these libraries were stored not just the treasures of the Islamic world, but the classics from ancient Greece and Rome as well. Second, the expansion of Islamic empires in the Mediterranean Sea cut Europe off for centuries from the Indian Ocean, the dynamic center of world trade. It was said that as long as Muslims dominated the Mediterranean, Europeans "couldn't even float a plank on it." To that extent, the flourishing of the Islamic world contributed to the withering of trade within Europe and to its self-described "Dark Ages."

Soon, however, central political control over the Islamic empire began breaking up, with numerous areas asserting effective independence and a new, more stable Islamic dynasty, the Abbasid, with its capital at Baghdad, effectively governing a core region and claiming to be the authoritative center for dar al-Islam. Those areas that had broken free of this central control, though, remained Muslim, as with the Emirate of Cordoba on the Iberian peninsula. In 1258, though, Mongol forces captured and destroyed Baghdad, killing the last Abbasid caliphs and severely disrupting the established Islamic world. Out of this disarray, three new Islamic empires arose: first the Ottoman, which inherited much of the western part of the Islamic world, and then in the early 1500s the Safavids established their rule over Persia, and the Mughals conquered most of India.

The Ottoman empire originated in the late thirteenth century when Turkish nomads, led by Osman Bey (from which the term "Ottoman" comes), began consolidating their power on the Anatolian peninsula (current Turkey). Then, in the 1300s, when Osman's successors constructed an impressive military machine built around the new technology of gunpowder weaponry and a slave-based army called the Janissaries, they ousted the Mamluks from Egypt. Fueled by a desire to be *ghazi* (Muslim religious warriors), the Ottomans pressed hard against the Balkan lands of Christendom held by the Byzantine empire, taking Serbia in 1389 and by 1400 reaching the Danube.

The real prize, though, was the city of Constantinople, the capital of the Byzantine empire and the eastern outpost of Christendom, albeit Eastern Orthodox, not Roman Catholic. Constantinople sat astride the Bosporus Strait and controlled trade in the eastern Mediterranean and on the Black Sea. For centuries, Eastern Orthodoxy and the Byzantine empire had checked the western advances of the Ottomans and Islam. But Ottoman forces besieged Constantinople in the middle of the fifteenth century, and when it fell in 1453, the Ottomans made it their capital (later renaming it Istanbul), and turned St. Sophia's cathedral into a mosque. From there the Ottomans completed their conquest of the Balkans, including Greece and Albania, took the island of Crete, captured Genoan ports in the Black Sea, and planned to take Rome.

The fall of Constantinople in 1453 was a huge blow to Christian Europe. The eastern outpost of Christianity in the Mediterranean, Constantinople had served as a launching pad for some of the crusades into the Levant and represented the hopes of many Christians for an ultimate recapture of Palestine and Jerusalem. But when Constantinople fell to Ottoman rule, it served as a stern reminder that the forces of Islam were not spent and that Europeans could become even more marginalized in the world than they already were. The Ottomans blocked European access to the eastern Mediterranean and hence the trade circuits to China and the Indian Ocean, forcing Europeans to search for alternative routes to gain access to the riches of Asia.

Africa

Ibn Battuta's travels point out the extent and power of the Islamic empires in the early modern world, even into Africa. Indeed, North Africa, Sub-Saharan Africa, and East Africa were all part of dar al-Islam. When Ibn Battuta traveled in Africa, he was visiting not just places in "the abode of Islam" but highly developed civilizations with all that that included: productive agriculture, cities, ruling and subject classes, regional trading systems, and advanced mining industrial activity, including an iron industry. By 500 CE, the social, economic, and cultural complex characteristic of highly civilized people had spread throughout Africa, and great empires soon arose, the largest of which was Ghana in West Africa. Situated at the juncture of three different ecosystems—the savanna, the tropical rain forest, and the Sahara desert—and therefore able to take advantage of the products from all, Ghana was the most strategically located state at the time of the Muslim arrival in North Africa. After the explosion of Islam across the Mediterranean in the seventh century, all of the African empires that traded north across the Sahara converted to Islam between the tenth and twelfth centuries CE.[15]

After the kings of Ghana converted to Islam, their kingdom continued to expand. The kingdom of Ghana produced some gold itself, but the Muslims' demand for it proved sufficiently strong, and the goods they brought to trade were in sufficient demand in West Africa (cotton cloth from India, horses, beads, mirrors, and, most important, salt, which was not locally available) that gold flowed into the capital of Ghana, Koumbi-Saleh, fueling an already thriving trade.

Even more extensive than Ghana was the Mali empire that replaced it. From the 1200s to the early 1400s, Mali controlled and taxed almost all the trade in West Africa, which was indeed substantial. Huge caravans of up to 25,000 camels stretching for miles across the desert brought gold and slaves out of Africa and Indian cotton textiles (among other goods) into Mali. The cities of Mali prospered, and not just the capital city of Niani. Commerce turned Timbuktu into a great center, attracting scholars, architects, poets, and astronomers to its university, and Muslim theologians went there to the more than one hundred schools established to study the Quran.

The height of Mali wealth and influence came during the reign of Mansa Musa (1312–37), a Muslim who made the pilgrimage to Mecca in 1324–25 with a huge procession and amount of gold; it was said that when he sojourned in Cairo he gave away so much gold to all whom he met that its value plummeted 25 percent. Most of the gold from Africa found its way first to Cairo, the great trading port linking Asia with the Mediterranean and northern Europe, and from there via trade to India and to the Italian city-states of Venice and Genoa, who then took it farther north into western Europe. In the fourteenth and fifteenth centuries, access to African gold was crucial for Europeans: in the view of one scholar, it was "absolutely vital for the monetization of the Mediterranean economy and for the maintenance of its balance of payments with [India]."[16]

The other route Islam followed into Africa was along the maritime trade routes south from Cairo and the Red Sea along the east coast of Africa to the trading cities of Mogadishu, Malindi, Mombasa, Kilwa, and Sofala. Even during Greek and Roman times, ships had called at East African ports, so the arrival of Muslim traders was not a major change, except that in addition to goods, they brought Islam, and gradually the peoples of East Africa converted. These cities, though, were so cosmopolitan—traders coming from inland Africa, Arabs, Persians, South Asians, Malays from Indonesia, and even Chinese (some of whom may have stayed behind when Admiral Zheng

He's ships departed)—that people intermarried, giving rise to a new coastal culture and language called Swahili, a dialect with strong Arabic influence. Like West Africa, East Africa was a great source of primary products for the world economy, in particular ivory, animal skins, gold, and slaves.

The existence of large empires in Africa, though, should not obscure the larger fact that political power throughout most of Africa was highly fragmented, with hundreds of "mini-states"—territories with less than four hundred square miles and just 3,000 to 5,000 inhabitants—in West Africa alone. Medium-size states may have been ten times as large, but there were fewer of them. Although there was much warfare between and among African states, there was not much pressure within African society for warring states to expand their territory at the expense of their neighbors. The reason, according to historian John Thornton, is that land was not considered private property, and land was not the basis of wealth in African society.[17] Rather, and in sharp contrast to China, India, or Europe, in Africa control of labor was the source of wealth. It is in this context that we must understand the institution of African slavery.

Slavery

Slaves were used in virtually every society discussed so far in this book: Europe, the Islamic empires, China, and India all had them. Mostly, slaves were used as domestic servants in the households of the wealthy and powerful, and slave status had nothing to do with skin color. Indeed, one of the major sources of slaves was eastern Europe, especially the areas around the Black Sea inhabited by a Caucasian people called Slavs, giving us the word "slave." One of the major "commodities" that Venetian merchants traded to the Mamluk empire in Egypt in fact was these "Slavs," sold for spices and gold in the markets of Cairo. In short, there was a world market for slaves, and European and Muslim traders were eager to supply it.

Africans too kept slaves. Because land was not owned privately and hence was not a source of wealth and power, elite Africans (political heads and merchants mostly) owned labor, that is, slaves. This absence of private property in land made slavery pervasive in Africa. Slaves were used as domestics in households, for agricultural labor, as the mainstays of the armies of several states, and in commerce. Slaves were not necessarily given the most degrading or demanding work in the society, and mostly they were considered as "permanent children," albeit ones who could be inherited by one's real children. Within Africa there was thus a huge indigenous market for slaves, many of whom were acquired in wars between African states.[18] In the centuries from 750 CE to 1500 CE, scholars have estimated that as many as ten thousand Africans were enslaved annually, and the total over those 750 years may have reached five to ten million individuals.[19] Of course, a major part of the story of African slavery is connected to Europe's Atlantic slave trade to the Americas, and that will be taken up in the next chapter.

By the fifteenth century, Sub-Saharan Africa was composed of cultured landscapes that supported a human population of some forty million people. That was slightly less than Europe, probably the same as the Americas, but half the size of China or South Asia. Moreover, because Africa is so huge—at thirty million square kilometers, it equals the continental United States, China, India, Europe, and Argentina combined—the population density was comparatively low. Despite the low population density, urban centers, social hierarchies, and central states did develop in Africa: based upon fertile and productive agriculture in Nubia on the upper Nile and in Eritrea and Ethiopia; in West Africa where trade routes across the Sahara linked Ghana and its successor states of Mali and Songhai to the Mediterranean world; and in East Africa where Swahili trade ports connected Africa to the Indian Ocean world, especially after the expansion of Islam there from about 900 CE on. Nevertheless, Africa's environments presented many obstacles to human population growth: poor soils, debilitating diseases, and dangerous large animals.[20] And that was before transatlantic slavery took millions more Africans to the Americas, a story that will be taken up in chapter 3.

Although there is much that is interesting and significant to know about Africa, for our purposes two things stand out. First, African people had constructed large and successful empires, extensive internal trading networks (see map 2.2), and productive agriculture and industry, especially mining and refining, long before Europeans arrived on the scene in the fifteenth century. Second, Africa already was an integral part of the world system, supplying gold and slaves and purchasing in return manufactured goods, many of which originated in Asia, such as brightly colored cotton textiles from India and porcelain from China. Although Africa was not an engine propelling the global economy, unlike India or China, neither was Europe.

Europe and the Gunpowder Epic

Although I have used the terms "Europe" and "China" as if they were similar units of comparison, politically they were not at all alike. For most of its long imperial history, China was a unified empire ruled by a single sovereign, as large as the United States today and in 1400 with eighty-five to one hundred million people. "Europe," on the other hand, is just a convenient shorthand to name the westernmost peninsula of the Eurasian continent.[21] Though I have been using the term "Europe" as if there were some unity to it, the truth is that Europe in 1400 was divided among hundreds of political units, from city-states (like Venice or Genoa) to principalities, bishoprics, duchies, kingdoms, and even a Muslim caliphate on the Iberian peninsula, each suspicious of the others, most at war at one time or another with their neighbors, and all trying to build armies and navies for their own protection if not gain at the expense of another.

This system of fragmented sovereignty in Europe was a legacy of the breakup of the Roman Empire by the end of the sixth century and the spread of Islam in the eighth century. After the fall of Rome and the loss of access to Mediterranean trade, much of what we now call Europe had regressed into a rural protectionist mode, with a nobility resident in castles for protection against invaders and marauders, collecting dues from an enserfed peasantry tied to the land. Military force was used for protection against outsiders, against other untrustworthy nobles, against subordinates who wanted power, against serfs if they rebelled, and in the Crusades against the "Infidel," the Muslims who had taken the Holy Land. In this world, holding ("owning") a piece of land (and the agricultural produce from its serfs) was the primary objective, and a castle was the main means of securing it.

With swords, knives, lances, pikes, and long- and crossbows being the most lethal weapons available to medieval Europeans, an area could be held by these stone-built castles high on hills overlooking fertile river valleys. By the eleventh century, the usefulness of these essentially defensive structures proved sufficiently effective that they proliferated throughout western Europe. For the next three centuries, defeat of an enemy meant capture of a castle, a feat that usually entailed lengthy sieges. What towns there were—and they were beginning to develop in various places—also built walls for protection, the most famous in northern and central Italy.

It was into this situation of almost constant warring, castles, and fortified towns that a new military technology was introduced in the late fourteenth century: cannons fired by gunpowder.[22] Exactly when cannons became available to Europeans for use in their wars is not clear, but the means by which they got there are. The Mongols not only transmitted the Black Death to Europe in 1347, but sometime in the preceding century Europeans learned about cannons from them too, for by 1327 we have pictorial evidence of an early European cannon.

Gunpowder and cannons had been invented by the Chinese in a process beginning around 1000 CE when Chinese sources describe "fire lances" and other weapons, including bombs, rocket launchers, flame throwers, land mines, and poison smoke. Unfortunately for the Chinese, the Mongols gained access to this new technology, improved it with the development of early cannons called "bombards," and then used those bombards against besieged Chinese cities in their final campaign of conquest in the late 1200s. The Mongols used these devices in their attacks against Europeans in the 1200s as well, and some enterprising (or frightened) European stole or bought the technology from the Mongols.

Bombards were not particularly effective at hurling projectiles far or with much accuracy; indeed, they were used initially mostly to scare horses. But Europeans quickly improved them. First to be improved was the shot, at first made of rounded stones but then later of cast iron. Next, European rulers were fortunate to have within their realms craftsmen expert in casting huge bronze church bells. The technology to make cannons was essentially the same, and soon bell casters were hard at work improving cannons, making them stronger, smaller, lighter, and hence more mobile.[23] In the context of nearly constant warfare among European rulers, this new military technology was to prove very useful.

From 1000 to 1500, the major activity of European rulers was warfare: preparing for war, paying for war, recovering from war. This circumstance, plus the fact that wars became even costlier with the introduction of cannons and other guns, drove European polities toward a common form: a territorial state with sufficient wealth generated in towns and cities, and a population sufficiently large to sustain armies. For a while, states that were small but wealthy (such as the Dutch) could hire mercenaries, while those that were large but poor (such as Poland) could conscript serfs into their armies and force them to fight. But by and large the combination that was to prove most successful in the European system of warring states was one with both urban wealth to pay for wars and young men from the countryside to fight in them. Those who had these weapons could claim to be sovereign within their territories and then by force, if necessary, make others subject to them. In the fifteenth century, the consolidation of political power—not just by European rulers— proceeded apace as cannons blazed the way.

In 1453 the Ottoman Turks used cannons to capture Constantinople, and by the same year the king of France had used cannons to drive the English out of France by leveling their fortifications and pushing them back across the English Channel, thereby bringing the Hundred Years' War to an end.

By 1453, cannons had proved their worth to the leaders of the hundreds of various-sized political entities spread across Europe. A few decades later in Spain, the "Catholic Kings" Ferdinand and Isabella used a siege train of 180 guns to drive the Muslims from Granada, their last stronghold on the Iberian peninsula.

Because Europe was so fragmented politically, no one leader could get or maintain a monopoly on these new weapons and use them to establish an empire in Europe, although there was a brief moment at the end of the 1400s when that might have been possible, had it not been for the defensive inventiveness of the Italians. The French kings used their new military power to consolidate their grip on Burgundy and then Brittany, before deciding in 1494 to expand their territory by invading Italy. Italian city-states had long been at war with one another, and when Florence attacked Pisa in 1500 with the new cannons, they discovered that behind the stone fortifications lay a new wall—a berm, actually—of soft dirt dug up from a trench. Cannonballs harmlessly hit the dirt, and the fortifications of Pisa held. Soon news of this new defensive maneuver spread throughout Europe, and once again sieges became a prime feature of European warfare.[24] Neither the French kings, the Holy Roman emperor, nor Ferdinand and Isabella of Spain now had the military power to sweep away all the small territories and successfully reunite Europe into an empire, although the attempt would be made again, as we will see, in the not-too-distant future.

Armed Trading on the Mediterranean

The reason for much of this warfare was the attainment, maintenance, and enhancement of wealth and power. Although the understandings of those two concepts meant different things in different times and places, the fact is that most rulers (and others) found the accumulation of wealth to be a good thing. The problem for fifteenth-century Europeans was that their part of the world was relatively poor. Sure, one ruler might be able to take the land of a neighbor by force, but that land and the people on it for the most part were as poor as their neighbors. The land was sparsely populated, with much of it given over to pasturage and raising horses used to pull the plows through the heavy soils. Among the various problems that European farmers had was that they just did not have enough feed to keep all their animals alive through the winter, so they usually slaughtered a fair number of their draft animals. But to prevent that meat from going to waste, Europeans had to find a way to preserve it, and for that salt and especially pepper were critical commodities. Salt could be obtained locally, but pepper came only from India, and it was exceptionally expensive. For the most part, Europeans had little to sell in exchange for the pepper.

But Europeans did fight constantly over who would have access to those spices from Asia, in particular the northern Italian city-states of Genoa and Venice, both seaports on the Mediterranean. For centuries, Venice and Genoa competed for access to Asian goods that could be traded within Europe. The competition was not only economic but military as well. Preying on each other, and seeking protection from North African "pirates," each side began building warships to protect their merchant ships, and ships left port not singly but in convoys. The government of each city provided the protection, paid for by the creation of public debt. Furthermore, all the sailors were expected to be fighters as well. Trade on the Mediterranean thus was armed trade.

A series of events in the thirteenth and fourteenth centuries enabled Venice to gain the upper hand, by 1400 securing for its merchants a virtual monopoly on access to Asian spices and textiles.[25] The Venetian victory and use of military force also kept other Europeans out of the Mediterranean. Nonetheless, seafaring Europeans had long fantasized about a direct route to Asia, outflanking the Muslims who stood in the way and avoiding the Venetian monopoly on spices. The Mongols had made an overland route available for a while (which enabled Marco Polo to get to China), but that ended with the collapse of the Mongol empire in the late 1300s. By the 1400s, only one route to Asia existed for Europeans: the Venetian-monopolized connection through Egypt.

Portuguese Explorations of the Atlantic

The Islamic world thus blocked European access to the spices and manufactured goods of Asia, except through the hands of Egypt's Venetian collaborators. To find a different sea route to Asia around these obstacles, Portuguese mariners on the Atlantic coast of Europe under the leadership of Henry of Avis, better known as "Henry the Navigator," began probing southward in the Atlantic, well aware that Muslim navies still patrolled the Strait of Gibraltar. He was also aware of the Arab belief that at the southern tip of Africa was a cape that could be rounded, leading directly to the Indian Ocean. He was determined to find that route, both to establish direct trade with Asia, thereby cutting out both the Venetians and the Egyptians, and to outflank the Muslims, thereby continuing the work of the crusaders in driving Muslims from the Mediterranean and the Holy Land.

In 1415 Henry the Navigator began his quest with an attack on Muslim positions and every year thereafter sent ships to explore the African coast. By 1460, when Henry died, Portuguese ships had reached Sierra Leone, near the equator, and established trading relations with Africans. The Portuguese found both gold and slaves in Africa, which they obtained by trading textiles and guns. They also "Europeanized" several of the islands of the Azores, Madeiras, and the Canary Islands off the West African coast, producing sugar and other commodities for the European market (we will learn more about these ventures and their environmental consequences in chapter 3). But the big prize still was Asia via the Indian Ocean, and the Portuguese pressed farther south until 1488, when Bartholomeu Dias finally reached and rounded the Cape of Good Hope.[26] The prize was nearly in Portuguese hands, and so, when a Genoese sailor named Christopher Columbus approached the Portuguese crown with his idea to reach Asia by sailing west across the Atlantic, he was rejected. As is well known, the Spanish rulers Ferdinand and Isabella ultimately granted Columbus his commission. When news of Columbus's success reached Spain (and Portugal) in 1493, the Portuguese redoubled their efforts to get around the cape, in 1497 sending a new mission under the command of Vasco da Gama (see map 2.1).

By the time Henry the Navigator began his voyages in 1415, Admiral Zheng He had already established Chinese dominance throughout the Indian Ocean. Had the Chinese themselves decided to round the Cape of Good Hope and head north along the African coast—which they could have done, having the technology and the ability to learn the tricky winds off the West African coast—they would have encountered the Portuguese in the 1420s making their way down the coast of Africa, but it is hard to imagine that the Portuguese would have presented much of a threat to the Chinese fleet. Thus, it might have been the Chinese, not the Portuguese, who established a direct water route between Asia and Europe, reaping the profits from that trade and keeping the Europeans close to home. As it turned out, of course, the Chinese instead decided to call their navy home, leaving the Indian Ocean an open and peaceful place. Rather than encountering a formidable Chinese navy that could have turned them back with little difficulty, the Portuguese in 1498 instead sailed into an Indian Ocean remarkably free from naval power or port cities protected by walls or bastions, a contingent outcome they neither understood nor appreciated.

Armed Trading in the Indian Ocean

After rounding the Cape of Good Hope in 1498 and taking on an Arabic-speaking pilot, Vasco da Gama set sail for Calicut on India's west coast (the same destination, it might be remembered, of Admiral Zheng He), and on May 18 he dropped anchor. Upon his return to Lisbon, Portugal's capital, in 1499, the Portuguese crown knew he had pioneered the way to the riches of Asia and quickly sent another expedition, this time under the command of Alvares Cabral. Armed with cannons and instructions to expel the Muslims from Calicut, Cabral bombarded Calicut for two days, targeting Arab ships as well. Then in 1502–3, according to Arab chroniclers, "the vessels of the [Portuguese] appeared at sea en route for India, Hormuz, and those parts. They took about seven vessels, killing those on board and making some prisoner. This was their first action, may God curse them."[27]

The Portuguese had introduced armed trading into the Indian Ocean and, in the words of one historian, "abruptly ended the system of peaceful oceanic navigation that was such a marked feature of the region."[28] By 1515, the Portuguese had taken by force several trading cities, including Melaka and Hormuz. To consolidate their grip in the Indian Ocean, they had defeated a combined fleet of Egyptian and Indian ships trying to break the Portuguese blockade of the Red Sea. Even though their numbers were small and they could not possibly control much land, they could (and did) capture the sea-lanes, first by force and then by creating a protection racket, selling passes to Indian traders. The Portuguese used force to take up a prominent position in the Indian Ocean, although they were never able to control or monopolize trade there.

After taking Melaka, the Portuguese moved into the South China Sea, sparring with the Chinese in order to get rights to trade at Guangzhou, eventually obtaining from them a territorial concession at Macao on the southern edge of China. The Portuguese traded with Japan, and because Japanese trade with China had been banned, they profited handsomely by taking silver and gold from Japan to China and returning with silks. Bolstered by the pope's 1494 division of the world into Spanish and Portuguese halves, for most of the sixteenth century the Portuguese ruled the roost in the Indian Ocean, even though their objective of obtaining a monopoly on the spice trade to Europe remained elusive.[29]

Having felt the effects of the European style of armed trading, some Asian rulers of coastal trading cities responded by walling their territories and purchasing their own cannons and guns. This was especially true of the Islamic rulers in the Spice Islands, in particular Aceh on the northwestern tip of Sumatra. There the Islamic ruler in the early 1500s built a formidable navy for the dual purpose of running the Portuguese blockade and capturing their ships and arms. Later in the 1500s, through its contacts with the Ottoman empire, Aceh imported several large and well-made Ottoman guns, sufficient not just to defend themselves from the Portuguese but to threaten Portuguese-controlled Melaka. Portuguese armed trading may have altered much in the Indian Ocean, but dar al-Islam continued to limit what Europeans could and could not do in the world.

Conclusion

In the introduction I wrote that the early modern world was polycentric and not dominated by any one region or state. This chapter has taken us through China, to India and the Indian Ocean, the Islamic world, Africa, and then to Europe to explore the interactions and interdependencies of those parts of the world with each other. With the exception of the Americas, southernmost Africa, and most of Oceania, the world's societies in the fifteenth century had extensive and systematic interactions and linkages forged by trade. This early modern world system was made possible by three factors.[30] Some parts of the world, in particular China and India, had a *technological advantage* over the rest, and hence were able to produce industrial goods cheaper and better than anyone anywhere else, in particular silk and porcelain in China and cotton textiles in India. Second, *climatic and geographic constraints* limited some natural products to one or a few places on Earth; examples include spices from the Indonesian archipelago, ivory from Africa, certain kinds of incense from the Middle East, or gold from Africa and silver from Japan. And third, *consumer tastes and social conventions* shaped demand for luxury items (e.g., silk, spices, pearls and raw gems, etc.), increasingly mass-market items like cotton textiles, and precious metals as the foundation for a monetary system (e.g., silver in China). The trade linkages among the various parts of the world emerged as an outcome of the complex interplay of these three factors.

Moreover, the linkages that did exist, especially in the Indian Ocean, were for the most part mutually agreeable and peaceful. No one part of the world attempted to seize or impose control over the whole system, even though the expansion of Islam in the seventh and eighth centuries did result in the conversion of huge numbers of people to that religion. The fifteenth-century voyages of Admiral Zheng He briefly extended Chinese influence over much of the Indian Ocean. The world was polycentric, with three major regions centered around China, India, and the Islamic world, and others connected to one or more of those powerhouses.

Most societies could participate in this world system by producing and trading something that others wanted. Europeans, however, were particularly handicapped by the fact that they had little to trade with the rest of the world, with the possible exceptions of wool and, with Africa, firearms. Mostly what Europeans possessed were peculiar forms of armed trading that allowed first the Portuguese and, as we will see in the next chapter, then the Dutch, English, and French to muscle in on the otherwise peaceful trading in the Indian Ocean. In finding a route around the Cape of Africa and across the Atlantic, Europeans had developed into true blue-water sailors; that is, they could sail out of sight of land, a capability that gave them significant advantages in the Indian Ocean. And, oh yes, in one of the greatest accidents in world history, Europeans were to stumble across huge stores and mines full of silver in the Americas, which allowed them, in the words of one analyst, "to buy a ticket on the Asian train."[31] How that happened is the story of the next chapter.

CHAPTER THREE

Empires, States, and the New World, 1500–1775

In the period from 1500 to 1775, many of the ways the world was organized began to change. First and foremost, most parts of the world were drawn into regular, ongoing contact in ways that had never happened in the past. Where previously there had been several "worlds" in the world—the Chinese world, the Indian Ocean world, the Mediterranean world, and the Americas, as yet unknown to Europeans, Asians, or Africans—after 1500 two new links drew the entire globe into a single world for the first time. The voyage of Christopher Columbus in 1492 opened up the New World and established new relations among the Americas, Europe, and Africa. But there was also a less well-known Pacific route linking the New World to China after the Spanish established a colony in the Philippines in 1571.[1] These new linkages led to the exchange around the world of commodities, ideas, germs, foods, and people, in the process creating a dynamic but also very peculiar kind of New World, quite different from the Old (that is, Afro-Eurasia). We can easily think of these sixteenth-century developments as the "first globalization." They were contingent on the withdrawal of the Chinese navy from the Indian Ocean and the historical accident of an Asia-seeking Columbus landing in the Americas.

A second large process was the continued growth and vitality of empires throughout Eurasia. In the sixteenth century, empires remained the most common political form for bringing large parts of the Earth under human control. Of all the various kinds of political and economic systems that humans have devised to draw sustenance from the land and to increase our numbers, by far the most successful was the empire. Why we are not now living in empires instead of nation-states is worth pondering. We aren't because a new kind of state system developed in western Europe, and the resulting nation-state and a world based around nation-states has come to structure the modern world. Formal empires no longer exist. To be sure, Spanish control of much of the New World initially gave them the resources to attempt to establish an empire, but that attempt also elicited fierce resistance among other European states, both killing the prospects for an empire in Europe and launching a new kind of international political order.

The third major process concerns the growth of a system of sovereign states in Europe and the linkage between that process and war. In comparison with Asian empires, the European states appear to be small and rather fragile constructs that could not possibly compete with the larger empires. Their rulers were so poor that they constantly had to seek loans to maintain their militaries. They were so small that they did not have within their borders all the resources necessary for their own defense, and, had the Spanish succeeded in establishing an empire in Europe and eliminating interstate war, independent European states might not have developed at all. As it was, the system of European interstate war favored a particular kind of state that developed in England and France in the sixteenth and seventeenth centuries, leading to conflict between those two for much of the eighteenth century.

Fourth, these developments unfolded in the context of a seventeenth-century "Global Crisis," a period when a global climatic event called the "Little Ice Age" interacted with wars and civil wars to decrease human populations around the world, and to influence the ways rulers and their subjects viewed the purpose of states and political order. The Little Ice Age probably had commenced as early as the fourteenth century, caused by several natural factors that reduced the amount of solar energy reaching the Earth's surface, and may have lasted until the early nineteenth century. The human crises of the seventeenth century lasted a much shorter period, but certainly were intensified by the adverse effects a cooling climate had on harvests and by the tax revenues rulers of states could extract from their subject populations to prosecute their wars. Historian Geoffrey Parker calls this conjuncture of climate change and social crises in the seventeenth century a "fatal synergy" that had many outcomes important for understanding the emergence of the modern world.[2] By the late eighteenth century, England would emerge on top of the European state system. In Asia, the dynamics of empires in India and China would lead to the weakening of India and the strengthening of China. From a global perspective at the end of the eighteenth century, it is not too much to say that two very differently organized worlds would come to confront each other: a China-centered East Asian world system, and a British-centered Euro-American world system.[3] That the nineteenth century would see the balance of power tip in Britain's favor is part of the story that is told in chapters 4 and 5; here we need to examine the four processes introduced above.

Empire Builders and Conquerors

Across Eurasia, five empires expanded dramatically after 1500, remaking the political demarcations of the continent and all but ending the role of nomadic warriors there: China in the east, Russia in the center, Mughal India in the south, Safavid Iran in the southwest, and the Ottoman empire in the west. Although they did not all expand at the same time or rate, and one or the other experienced significant setbacks at one time or another, the expansive thrust of these empires was so great that by 1775 nearly all of Eurasia—except for the European far west—was under the control of one or another of these empires. Why nation-states ultimately eclipsed these empires is central for understanding the origins of the modern world.

Russia and China
The two most dramatic cases of empire expansion were Russia and China, the former more than quadrupling its size from 1500 to 1800 and the latter more than doubling its size. The Russian empire expanded from the principality of Moscow, which in 1300 was little more than a stockade (called a "kremlin") surrounded by a few thousand square miles of forest interspersed with farms. Over the next 150 years, Muscovite rulers expanded their territory by conquering other Russian-speaking principalities. The most dramatic expansion came in the 1500s when the Muscovite ruler Ivan IV ("the Terrible," r. 1533–84) pushed his empire east to the Ural Mountains, north to the Barents Sea, and south to the Caspian Sea. Following a "time of troubles" during the global crisis of the seventeenth century, the new Romanov dynasty (which ruled Russia until 1917) expanded the Russian empire east into Siberia and then all the way to the Pacific Ocean. Eighteenth-century rulers Peter the Great (r. 1682–1725) and Catherine the Great (r. 1762–96) also extended Russian boundaries to the west, taking the Baltic nations, partitioning Poland, and crushing resistance to Russian rule in Ukraine and Crimea.

China had the world's longest tradition of empire, a 2,100-year stretch beginning around 200 BCE and lasting until the early twentieth century.

Although experiencing significant periods of disintegration and conquest by non-Chinese forces, the traditions and techniques of imperial rule perdured. In 1500 China had been ruled by the Chinese Ming dynasty since 1368. During the seventeenth century, political decay of the Ming dynasty coupled with sharp declines in harvests and tax revenues brought about by the cooling climate of the Little Ice Age created conditions favorable for the Manchus from north of the Great Wall to invade and, in a forty-year war of conquest, establish themselves as China's new ruling Qing dynasty.[4] The new Qing dynasty soon set out on a series of military campaigns, especially under the leadership of the Qianlong emperor (r. 1736–95). The Qianlong emperor campaigned in the northwest and west, defeating several non-Chinese peoples, in particular the Muslim Uigurs and the Tibetans, and incorporating them and their lands into the empire. By the time he was finished in the 1770s, the size of the Chinese empire had doubled with the incorporation of Tibetan, Mongol, and other peoples, although the new territories were sparsely populated steppe, semi-desert, or mountainous regions.

China was the center of its own "tribute trade system," which included most of East Asia, including neighboring areas that were not formally incorporated within its empire. To the north, west, and southwest, stateless peoples of various ethnicities paid tribute, both literally and figuratively, to China's emperor by sending periodic missions to the capital in Beijing. China's rulers also considered neighboring states, such as Vietnam, Korea, Java, and even Japan, to be tributary and expected to receive tribute missions from them as well. The tribute missions not only recognized the dominant position of China within East Asia, but also provided lucrative official and private trade opportunities linking China and the tributary states. China thus exercised substantial direct and indirect influence over a territory much greater than that directly governed, incorporating most of Southeast Asia within its tribute trade system.[5]

Mughal, Safavid, and Ottoman Expansion

The Mughal, Safavid, and Ottoman empires, which together spanned the southern and southwestern portions of the Eurasian continent, shared many similarities. First, they all had Turkish ruling dynasties. Originally, the Turks had been one of the nomadic peoples of Central Asia, developing sufficient military strength to conquer the more densely populated agricultural regions of north India, the Persian peninsula, and the Anatolian highlands. I already discussed the origins of the Ottoman empire in the previous chapter. Here, suffice it to say that after conquering Constantinople in 1453, the Ottomans continued to expand their empire around the Mediterranean Sea, including Greece and the Balkans on the northern coast; Syria, Lebanon, and Palestine in the Levant; and the entire southern coast from Egypt to Algeria. Similarly, in the early 1500s leaders of Turkish bands conquered Persia, establishing the Safavid dynasty, and India, establishing the Mughal dynasty.

Second, these three dynasties all embraced one branch or another of Islam. The Ottomans were staunch Sunni believers, the Safavids were Shiite, and the Mughals (a Persian word for "Mongol"), initially at least, were quite tolerant not just of the various branches of Islam but of Hindu practices and beliefs as well. These three empires, then, were all successor states of the first great Islamic empire that arose in the eighth century. Nonetheless, the doctrinal differences between the Sunni Ottomans and the Shiite Safavids were so great that they clashed militarily, first in the Battle of Chaldiran in 1514, and then intermittently for the next two hundred years.

Third, these Islamic empires had similar political and economic structures. The conquering rulers established dynasties in which their sons ascended to the throne following their death in a way very similar to the Chinese system. Also like China, the Islamic successor states ruled their territories through a bureaucracy of officials posted throughout the realm and responsible to the emperor. These empires all rested on productive agricultural economies that produced a surplus the rulers could tap by taxing the peasant producers or larger landowners.

The Dynamics of Empire

Although all of these empires faced difficulties, especially arising from "the global crisis of the seventeenth century,"[6] the fact is that, even with their ups and downs, they were expansive and successful forms of organizing political economies over vast territories in the period from 1500 to 1775. What they showed they could do was mobilize resources within their control to augment and extend the power of the ruling dynasty into new areas. Indeed, by 1700 most of the Eurasian continent was under the control of an empire of one kind or another. Ironically, since all of these empires except the Russian had been established by conquerors from the steppe, these expansive empires ended any further nomadic threat to their existence by placing the remaining nomads under their control. To be sure, even into the nineteenth century these pastoral peoples and others could "revolt" and cause substantial disruption, but the power of the large empires was rolling over that of the nomadic pastoralists. One of the previous dynamics of empires—nomadic invasions causing collapse or strain—was thus extinguished during the eighteenth century.[7]

But other dynamics internal to particular empires continued to account for their rise and decline. In India, the peak of Mughal power was reached under the rule of Aurangzeb (d. 1707). Shortly after his death, various Indian princes challenged Mughal power and effectively asserted their independence, fragmenting political power and leaving openings, as we will see in the next chapter, for Europeans to establish footholds in India. China's power during the eighteenth century seemed to be quite well established, although in retrospect we now know that corruption at the highest levels was beginning to sap political will, and population growth coupled with economic difficulties fueled a large rebellion at the end of the century. The costs of suppressing the White Lotus Rebellion caused other problems to begin surfacing in the early nineteenth century.

Throughout most of the Eurasian continent, empires flourished over the centuries from 1500 to 1800. Although they each had their own particular histories and cultures, they did share commonalities. Mostly, empires were political systems encompassing large territories over which a single person (usually called "emperor") claimed sovereignty. Empires tended to be so large and encompassed so many peoples speaking different languages that emperors ruled indirectly through intermediaries rather than through centrally appointed local officials (although the Chinese emperor did try to rule that way). Empires proved to be quite effective in ruling people, so it is not surprising that they developed and were used elsewhere in the world too, especially in western Africa and in the pre-Columbian Americas, and that even Europeans, as we will see, harbored dreams of a unified empire. In chapter 2, I discussed the West African empires; here I will bring the Americas and Europe into the story.

The Americas

North and South America prior to the arrival of the Europeans was populated by peoples who had constructed varying kinds of social and economic systems, ranging from hunting-and-gathering societies to highly developed agrarian societies and exceptionally creative uses of the Amazon rain forest for agriculture,[8] in the centuries after humans first migrated into the Americas around 15,000 BCE.[9] It thus should not be too surprising that these people could also create the highest form of political organization in the biological old regime, an empire. Two in particular are important to our story: the Aztecs in central Mexico and the Incas in the mountains of what is now Peru and Chile (see map 2.1).

The Aztecs

The valley of central Mexico had long sustained impressive civilizations, starting with the Olmecs about 1500 BCE. On the Yucatan peninsula, the Mayas had built a magnificent civilization with cities, large pyramids, and a highly productive agriculture that peaked around 600–900 CE, after which the Mayan state dissolved into numerous smaller agglomerations. By 1100 CE, the Valley of Mexico was dominated by the Toltecs, who had a capital at Tula at the northern end of the valley. With rich soils and regular supplies of water from snow-fed rivers originating in the surrounding mountains, the Valley of Mexico was agriculturally rich and attracted peoples from all over North America.

Among those migrating into the Valley of Mexico around 1350 were a people called the Mexica, also known as the Aztecs.[10] As latecomers with dubious civilizational achievements and agricultural competence, the Mexica were shunted off into the worst land—swamps and a lake, to be precise—and were considered to be subordinates of others. After making the mistake of sacrificing the daughter of one of their superiors, the Mexica were exiled to some islands in Lake Texcoco. Dredging up fertile muck from the lake bed into small floating plots called *chinampa*, the Mexica gradually created an island in the middle of Lake Texcoco upon which their city, Tenochtitlán (the site of modern-day Mexico City), ultimately arose. Being interlopers and forced to defend themselves, the Mexica became excellent warriors, sometimes working for others but all the while building their own defenses and power.

By 1400, the Valley of Mexico was studded with numerous warring city-states. Three or four were major players, while the Mexica were mercenaries and minor players until 1428, when they established a Triple Alliance with two other groups. The Mexica then were powerful enough to begin conquering and subduing their neighbors and demanding that they send tribute to the capital at Tenochtitlán. Two Mexica rulers in the mid-1400s—Itzcoatl (1428–40) and Moctezuma I (1440–69)—led the alliance, which came to control all of the Valley of Mexico and beyond. At the peak of its power in the early 1500s, the empire ruled over some 489 subject territories totaling twenty-five million people, all of whom were expected to pay tribute to the Mexica at Tenochtitlán.

The Mexica rulers thus accumulated considerable wealth from their tributary states. Food, textiles, jewelry, furs, rubber balls, precious stones, gold, and silver flowed to Tenochtitlán, not because the conquered peoples wanted to send these items, but out of fear of retribution if they did not. The Mexica ruled their empire not through a bureaucracy or assimilation, but through terror, and used the least sign of resistance as a pretext for war and the taking of prisoners for sacrifice to their gods.[11] The Mexica thus constructed a large empire built upon the extraction of tribute from subject peoples, periodic wars, and the daily sacrifice of hundreds if not thousands of captives. Tenochtitlán may have been an exceptionally wealthy city, but the foundations of the empire itself were not strong, resting largely on the fear the Mexica instilled in their subjects.

The Inca

The same could not be said about the other empire being built in the Americas by the Inca. Unlike the Mexica (and the Maya), the Inca did not develop a written language, so most of what we know about them comes from accounts compiled in the early 1500s by European conquerors. Nevertheless, the story is impressive. Settling in the highlands of Peru around Lake Titicaca in the mid-1200s, the Inca (the name originally referred to the title of their emperor, but later European usage expanded it to refer to the people as well) launched military campaigns in the 1400s that created a huge empire, stretching some 2,500 miles from modern Quito in the north to Santiago in the south.

Unlike the Mexica, the Inca consciously incorporated the conquered peoples into their culture, forcing them to adopt a common language (Quechua) and directly governing them with professional administrators. Besides being exceptionally long, covering most of the Pacific highlands of South America, the Inca empire was also "vertical." The Peruvian mountains reached to 13,000 feet, some cities sat at 9,000 feet, and Incan villages were scattered all the way up and down the mountains and the valleys. Besides a challenge to governing, verticality was also a challenge to growing food; because of the vast changes in ecosystems arising from the different altitudes, different crops had to be grown in different locales. To ensure the unity of such an unusual empire, the Incas paved mountain roads with cut stone for imperial runners and armies.

Surprisingly, for such a large empire, the Inca did not have a true writing system, but instead developed an ingenious system of colored, knotted cords that allowed the rulers to keep track of vital information (population, taxes, labor services owed the government) to keep the empire together. Movement from one's village was prohibited, and the absence of money and private trade limited the development of private property and wealth. Nonetheless, the empire itself was wealthy, ruling over sixteen million people.

Like the Mexica empire, though, stresses had built within the Inca empire as it expanded. The Inca believed that their ruler was descended from the sun god, and to keep him happy (and the crops growing) after death, the ruler was mummified in order to be taken out for all important occasions or decisions, thereby maintaining the link to the sun god. Moreover, the mummified leader's direct descendants were given all his land and possessions in order to sustain this activity. A new Inca ruler thus came to the throne land poor and had to conquer new lands and peoples of his own, thereby giving a certain dynamic to Incan imperial expansion. When that expansion slowed, as all available lands were conquered or the Incan armies suffered defeat—as they did when they went down the east side of the Andes into the Amazon rain forest, where they were then driven out—tensions within the royal family began to run high and soon exploded when an Incan emperor died in 1525, leading to a succession crisis and contest for the throne between two half brothers.

By 1500, both the Aztec and Inca empires were well established and quite powerful, although each had weaknesses. The Aztecs had constructed an empire based on forced extraction of surplus from subjugated people, while the Incas had a system that required expansion in order for the new ruler to obtain new lands to support his family. Then, the arrival of the Spanish, first Columbus in 1492 of course, but more importantly Hernan Cortéz in 1519 and Francisco Pizarro in 1531, changed everything.

The Conquest of the Americas and the Spanish Empire

In 1500, Tenochtitlán, the capital of the Aztec empire, had a population of 250,000, making it one of the largest cities in the world. The city boasted pyramids, botanical gardens, canals, zoos, a sewage system, and streets that were cleaned daily by about one thousand men. Tenochtitlán was an impressive place. Aztec warriors instilled fear in the people they conquered, ensuring the flow of food and goods into the capital. Yet this large, complex, and powerful empire was brought down by just six hundred Spanish "conquistadors" led by Hernan Cortéz; an even smaller "army" under Francisco Pizarro conquered the Incan empire in the 1530s. How did that happen? The conquest was contingent on several factors.

In 1519, after Cortéz landed on the coast of Mexico near what would become the city of Vera Cruz, he heard stories of vast amounts of gold inland and that various people the Aztecs had conquered would help him by providing intelligence, food, canoes, and warriors. The Aztec emperor, Moctezuma II, at first believing that Cortéz was a returning god, sent gifts of gold to appease the Spaniards, hoping they would go away. But, according to Cortéz, "we have a disease of the heart that can only be cured with gold," and so began the expedition overland to Tenochtitlán.

Exploiting the feelings of hatred the conquered peoples had toward the Aztecs, Cortéz enlisted their help both in getting to Tenochtitlán and then in war against the Aztecs. Even though the Aztecs were fierce warriors who had developed many instruments of war that worked well in the Valley of Mexico, ultimately the Spaniards had a huge technological advantage. Where the Spaniards had steel swords and armor, the Aztecs had bronze weapons and cloth armor; where the Spaniards had cannons, the Aztecs had none; where the Spaniards had wheels, the Aztecs had none; where the Spaniards had horses, the Aztecs had none; where the Spaniards had "the dogs of war," the Aztecs had none; where the Spaniards fought to kill and to conquer territory, the Aztecs fought when equally matched and did not kill all their enemies. And finally, the Spaniards unwittingly brought the smallpox virus, which unleashed an epidemic in the summer of 1520, killing over half the residents of Tenochtitlán, demoralizing the Aztec warriors, and enabling the disciplined Spanish soldiers to take advantage of the moment to seize Tenochtitlán.

A similar combination of factors allowed Francisco Pizarro's small band of men to conquer the Incas.[12] In this case, though, the smallpox epidemic had already spread to Peru from Mexico in the 1520s, decimating Andean Indian populations long before Pizarro arrived. When he did, he exploited differences among Incan claimants to the throne, lured them into a trap, and then killed almost all, initially sparing the last Incan ruler until he delivered a sufficient amount of gold but then strangling and decapitating him.

Although we use the word "conquest" to describe what happened to the Aztecs and Incas in the sixteenth century, the fact is that Spanish victory was neither swift nor complete, for the native peoples of the Americas put up a long and valiant struggle against European invaders and colonizers. The Incas resisted for another century, the Spanish in fact faced several defeats at the hands of the Seminoles in Florida. Indeed, in some ways Native American resistance has not yet ended, as the events in Chiapas, Mexico, in the 1990s serve to remind us. However, if not fully defeated and if continued resistance allowed Native Americans to negotiate or win concessions at the margins, the fact is that ultimately Europeans and Africans replaced the Native Americans as the most populous peoples in the Americas, as we will see in more detail below.

The Columbian Exchange

The conquest of the Americas led to a global exchange of peoples, pathogens, natural products, and foodstuffs, especially of New World foods to the Old World agrarian economies that changed the world. Maize (corn), potatoes, tomatoes, chilies, and other foods spread rapidly throughout Eurasia, enriching the diets of commoners and elites alike. Sweet potatoes, for instance, reached China by the early 1500s, making it possible for peasants there to sell their rice rather than eat it. Certainly, the spread of New World crops into the Old World made it possible for populations there to increase above what would have been possible on the basis of the existing basket of foods.

But the Columbian Exchange was a two-way exchange, and it seems that the native peoples of the New World were the losers, for the encounter between the Old and New Worlds brought two hitherto separate disease pools into contact. The Native American ancestors had migrated into the Americas during the last Ice Age when a land bridge linked Alaska to Siberia, thousands of years before the agricultural revolution in Eurasia brought people and domesticated animals together in a rich recipe for the transfer of animal pathogens to humans, leading to a whole range of human diseases, including smallpox, chicken pox, and influenza. Eurasians contracted these diseases and over time developed some immunities to them; New Worlders did not have a chance to do the same. When the Ice Age ended and the melting glaciers raised the ocean level above the Bering Strait land bridge, the peoples in the Americas were isolated from the diseases that then became an everyday part of the material world in Eurasia, rendering some of them "childhood" diseases from which most people easily recovered. The diseases for which Europeans had developed immunities over the centuries proved to be deadly to those in the Americas (and later the Pacific Islands too) without such acquired immunity.[13]

The Great Dying

The smallpox epidemics that weakened both the Aztecs and the Incas, paving the way for the Spanish conquest of both empires, were just the beginning of a century-long holocaust that almost wiped out Native American populations, bringing the pre-Conquest population, variously estimated at forty to one hundred million, down to just eight million. From 1518 to 1600, seventeen major epidemics were recorded in the New World, spanning a territory from what is now Argentina in the south to what is now Texas and the Carolinas in the United States. Not just smallpox, but other killer diseases—measles, influenza, bubonic plague, cholera, chicken pox, whooping cough, diphtheria, and tropical malaria—ravaged American populations.[14] Disease was not the only cause of the depopulation of the Americas in the century after the Spanish Conquest. The Conquest itself, war among the American natives, oppression by the conquerors, the forced requisitioning of Indian labor, lowered fertility, and depression among the surviving native population all contributed to the disaster.[15]

In Mexico alone, where there had been twenty-five million people in 1519, fifty years later there were 2.7 million, and a hundred years later there were but 750,000, or 3 percent of the original total. Similar fates befell the Incas, the inhabitants of the Caribbean Islands (starting with the Arawak on Española), and the Indians of (what is now) the southeastern United States, although at different rates. Whether or not European-introduced diseases ravaged the Indians of the American Northeast, the upper Mississippi, or the Northwest before the 1600s is open for scholarly debate, but after permanent European settlements were established in North America, diseases afflicted those natives too. In short, in the century after European contact with the New World, vast regions were depopulated, losing 90 percent of their pre-1500 numbers, even if we do not know with certainty what the pre-contact population of the Americas was.[16] Nonetheless, it does seem certain that by 1600 tens of millions of people across the Americas had vanished.

Climatologist William Ruddiman thinks the Great Dying may well have contributed to the global cooling of the Little Ice Age. Without those millions of people to tend their farms and to periodically burn trees, forests returned to cover the Americas. That much tree growth, Ruddiman argues, took enough carbon dioxide—what we now know as a "greenhouse gas"—out of the atmosphere to contribute to the cooling of the planet. Well before the problem of human-induced global warming of the twentieth century, human action—or the consequences of it—may have contributed to the opposite human impact on climate—its cooling during the Little Ice Age.[17]

Labor Supply Problems
Even without the Great Dying, the Spaniards would have had a labor problem in the New World because they themselves were not inclined to do manual labor, and getting the native Indians to work for them voluntarily proved

problematic. Enslaving the Indians was also ruled out after a debate within the Catholic Church settled the issue of whether the Indians had souls (ruling that they did). Although not slaves, Indians were compelled by Spaniards to work their fields or their mines in return for providing food, shelter, and Christianity in a system known as the *encomienda*. After the Conquest and the Great Dying, the *encomienda* system was supplemented by another, the *repartimento*. With Indians few and far between, the *repartimento* forced them into small towns laid out in the grid pattern familiar to Spaniards. The combination of these two institutions provided food and clothing for the conquistadors and their followers.

Silver

The "discovery" of the Americas was of course an accident. Columbus sailed west to get to Asia, and on the way stumbled across a huge new continent. But the reason he sought Asia was shared by those who followed him to America: to get rich. Not only did the Spaniards stumble onto America, they stumbled across huge amounts of gold and silver that the Aztecs and the Incas had fashioned into works of art, power, and utility that were theirs for the taking after the Aztecs and Incas had been defeated.

A shortage of Indian labor was not a problem when all the Spaniards had to do was loot the silver and gold already collected in Tenochtitlán and Cuzco (the former Inca capital in Peru), melt it down, and ship it off to Seville. The Great Dying thus was accompanied by a Great Plundering, and that is what characterized the Spanish approach to the New World economy for several decades after the conquest. But that soon changed with the discovery of huge deposits of silver ore in the former Incan empire (now in western Bolivia) and also in Mexico.

The biggest strike was at Potosí in 1545, which soon became a boomtown (at an elevation of more than 13,000 feet) with 150,000 people by 1570. Over the next century, thousands of tons of silver came out of Potosí, especially after the introduction of the mercury refining process. Indians worked in the mines and refined the ore, either because they were forced to do it or because they were drawn to the work and were paid wages. Where to the Spaniards Potosí was a source of fabled wealth ("to be worth a Potosí" became a stock phrase for being rich), to the Indian laborers it was "the mouth of hell." Mining was especially dangerous to begin with, but working with mercury was deadly (it is a poison); over the three centuries that Potosí was operating, it is estimated that eight million Indians—seven out of every ten working the mines—died.

Huge amounts of silver flowed out of the New World, half of it coming from Potosí alone: from 1503 to 1660, over 32 million pounds of silver and 360,000 pounds of gold were exported. But where did it all go? Who provided such an enormous demand for silver that Potosí would sprout in the middle of nowhere and Spaniards were willing to work eight million Indians to death to get their hands on it? After all, the conquistadors had wanted gold, not silver. And yet here they were pumping out silver. Why? There are two parts to the answer to that question.

The Spanish Empire and Its Collapse

With vast sources of newfound wealth apparently at their fingertips, Spain's rulers attempted to bring all of Europe under their dominion. The idea (and ideal) of empire was never far from the surface in sixteenth-century Europe. Indeed, ever since the fall of the Roman Empire, some Europeans had pined for the reestablishment of a universal political order based upon Christianity. For a very long time, hopes rested with the Byzantine empire in the eastern Mediterranean, the defenders of Eastern Orthodox Christianity. But those hopes were dashed when the Ottoman Turks took Constantinople in 1453 and made it into a Muslim city.

Within western Europe, the idea of empire was enshrined in the Holy Roman Empire. More name and hope than reality, the title was revived in 962 when a semi-barbarian Germanic invader took Italy and was crowned "Holy Roman emperor" by the pope. The title, mostly associated with Austria and Germany, persisted until 1806, even though Germany itself was politically fragmented even more than Italy.

But in the early 1500s, it looked like the Spanish might just succeed in creating a real empire in Europe. Ferdinand and Isabella's grandson, Charles V, inherited not just the Spanish crown but claims to Habsburg lands spread throughout Europe (Austria, the Netherlands, Sicily, and Sardinia) as well as New Spain (Mexico) and New Castile (Peru) in the New World. The New World wealth that started flowing into Spain, at first from simply looting Aztec and Inca treasuries, but regularly after the mines at Potosí started operating, gave Charles V and then his successor, Philip II, the resources to attempt to unify their lands. Between the Spanish monarchs and their attempts to unify their lands stood France and the Protestants in the Spanish-claimed territories in the Netherlands, with the English helping Spain's enemies as needed.

War followed war between Spain and France, and the Dutch war of independence (the Protestant Dutch versus the Catholic Spanish, especially heavy in the 1570s) too sapped Spanish strength. Despite the massive amounts of New World silver flowing into Spain, the wars proved so costly that the Spanish crown declared bankruptcy not just once but several times (first in 1557 and 1560, and numerous times thereafter). The English defeat of the Spanish Armada in 1588, followed by further Spanish defeats in Europe (the Thirty Years' War, 1618–48) and in the New World too, sealed the fate of the Spanish attempt to create a European empire. Something new—a competitive system of sovereign nation-states—would take its place, and Spain would not be at its center. Many historians consider the end of the possibility of empire and the emergence instead of nation-states to be one of the critical turning points in West European history.[18] We will come to that later in this chapter. Now we need to return to the second part of the answer to why there was such an interest in digging silver out of the New World.

China's Demand for Silver

Columbus risked the unknown of the Atlantic and Vasco da Gama charted new waters around the Cape of Good Hope to get direct access to the riches of Asia, bypassing the Ottomans and the rest of the Muslim world that controlled the overland routes from the eastern Mediterranean to Asia. Of course, Columbus never got to Asia (although he did think he got there, calling the Native Americans "Indians"), and when the Portuguese sailed into the Indian Ocean and the China Sea, they discovered they were poor and had little money with which to buy Asian spices and manufactured goods (so they extorted the goods with their "armed trading" protection racket). But when the Spaniards stumbled onto the silver of the New World, they found the key to accessing the wealth of Asia. Sort of.

The problem was the Spanish "owned the cow but did not drink the milk," as the saying went. True, the silver flowed from the New World to Seville. But the Spanish monarchs, especially Charles V and Philip II, were constantly warring in their efforts to unite Europe under their empire. The silver thus flowed out of Spain and into the hands of Dutch arms merchants and English and Italian financiers, who then used their newfound silver wealth to finance trade missions to China and the Indian Ocean. Moreover, the Spanish lacked direct access to Asia in any event, those routes being held by the Portuguese, the Dutch, the English, and the French, at least until 1571 when the Spanish seized Manila in the Philippines, established a colony there, and sent galleons loaded with silver directly from Acapulco to Manila.

All told, "approximately three-quarters of the New World silver production" over the three centuries from 1500 to 1800 eventually wound up in China.[19] The reason is that China had a huge demand for silver, both to serve as the basis of its monetary system and to facilitate economic growth. Because the Chinese valued silver, it was expensive there and relatively cheap in the Americas (after looting it, its cost was the cost of production, and that was very low as the deaths of the eight million Indian miners attest). Silver thus flowed from the New World, both through Europe and across the Pacific to the Philippines, to China. As the largest and most productive economy in the world, China was the engine that powered much of the early modern economy, with New World silver providing the energy. It is not too much to say that without China, there would have been no Potosí (or at least a much smaller one). And without Potosí, the Spanish would not have attempted to create an empire in Europe. In short, silver "went around the world and made the world go round," in the words of a recent world historian.[20] Chinese acted, and Europeans reacted. Which, then, were the real agents in the making of the modern world?

In the period from 1500 to 1800, the bulk of the world's population, economic activity, and trade remained Asian, despite the new beginnings made by Europeans in the New World and Asia.[21] In fact, Asia's proportion of the world population rose from about 60 percent around 1500 to 66 percent in 1750 and 67 percent in 1800. Two-thirds of the world's population was Asian as late as 1800, with the bulk of that in China and India. As discussed in chapter 1, in the biological old regime, a growing population is evidence of success in developing additional resources to sustain the larger population.

But not only was Asia's population growing, so too was its economic production and productivity. In 1775, Asians produced about 80 percent of everything in the world, probably an increase from 1500. In other words, two-thirds of the world's population—Asians—produced four-fifths of the world's goods. Seen from another perspective, Europeans, at one-fifth of the world's population in 1775, shared production of one-fifth of the world's goods with Africans and Americans. Asia thus had the most productive economies in the three centuries after 1500.

Evidence for that can be seen in some surprising places, including the New World. In the 1500s, Chinese manufactured goods were so much better and cheaper than European ones that "they quickly ended the domination of markets there by commercial interests in Spain." The Spanish viceroy of Peru thus complained in 1594 to the authorities in Madrid:

Chinese merchandise is so cheap and Spanish goods so dear that I believe it impossible to choke off the trade to such an extent that no Chinese wares will be consumed in this realm, since a man can clothe his wife in Chinese silks for 200 reales [25 pesos], whereas he could not provide her with clothing of Spanish silks with 200 pesos.

In Lima, the citizens also wore Chinese silks, and in Mexico City women wore dresses known as *China poblana*, which were, and remain, the "national dress" of Mexican women. Indeed, Chinese imports were so well made and cheap that they destroyed the Mexican silk industry, even as silk weaving increased because of cheap silk thread imported from China.[22]

The English too found cheap cotton textiles from India to be so superior to anything they could buy locally (either woolens or linens) that Indian imports climbed steadily during the seventeenth century. Indeed, the British were importing so much finished cotton from India by 1700 that it appeared to British textile manufacturers that their industry was doomed by the competition. So, instead of becoming more efficient producers to compete with India, in 1707 they successfully pressured the British government to embargo the importation of Indian cotton. French women found brightly painted Indian calicoes to be so fashionable that laws were passed in 1717 against wearing Indian cotton or Chinese silk clothing in order to protect the French home industry. One Paris merchant went so far as to offer to pay anyone 500 livres who would "strip . . . in the street, any woman wearing Indian fabrics."[23]

I will have more to say about the place of textiles in the story of industrialization in the next chapter. Suffice it to say here that in the global economy, and despite the wealth extracted from the New World, Europeans at the turn of the eighteenth century still were at a competitive disadvantage to Asians. In fact, one way to think about the global situation is that Europeans were so poor relative to Asia and still so peripheral to the real generators of industrial wealth and productivity that they competed mightily among themselves merely to gain the upper hand in dealing in Asian markets. Europe's peripheral position, in other words, heightened competition among European states, leading to attempts to find ways to accumulate wealth and power in a world still dominated by Asia. That is where the New World fits in again.

The New World Economy

Sugar, Slavery, and Ecology

Contributing to the making of the New World economy was the establishment and growth of a plantation system using imported African slave labor, initially for the production of sugar[24] but eventually adapted to tobacco in the seventeenth century and cotton in the eighteenth century. The Portuguese played an essential role in this process by experimenting with the best way to exploit their colonial possession in Brazil. With so few Portuguese willing to migrate to Brazil, the Portuguese had no choice but to rely upon the native Tupi, who, to put it mildly, had little desire to work on farms and instead fled into the forest. Even enslaving the Tupi did little to resolve the Portuguese labor shortage, which became acute after the introduction of European diseases further reduced the Tupi population. The solution was the use of African slaves.

Even before the discovery of the New World, the Portuguese had already worked out a slave-based plantation system for sugar production on the islands off the coast of Africa they had conquered in their quest for a sea route to Asia (borrowing from even earlier Spanish and Genoan success in the Mediterranean). The story of how that happened from the 1420s on is quite instructive for what happened later in the New World, for it involved the massive ecological change of tropical forests into sugar plantations, the enslavement and extermination of a native people (the Guanches), and then the importation of African slaves to work the sugar plantations.[25] All of this happened before Columbus stumbled on the Americas, but it did give the Portuguese experience in slave-based plantations, which they quickly adapted to the depopulated New World; by the 1580s, slavery and sugar plantations were dominant features of the Portuguese colony in Brazil.

The French and the English also created slave-based sugar plantations on Caribbean islands. Soon after the British took Barbados, in 1640, settlers started clearing the land for sugar plantations, with sugar exported to the home country in the 1650s. The sugar industry expanded rapidly, especially after Britain took the island of Jamaica—thirty times the size of Barbados—from the Spanish. The French also established sugar plantations in the Caribbean, starting on Martinique, exporting sugar back to France. By the late seventeenth century, so much English and French sugar was being exported back to the home countries that the competition drove Brazilian sugar from northern Europe. Ultimately, the British and French had so totally deforested several Caribbean islands for sugar that erosion wrecked the fertility of the soil (as in Haiti) and changed local climates as well.[26]

The ecological changes wrought by the sugar plantation complex had further unintended consequences, in particular for the spread of the deadly mosquito-borne diseases of yellow fever and malaria, neither of which had existed in the Americas prior to 1492. Each is caused by a virus spread to humans through the bites of particular kinds of mosquitoes. Neither the yellow fever virus nor its mosquito carrier had existed in the Americas, so for it to get established and spread disease to humans required that both be transmitted to the Americas. For malaria, there were at least three host genera of mosquitoes already in the Americas—all that was missing was the malaria virus.

The common causal factor in creating these disease ecologies in the Americas was the sugar plantation. Cutting down forests in Brazil and on Caribbean islands created ditches and other lowland sources of fresh water; cattle and other hooved animals left indentations in the ground that filled with rainwater. African slaves brought with them in their bodies the malaria virus, so that when bitten by one of the indigenous mosquito species that could carry the virus, it could be passed to other humans when bitten by the same mosquito. For yellow fever, the mosquito itself was transported to the Americas in the casks of drinking water on European ships. Further spreading ecologies favorable to malaria was the building of rice paddies to provide food for slaves.

Historian John McNeill argues not just that these diseases spread to the Americas as part of the Columbian Exchange, but that their existence played important historical roles in the outcomes of wars and revolutions in the Americas. The reason, he argues, has to do with the fact that survivors of yellow fever had acquired immunity to the disease, while Africans already had acquired resistance to malaria, and every time they were reintroduced to the virus, that immunity was renewed. The importance here is that populations not immune or resistant—such as armies composed of northern Europeans—could be severely affected. This fact, McNeill thinks, explains why the Spanish empire in Mexico and the Caribbean could resist English or French attacks and last for so long—with the help of these diseases. Similarly, American rebels in the southeast had acquired immunity to malaria, whereas the British Redcoats had not, and the African, largely urban, leaders of the Haitian Revolution (1791–1804) were immune to yellow fever, but the French were not. Certainly, the story behind all of this is much more complicated, interesting, and contingent than this very brief overview can possibly convey, but it does show how complex the interactions among all of the various elements of the story behind the history of the Americas after 1492 truly were.[27]

The number of African slaves taken to work the New World plantations is astounding, numbering over twelve million people by the time the slave trade ended in the 1800s; by 1650, "Africans were the majority of new settlers in the new Atlantic world."[28] For nearly three hundred years, European slave traders, at first Portuguese and Dutch but eventually mostly British, took thousands of African slaves every year to the Americas, leaving a lasting impact not only on African but on American (North and South) society as well. Although those effects are historically important,[29] here we are mostly interested in how the slave-based plantation system fit in with the world economy.

Two triangles of trade linked the Atlantic world, arising in the seventeenth century and maturing in the eighteenth century. The first, and by far the best known, linked England to Africa and the New World. Commodities from the Americas (not just sugar but timber and fish from North America too) went to England (and from there to its trading partners); finished goods (increasingly cotton textiles from India) were taken to Africa, where they were exchanged for slaves; and slaves were taken to the Americas. The other triangle went in another direction. From England's North American colonies, rum went to Africa in exchange for slaves; slaves went to the Caribbean; and molasses (from sugar refining) went to New England to produce more rum.[30]

In all of these transactions, Europeans and North American colonists made money and accumulated wealth. Indeed, the Atlantic trade was three times as large as Europeans' trade with Asia.[31] The question of the extent to which slavery and the plantation economy benefited Europeans and allowed them to compete more effectively and in the world economy will be taken up in more detail in the next chapter. For now, we need note only that seventeenth- and eighteenth-century Europeans competed not only in a world economy dominated by Asian manufactures, but among themselves as well. The end of the Spanish attempt to create an empire in Europe soon led to the creation of a new system linking European states and pushing the development of the state and its power.

Human Migration and the Early Modern World

Humans have been migrating from one part of the world to another since we first evolved as a species some 200,000 years ago in eastern Africa.[32] From there, in the words of historian Patrick Manning, "Our ancestors dispersed progressively as they colonized the African continent, then all of Eurasia, Australasia, the Americas, and ultimately every piece of land on earth."[33] Almost everyone on Earth is descended from relatives who have moved from one place to another. People have migrated for various reasons, including improvement of their or their families' economic, social, or political standing, spreading religious ideas, fleeing environmental or climatic disasters,[34] or just seeing the world. Sometimes those decisions are freely made by individuals or family heads, and at other times the decision to migrate was made by others and forced on people, as in the case of slavery, or when wars send people fleeing. And when people migrate to other parts of the world already inhabited by others, that usually requires learning new languages and cultures. In the early modern world, most of the migration has been of the latter type, which Manning terms "cross-community migration."

In the early modern world, the movement of people was facilitated by the new and improved maritime technologies that made the voyages of Zheng He, Columbus, and da Gama possible. Behind nearly all of the historical processes discussed in this chapter lay the migration of people, forced or otherwise. The expansion of the Mongol, Chinese, Russian, Ottoman, Portuguese, and Atlantic world empires caused people to move within the borders of these empires, and sometimes to flee them as well. The knitting together of a single global world by explorers, conquerors, and merchants permanently changed the world as all parts of the inhabited world came into regular and sustained contact with each other. Migration and globalization proceeded hand in hand.[35]

Migrants established settler colonies of various kinds in the Americas, the South African Cape, Melaka, Singapore, and Manila, among other ports and outposts. Mostly, these migrants were free men (as in Spanish and Portuguese America) who often had children with local women, creating mestizo cultures and communities and the exchange of languages, religions, tools, and foodstuffs, among other things. These communities were the result of the actions of colonizers upon the colonized and enslaved, and their creation was accompanied by much violence, trauma, and oppression. In Latin America, native cultures were not obliterated by the conquest and the forced in-migration of African slaves, but by a two-way process of "transculturation" created new cultures.[36] Migration of English settlers to New England in North America was unusual in that mostly the migrants were existing family units. Throughout the world, wherever sailing ships could reach, creole societies—a combination of migration and colonial rule in the Americas, Africa, and Asia—developed, and because most of the ships sailing under European flags had Christian kings or queens, missionaries and proselytization accompanied merchants and trade.[37]

Throughout this chapter, we have seen how ocean-crossing voyages led to vast amounts of new trade between and among the parts of the world, but also to the conquest of the Americas, the Great Dying and much more human suffering, the Columbian Exchange, and the enslavement of Africans. Indeed, in the early modern world the greatest migration of people was that caused by slavery. For three centuries, up to 100,000 enslaved Africans annually were shipped to the Americas to work in the plantations and mines.

The slave trade was racialized and gendered, with two-thirds being young African males, affecting African communities in both the Americas and Africa. Although enslaved, Africans brought with them their languages, religious practices, and skills, and created their own cultures despite the repression and dehumanizing practices of slave owners, as a pioneering study showed.[38] Insights into the mostly horrific lived experience of American slaves comes from slave narratives; two notable memoirs are by Olaudah Equiano who purchased his freedom,[39] and another by Solomon Northup, a free Negro in Massachusetts who was kidnapped and sold into slavery;[40] a film based on his memoir, 12 Years a Slave, won three Academy Awards in 2014. As we will see in chapter 5, the end of American slavery after the Civil War (1860–65) spawned another mass migration of former slaves out of the southern states.

Migrations large and small in the early modern world crossed borders, but mostly linguistic and cultural ones. Boundary lines between empires were somewhat fuzzy but not necessarily porous. In East Asia at least, China's Qing empire negotiated its northern border with Russia and then established outposts to patrol it,[41] and in Japan the Tokugawa regime (1600–1868) enforced a "closed country" policy. In both cases, Europeans were permitted coastal enclaves from which they were allowed to conduct trade on a very restricted basis.

Overall the cultural, biological, and genetic contact facilitated by maritime ventures certainly was new, and in many ways it permanently changed the world order, especially because of the Columbian Exchange not just between the Americas and Europe but Asia too. The world was becoming permanently interconnected, and migrants were the living tissue that held it together. Globalization was more than just an economic process; it was composed of people who certainly benefited from the opportunities that sailing ships and military power brought, while for other people globalization brought misery, whether as enslaved Africans working sugar plantations or as indentured European servants tending tobacco patches.

The Global Crisis of the Seventeenth Century
and the European State System

Historians have long known that in the seventeenth century many of the states in the world had become embroiled in rebellions, revolutions, social crises, population declines, and sharp economic downturns known as the "general crisis of the seventeenth century," a vast conjuncture of human and natural forces. We now know as well that that crisis was linked both causally and temporally with the cooling of the global climate known as the Little Ice Age.[42] Many of the Eurasian empires discussed in this chapter—China, Russia, and the Ottomans especially—were thrown into crisis in the seventeenth century. Cooler to cold climatic conditions accompanying the Little Ice Age sent harvest yields tumbling, throwing rural populations into crisis mode. Civil wars in China and Russia intensified the downward pressure on food supplies as rulers of those states refused to acknowledge the declining food supplies and instead continued to extract taxes to pay for their wars and to feed strategically important urban centers. Not surprisingly, the combination of climate change and warfare killed off huge numbers of rural people. Those living through the carnage—variously estimated at a third to a half of their populations—died of famine and starvation. Among the Eurasian empires, the only rulers who recognized that cooling temperatures put their rural subjects in danger from food shortages were the Mughals ruling India, who not only held off collecting taxes in those circumstances but actually provided tax relief.[43]

Nearly all European states not only had internal crises comparable to those of the Eurasian empires, but also engaged other European states in warfare. The Thirty Years' War (1618–48) embroiled nearly all European states in war, and the short-sightedness, greed, or fear of their rulers meant that all of Europe suffered not just from declining harvests brought on by the cold but from heightened taxes to pay for the wars. The stupidity and venality of European rulers recounted by historian Geoffrey Parker in his study of the seventeenth-century global crisis, especially in Germany, where perhaps half of the population died of war- and climate-induced famine, highlights the immense costs Europeans bore on their way to the 1648 Peace of Westphalia that extricated Europe from the seventeenth-century horrors of war, famine, and death.[44]

Warfare thus defined the emerging European state system. Until the mid-seventeenth century, wars were mostly fought to stop the Spanish from establishing an empire or to support Protestants (in Holland and the German states) in their attempts to gain independence from the Catholic monarchs of Spain. Where the large Eurasian agrarian empires emerged from the depths of the crisis renewed or at least reconstituted, the European state system was significantly changed by the seventeenth-century crisis. From the 1648 Peace of Westphalia, which ended the Thirty Years' War, wars mostly involved France, whose fortunes had risen while Spain's declined, and then, from the late 1600s on, contests were mostly between France and England, culminating in the Seven Years' War (1754–63), or what Americans call the French and Indian War, leading to Britain's victory over France. The Treaty of Westphalia defined what it meant to be the "sovereign" of a state and began the process of institutionalizing the multistate system—albeit one defined by "the rules of war"—that came to define Europe.

There are many things that are historically significant about wars among European states in the period we are considering in this chapter (i.e., from 1500 to 1775). First, the wars involved virtually all European states, tying them in a single system, especially after the Peace of Westphalia. That can be seen quite clearly in two schematic charts prepared by the historian Charles Tilly (see figure 3.1).[45] In these charts, which represent two different periods (Europe ca. 1500 and ca. 1650), the thin lines represent one war and the bold lines two or more wars between the states connected. Where there were two subsystems in 1500, with the western one focused on Italy, by 1650 all European states were embroiled in a common set of entanglements defined by war.

Second, wars in Europe led both to consolidation into increasingly fewer political units and to the development of a particular kind of national state as the most successful form of European state. Tilly's work again supplies the basic data. Beginning around 1000 CE, the thirty million or so people who lived in the area we now call Europe lived in a bewildering array of political units headed by "emperors, kings, princes, dukes, caliphs, sultans, and other potentates." These titles, Tilly warns us, should not hide the fact of stupendous political fragmentation in Europe: in Italy alone there were two hundred to three hundred city-states. Five hundred years later, around 1500, "Europe's 80 million people divided into something like 500 states, would-be states, statelets, and state-like organizations." From then on, warfare reduced the number of European states until modern times when there were about thirty or so.[46]

Where the Spanish Habsburg empire proved to be too large and inefficient to mobilize its own resources against the English or the French, the wealthy city-states of Italy lacked the manpower to campaign outside of Italy

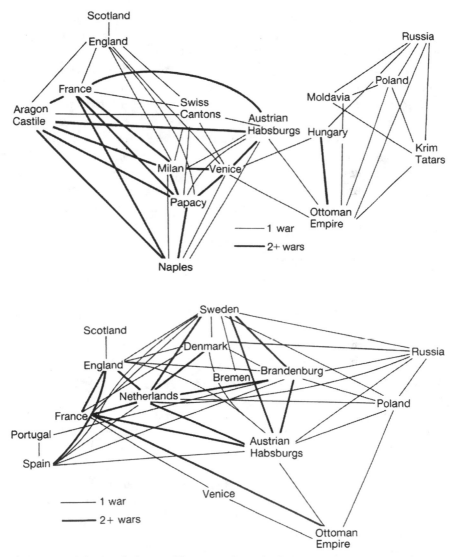

Figure 3.1. Joint Involvement of European States in Great Power Wars, 1496–1514 (top) and 1656–74 (bottom)

Source: Charles Tilly, *Coercion, Capital, and European States, A.D. 990–1990* (Oxford: Basil Blackwell, 1990), 176–77.

against larger armies. Similarly, the various principalities of Germany, while strong enough to fend one another off, found it hard to keep larger states from interfering in their affairs. Small states like Sweden or Holland, which had some resources that allowed them to be international players in the seventeenth century, fell by the wayside in the eighteenth century as larger states came to dominate European politics. On the other hand, some large and populous states such as Poland, with a small nobility ruling over a large enserfed peasantry, could not field large enough armies to compete; Poland thus was partitioned at the end of the eighteenth century.

In this context, the third interesting consequence of war was the way it affected the internal evolution of European states, favoring some kinds but not others. The rulers of European states were not rich, and wars were expensive. Basically, European rulers could tap two sources of revenue. First, they could tax, but taxes usually met resistance from landowners, who could pass those tax hikes along to their farming peasants, but at the risk of inciting rebellion. Hence, to gain the right to levy and use taxes, most European rulers had to negotiate with landowning elites, usually resulting in the establishment of some form of representative assembly that rulers were supposed to consult before imposing or raising taxes. Besides assemblies of landowners, the other institution growing up with taxation was the state bureaucracy necessary to assess and collect taxes from the known subject population, rather than "farming" the collection of taxes out to private parties. The tensions arising from both of these processes account for much of the internal political history of many European states in the centuries from 1500 to 1800.

A second source of revenue was loans from bankers or other wealthy people. The sixteenth-century Spanish monarchs, for instance, had to rely on loans to finance their wars, but much of the money came from bankers outside of Spain or Spanish control, an early form of the globalization of capital, if you will. All European rulers had to rely on both short- and long-term loans to prosecute their wars, and it thus became in their interest to encourage those with capital to reside in their cities. The English and the Dutch were most successful at this, in part because of their religious tolerance and willingness to take in wealthy Protestants and Jews unwelcome in Catholic lands. But even loans from one's own subjects had to be repaid, leading the British to institute "the national debt" in the late 1600s, an innovation of immense importance in enabling British power to expand.

England's national debt was in effect long-term loans secured by the Bank of England, or in other words "bonds." Other European rulers had often attempted to resolve their financial difficulties by consolidating short-term into long-term debt, but these were secured on the ability of the ruler to repay. The English innovation was to issue the bonds through the Bank of England, established in 1694, and to guarantee them with the subscribed capital of the bank. The national debt not only provided British rulers with ready sources of cash for their wars, but also gave investors a relatively safe investment instrument, thereby attracting even more deposits to the Bank of England.

In summary, the wars of European states drove their expenses well above the amount of silver that was left in European hands after it was used to buy Asian products, leading to standing armies and navies, taxation and state bureaucracies to collect it, representative assemblies of various kinds demanded by the taxed subjects so they could influence the level of taxation (even though Europe's "absolute monarchs" tried mightily to ignore or shut down these institutions), public indebtedness, and the institution of the national debt. All of these activities were part of a "state-building" process in seventeenth- and eighteenth-century Europe, the conjuncture of a process set in motion by the end of empire in Europe and the impact of the Little Ice Age on European states. The collapse of the Spanish attempt to impose an empire over western Europe, followed by the Thirty Years' War in the early seventeenth century, opened the way for a differently organized state system to emerge in the aftermath of the 1648 Treaty of Westphalia.

State Building

European rulers would resort to force, if necessary, to gain access to the resources needed to conduct war, but rulers considered it preferable if their subjects would more voluntarily render those resources to the state. Rulers thus made various claims to legitimacy, that is, the idea that subjects should willingly obey their ruler. In the sixteenth and seventeenth centuries, these claims to legitimacy rested on religious grounds, expressed as "the divine right of kings," that is, that the Christian God gave them the right to rule. During the global crisis of the seventeenth century, even while harvests declined and farming populations were pressed ever closer to the edge of hunger or famine, kings under their "divine right" to rule demanded their taxes to be able to press their wars, even though their subjects suffered. These religious claims also led European monarchs, in particular the Catholic ones, to expel non-Catholics from their territory. Spain's Ferdinand and Isabella's 1494 expulsion of the Jews and Muslims (whom they called "Moors") was an early example, but so too was the late-seventeenth-century French persecution of Protestants (the Huguenots). The Spanish Inquisition was also part of this process of ensuring that subjects throughout their realms in Europe and the Americas were Catholic and loyal.

In the aftermath of the seventeenth-century crisis, the European Enlightenment of the late seventeenth and eighteenth centuries challenged the idea of the "divine right" of monarchs to rule, positing more democratic ones based upon the construction of the rights of the individual. Expounded most forcefully by the French "philosophes" in their struggle against the absolutisms of the French state and the Catholic Church, these ideas began to broaden the legitimate basis upon which a state could be established to include the consent of the governed, the "citizens." By the end of the eighteenth century and in the aftermath of the French Revolution of 1789, these were the ideas the French used to justify the execution of their monarchs and the establishment of a republic.[47]

In the competitive, war-driven environment in Europe, some states thus had advantages that ultimately led a particular kind of state—one that had cities with large accumulations of capital and rural hinterlands with a population large enough to sustain armies—to become the most successful. For reasons that need not concern us, in the centuries after about 1000 CE, cities in Europe tended to develop in a band extending north from Tuscany in Italy, across the Alps to Ghent, Bruges, and London; Paris also grew. To this day, this band is Europe's most urbanized zone. Cities provided the rulers of states encompassing them with opportunities to tax urban-to-rural trade, to gain access to funding from banks and thereby to avoid reliance on rural nobility for support, and generally to strengthen themselves: in general, to command more resources of all kinds, but especially money and men, than less-blessed competitors farther away from cities.[48] The rulers of two states in particular—England and France—proved to be most able to build that kind of state, combining the capital resources to be found in London or Paris with the manpower that could be tapped from the rural population. And, having built powerful states, England and France came to be intense competitors by the late seventeenth century.

The English proved willing and able to use state power for economic ends. In their struggles against Dutch competitors, the English had passed a series of Navigation Acts in the mid-seventeenth century designed to restrict the trade of their colonies in the New World to England only and to enforce those acts with force if necessary.[49] The Glorious Revolution of 1688–89 brought Protestant monarchs to the English throne, who agreed to abide by the laws of a Parliament dominated by domestic manufacturing interests; in

1707 Parliament then passed laws restricting the importation of Indian cotton textiles into England in order to protect British manufacturers and to encourage the development of a British cotton textile industry. By the eighteenth century, England had a government that was prepared to use state policy to support textile manufacturing, and as we will see in the next chapter, coal and iron too.[50]

Mercantilism

For its part, France too was building a strong state, and under the guidance of Jean-Baptiste Colbert, its minister of finance in the late seventeenth century, it implemented economic policies that came to be known as mercantilism. European rulers always seemed to be short of money to pay for their wars. Even the Spanish complained in the 1580s that "experience has shown that within a month or two of the arrival of a fleet from the Indies, not a farthing is to be seen." An English businessman likewise complained in the 1620s of the "scarcity of coin."[51] The reason is that although Europe's stock of money increased (especially from 1580 to 1620), by 1620 it probably declined as silver mining in Europe collapsed, American silver declined, and the outflow to Asia increased. Not only were European states competing on the battlefield, they were competing to attract and retain as much silver and gold bullion as possible.

In the intensely competitive European context, it appeared that one state could gain only if another lost: it was a war of each against all in which "looking out for number one" was the highest principle. And the best way for a state to gain advantage, according to mercantilist theory, was to attract and then to keep the largest possible quantity of the world's stock of precious metals, especially silver (and later, gold). The reason for the need for bullion reserves was simple: wars were very costly, arms had to be purchased, in many instances from weapons makers outside the monarch's own country,[52] and campaigning in a foreign country required vast amounts of silver or gold. To keep precious metals in one's own state therefore required economic policies that prevented them from flowing out in payment for, well, anything imported, especially for goods consumed and not used in war.

European states therefore imposed duties on virtually all imported goods, required that all goods be transported in their ships, and forced European New World colonists to trade only with the mother country, even if smuggling made such a policy somewhat porous. Mercantilist ideas also led to policies that states should use their own raw materials to manufacture within their own borders anything that was imported, an action we saw the English

Map 3.1.   The World circa 1760

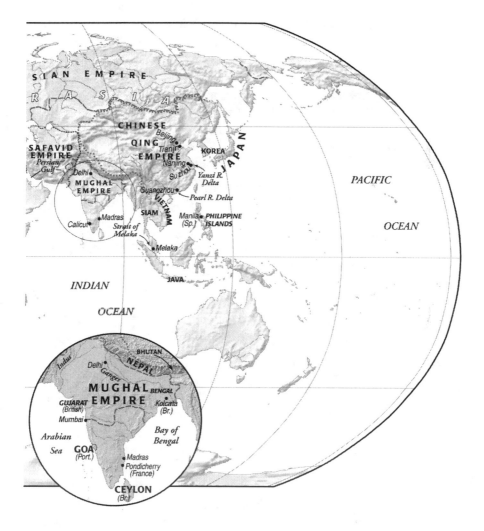

SIAN EMPIRE

E U R A S I A

CHINESE

QING

EMPIRE

Beijing

Tianjin

KOREA

JAPAN

Nanjing

Suzhou

Yanzi R.
Delta

Delhi

MUGHAL
EMPIRE

Guangzhou

Pearl R. Delta

SAFAVID
EMPIRE

Persian
Gulf

VIETNAM

Madras

SIAM

Manila
(Sp.)

PHILIPPINE
ISLANDS

Calicut

Strait of
Melaka

Melaka

PACIFIC

OCEAN

INDIAN

OCEAN

JAVA

BHUTAN

NEPAL

Delhi

Ganges

Indus

MUGHAL EMPIRE

BENGAL

GUJARAT
(British)

Kolcata
(Br.)

Mumbai

Arabian
Sea

GOA
(Port.)

Bay of
Bengal

Madras

Pondicherry
(France)

CEYLON
(Br.)

take in the early 1700s to keep Indian cotton textiles out. Although mercantilist policies did indeed lead to the establishment of industries in European
states, industrialization itself was not the object: keeping gold and silver from
flowing out of the state and enriching others was. European states were
obsessed with their silver stocks: "the more silver, the stronger the state" was
how a German once put it.[53]

In these inter-European wars, the fates and fortunes of various states rose
and fell. As we have already seen, by the end of the sixteenth century,
Spain's power had begun to wane, and Portugal proved to be too small to
mount much of a challenge to the French (or Spanish) in Europe, or to the
Dutch in Asian waters. The Dutch, being among the first Europeans to apply
vast amounts of capital to their trading enterprises in both Asia and the
Americas, saw their fortunes peak in the seventeenth century, just as the
French and the British were gaining power. Ultimately, though, the Dutch
did not have the manpower to build a standing army sufficiently large to
counter the French, and they ultimately allied with the British to offset
French power on the continent. By the eighteenth century, Britain and
France had emerged from the seventeenth-century crisis as the two most
powerful and competitive European states (see map 3.1).

The Seven Years' War, 1756–63

As the strongest and most successful European states, England and France
competed not just in Europe but in the Americas and Asia as well. In the
"long" eighteenth century from 1689 to 1815, Britain and France fought five
wars, only one of which Britain did not initiate. Their engagement (with
others) in the War of Spanish Succession was ended by the 1713 Treaty of
Utrecht, which established the principle of the "balance of power" in
Europe, that is, that no country should be allowed to dominate the others.
However, periodic wars between the British and French continued.

The most significant was the Seven Years' War of 1756–63, or what
Americans call the French and Indian War and interpret in terms of its
impact on the American War of Independence of 1776–83 against Britain.
To be sure, the spark that led to war between Britain and France came in
the American colonies, and it was in fact the twenty-two-year-old George
Washington who lit it.[54] But it became a global engagement—perhaps the
first real world war—with British and French troops fighting in the back-
woods of the American colonies, in Canada, in Africa, in India, and in
Europe. The outcome was disastrous for the French: they lost their colonial

claims in both North America (the British got Canada) and in India, leading to greater British power and position in both parts of the world.[55]

By 1775, therefore, the processes of state building in Europe had led to the creation of a system defined by war, which favored a particular kind of state exemplified by the ones built in Britain and France. Balance of power among sovereign states, not a unified empire, had become the established principle, and Britain had emerged as the strongest European state. But that does not mean that it was the strongest or richest state in the world—far from it. To be sure, Mughal power in India was declining in the early 1700s, and as we will see in the next chapter, the British were able to begin building a colonial empire there. But the British were still too weak to be able to contest China's definition of the rules of trade in Asia. When they tried, most famously in 1793 under Lord Macartney's mission, the Chinese emperor sent them home with a stinging rebuke, and the British could do nothing about it. However, the British Isles were fortunate enough to be the location for the start of the Industrial Revolution, which was gaining steam even as Lord Macartney was sailing back to London. And when the British learned to apply the tools of the Industrial Revolution to war, the global balance of power between Britain and China tipped. That world-changing conjuncture is the story of the next chapter.

CHAPTER FOUR

The Industrial Revolution and Its Consequences, 1750–1850

In 1750, nearly all of the world's 750 million people, regardless of where they were or what political or economic system they had, lived and died within the biological old regime. The necessities of life—food, clothing, shelter, and fuel for heating and cooking—mostly came from the land, from what could be captured from annual energy flows from the sun to Earth.[1] Industries too, such as textiles, leather, and construction, depended on products from agriculture or the forest. Even iron and steel making in the biological old regime, for instance, relied upon charcoal made from wood. The biological old regime thus set limits not just on the size of the human population but on the productivity of the economy as well.

These limits would begin to be lifted over the century from 1750 to 1850, when some people increasingly used coal to produce heat and then captured that heat to fuel repetitive motion with steam-powered machines, doing work that previously had been done with muscle. The use of coal-fired steam to power machines was a major breakthrough, launching human society out of the biological old regime and into a new one no longer limited by annual solar energy flows. Coal is stored solar energy, laid down hundreds of millions of years ago. Its use in steam engines freed human society from the limits imposed by the biological old regime, enabling the productive powers and numbers of humans to grow exponentially. The replacement—with steam generated by burning coal—of wind, water, and animals for powering industrial machines constitutes the beginning of the Industrial Revolution[2] and ranks with the much earlier agricultural revolution in importance for the course of history. The use of fossil fuels—first coal and then petroleum—not only transformed economies around the world but also added greenhouse gases to Earth's atmosphere. How and why this major transformation happened, and what consequences it had, thus are vitally important matters in world history and will be the focus of this and the following two chapters.

To understand the Industrial Revolution, we will use once again the tool of *conjuncture*, that is, the coming together at a particular point in time of otherwise separate historical developments and processes. In the case of the Industrial Revolution, the conjuncture involves the playing out around the world of growth potential in the biological old regime, the extension of European state conflicts around the globe, the peculiar nature of New World colonies, and the chance location of, and challenges for operating, coal mines in England. In particular, I will consider the ways cotton textiles and the British need for coal contributed to the Industrial Revolution.

Cotton Textiles

The Industrial Revolution is commonly thought to have begun in eighteenth-century England with the mechanization of the process for spinning and weaving cotton thread and cloth. The spinning jenny, the water frame, and the "mule" all have been taken as evidence of English inventiveness and hence contribute to a Eurocentric story line of the rise of the West. The problem is, while it is true that England was the first place to revolutionize cotton manufacture by using steam-powered machinery, how and why it happened can only be understood in a global context, and that explanation is what this chapter will provide.[3]

In the late seventeenth century, the English developed a strong desire for the Indian cotton textiles commonly known as calicoes. As one man observed: "On a sudden we saw all our women, rich and poor, cloath'd in Callico, printed and painted; the gayer the better." Another complained: "It crept into our houses, our closets and bedchambers; curtains, cushions, chairs, and at last beds themselves were nothing but Callicoes or Indian stuffs. In short, almost everything that used to be made of wool or silk, relating either to dress of the women or the furniture of our houses, was supplied by the Indian trade."[4] These observations by contemporaries around 1700 raise some interesting questions: Why were the English importing so much Indian cotton? How did it get there? How did they then create and industrialize their own cotton textile industry?

The reason the English imported so much Indian cotton around 1700 is it was of high quality and lower price than England's domestically produced textiles (in particular linen and wool). It felt good next to the skin, it was lightweight for summer wear, it could accept bright dyes for color, and most of all, it was less expensive than anything the English could manufacture themselves. Indeed, India around 1700 was the largest exporter of cotton textiles in the world and supplied textiles not just to meet English demand, but throughout the world as well. Southeast Asia, East and West Africa, the Middle East, and Europe were major export markets, in addition to the large domestic Indian market. No wonder that the demand for Indian cotton in the eighteenth century was "greater than all the weavers in the country can manufacture," and that India accounted for fully one-quarter of the world manufacturing output in 1750.[5]

Like so many things desired by Europeans and supplied by Asians—at first luxury items for the elite such as silk or porcelain, but increasingly products like tea from China for a mass market[6]—cotton textiles were produced well and cheaply in India. The British textile manufacturers focused on the "cheap" part and complained that with relatively higher wages, British manufacturers could not compete. India had a competitive advantage in the eighteenth century, being able to undersell in the world market virtually any other producer of textiles. Some thought the reason for cheap Indian textiles was a low living standard, or a large population earning depressed wages, but all of those claims have been shown to not be true: Indian textile workers in the eighteenth century had just as high a standard of living as British workers.[7] So, if it was not a low standard of living that gave India its competitive advantage, what did?

In a word: agriculture. Indian agriculture was so productive that the amount of food produced, and hence its cost, was significantly lower than in Europe. In the preindustrial age, when working families spent 60 to 80 percent of their earnings on food, the cost of food was the primary determinant of their real wages (i.e., how much a pound, a dollar, a real, or a pagoda could buy). In India (and China and Japan as well), the amount of grain harvested from a given amount of seed was in the ratio of 20:1 (e.g., twenty bushels of rice harvested for every one planted), whereas in England it was at best 8:1. Asian agriculture thus was more than twice as efficient as British (and by extension European) agriculture, and food—the major component in the cost of living—cost less in Asia. Thus although nominal wages may have been lower in India, the purchasing power—the real wage—was higher in India.

In the biological old regime, productive agriculture was Asia's competitive advantage, even in industry. The causal chain went like this: high per-acre yields → low-priced food → relatively low wages → comparative advantage. In England, the causal chain was like this: low per-acre yields → high-priced food → relatively high wages → comparative disadvantage. The question then becomes: How did the British begin to reverse this comparative disadvantage?

In part, as we saw in the previous chapter, they did it by raising tariffs on imports to Britain of Indian textiles, and the outright banning of the importation of some kinds of Indian cotton goods—that is, mercantilist protectionism. Had the British not done that in the early eighteenth century, there is little reason to believe they would have made much progress in competing against Indian producers and establishing much of a cotton textile industry in the first place.[8] But also, the British had colonies in the Americas and acquired their colonial "jewel" in India. Both became intimately connected with the story of the rise of a cotton textile industry in Britain.

India

Indeed, where England had very little by way of overseas empire in 1650, it soon began putting one together, preying on Portuguese and Spanish possessions in the East and West Indies (i.e., India and the Caribbean), competing with the Dutch in both regions of the world, and battling France in the eighteenth century. Curiously, though, the agents for this extension of European interstate conflict around the world were not at first the governments of European states but private trading companies, the first being the Dutch Vereenigde Oost-Indische Compagnie (VOC, East India Company), the English East India Company (EIC), and the Compagnie française des Indes occidentales (French West India Company).

Although each was formed at different times and had slightly different organization, all were private companies chartered by their governments and given monopoly rights to trade with Asia, all in keeping with mercantilist ideas. They also differed from mere trading expeditions in that they were formed with a permanent capital and stock that could be traded—to that extent, the East India companies are the forerunners of the modern corporation, and their success at organizing trade and raising profits meant that the corporation would play an increasingly important role in European industrialization. But in the seventeenth and eighteenth centuries, their purpose was to reap profits from trade with Asia.

The Dutch VOC, though, seeing itself as an extension of Protestant Dutch interests and hence deeply hostile to the Catholic powers of Spain and Portugal, saw trade and war as intimately connected. In a terse 1614 letter to his directors, the Dutch VOC governor-general observed: "You gentlemen ought to know from experience that trade in Asia should be conducted and maintained under the protection and with the aid of your own weapons, and . . . [s]o trade cannot be maintained without war, nor war without trade."[9] The Dutch then effectively pursued this strategy throughout the seventeenth century, taking Melaka from the Portuguese, seizing Java and making it into a sugar-producing colony, and trying to establish a colony on the Chinese island of Taiwan.

The English EIC, by contrast, was more interested in trade and the profits of trade than in war, at least at first. In the century after its founding in 1600, the directors insisted that "our business is trade, not war."[10] To avoid conflicts, the English EIC concentrated trade in India, where Indian states were weak and European competitors few, especially in Bengal and Madras. But by the late seventeenth century, that began to change as the French established forts nearby. And when the British and French warred in Europe, their forces (however small) clashed in India, with the French usually getting the upper hand because they began enhancing their war-making capability by enlisting Indians as regulars, known as Sepoys, into their army. In the 1750s the British EIC followed suit, and by the eve of the Seven Years' War, each had nearly ten thousand men in arms—mostly Indians—on the Indian coast.

In the meantime, the political and military power of the great Mughal empire had seriously declined. At its height of power it was capable of mobilizing perhaps a million troops; after the death of its last great leader, Aurangzeb, in 1707, the empire declined as regional political and military leaders asserted their independence from the Mughals. One of those leaders, the nawab of Bengal, took control of the British trading port at Kolkata (Calcutta) and demanded increased payments from the EIC for the privilege of trading there.

The British resisted, sent a force of some two thousand men under the leadership of Robert Clive and, together with other Indian forces opposed to Bengal, defeated the nawab's French-assisted forces at the Battle of Plassey in 1757. They captured and executed the nawab, got a more pliable replacement, and by 1765 received the right to collect tax revenue—a huge sum—from Bengal. In the meantime, of course, the Seven Years' War had begun, and British and French forces had at it up and down the Indian coast, with the British winning a decisive victory over the French at Pondicherry in 1760. This was the start of the British empire in India, and over the next fifty years the extent of British control widened, with the entire subcontinent becoming a formal colony in 1857 (see map 3.1).

The Seven Years' War—or more precisely, the British victory in the Americas and in India—is important to the story of how Britain became a cotton-textile-producing, rather than -importing, country. Recall that the British government had banned the importation of Indian textiles in 1707 for the purpose of allowing its domestic cotton industry to get going, which it did, in the area around the town of Lancaster. But because of technical difficulties in copying Indian dyeing techniques and because of its higher wages/higher prices, Lancashire (the region around Lancaster) produced mostly for the British home market, still being bested in the world market by Indian textiles traded by the EIC. For the British cotton textile industry to grow, it therefore needed export markets. And there was a growing market in the New World because of its peculiar institutions of slavery, plantations, and mercantilist trade restrictions.

The New World as a Peculiar Periphery

European New World agriculture from the beginning was export oriented. Throughout the Caribbean and South America, mostly all sugar, tobacco, and cotton was produced on plantations that used African slaves because of labor shortages caused by the Great Dying and the unwillingness of Europeans to migrate to the New World. Unlike peasants in India and China or serfs in eastern Europe, African slaves in America did not grow much of their own food. Food, especially fish and grain, had to be imported, mostly from the North American colonies. Slaves also had to be clothed, creating a demand for cheap cotton textiles. Additional quantities of Indian textiles were traded in West Africa for slaves who were then sold in the Caribbean. New World products—sugar, tobacco, raw cotton—were taken back to England.[11]

At each point in the triangular Atlantic trade, the English made profits and by colonial legislation tried to ensure that the New World would remain producers of raw materials only and consumers of the industrial products of Britain. Smuggling or trading with the enemy, whether Dutch or French, was pervasive, but by the early eighteenth century, "colonial trade conformed in almost every particular to the navigation system . . . [and] smuggled goods accounted for a tiny fraction of all quantities handled." Of course, the colonists in both the Caribbean and North America were Englishmen, and they too looked for ways to profit from a system that denied other nationals, especially the Dutch or the French, from getting a piece of Britain's colonial trade.[12]

This triangular trade and in particular the linkage between the slave trade and textiles fueled the growth of British shipping and established Lancashire as a center of cotton textile manufacture. Raw cotton was imported mostly from the Levant in the Ottoman empire and the British colonies in the Caribbean, and by the 1780s it was spun into thread in newfangled "factories" using water power and employing hundreds of workers in one place. As the Lancashire manufacturers became more proficient and the prices of their textiles declined, they even exported them to Africa, especially whenever Indian textiles were expensive. The real boom in British cotton textile production came after American independence in 1793 when Eli Whitney's invention of the cotton gin made it possible to use short-staple and much cheaper American cotton. With another series of innovations derived from the application of steam power, as we will see shortly, mechanizing both spinning and weaving over the years from 1815 to 1840, the productivity of the Lancashire textile factories surged again, resulting in ever lower prices and the ability to outcompete Indian textiles in the world market. Indian textile producers were the first ones to create a worldwide market for cotton textiles—the British then captured it from them.[13]

When that happened, the British became advocates of "free trade" and abandoned both mercantilist theory and practice and tariffs on imports. Indeed, "free trade" became the ideological mantra of imperial Britain at the height of its global power in the nineteenth century. Mercantilism, at least as it applied in the Atlantic world, had been dead since the victory of the Americans in their War of Independence from Britain. To the British, their former American subjects and colonists became "foreigners, subject to all the provisions of the Navigation Laws,"[14] which restricted the importation of raw cotton, potentially strangling the British textile industry and giving rise to calls for "free trade." Free trade with the new United States after 1783 showed the fallacy of the argument that British manufactures could grow only with a monopoly on colonial markets, and the American South with its cotton plantations worked by African slaves and their descendants became the major supplier of raw cotton to the mills of Lancashire.

Although this story of the rise to global competitiveness of the British cotton textile industry sounds Eurocentric, it really is not, for British success was contingent upon a number of worldwide developments that were not of their own making. In the first place, the British were at a competitive disadvantage to Indian producers and would have remained so except for several coincidences. The Glorious Revolution of 1688–89 brought to power a government willing to use state power to protect its domestic manufacturers; and the New World developed as a peculiar periphery that, by the accident of the Great Dying and colonial legislation, provided a market for British manufactured goods. In the second place, the British were fortunate to develop a usable coal-fueled steam engine, which further revolutionized cotton textile production, making it even more productive and its products so cheap that the British could undersell Indian textiles not just in Africa but, interestingly, in India as well. For that part of the story, we now look at the innovations in coal and steam engines.

New Sources of Energy and Power

Until about 1830, the story of cotton textiles for the most part remains one that unfolds within the biological old regime; that is, everything about it depended on the annual flows of solar energy and their capture by humans.[15] To be sure, the early British "factories" had begun to use water power, but there was a limit to how much that could increase cotton textile production. Indeed, there is every reason to think that cotton textile production would have reached serious limits within the biological old regime, leading not to an industrial revolution but to an economic dead end, had it not been for coal, the steam engine, and iron and steel production, which truly launched the Industrial Revolution and allowed Britain to break out of the constraints imposed by the biological old regime. To see how and why, we need to take a closer look at what was happening to the most advanced biological-old-regime economies, starting with China and then looking at England. What we will see is that all old-regime economies were beginning to push up against serious ecological constraints that would have stopped all of them from developing an industrial revolution. Except for a few chance occurrences and a vast global conjuncture, we all now might still be living in the biological old regime.

China

Two favored explanations of the Industrial Revolution in Europe have focused on population dynamics and the growth of free markets. By various techniques and practices, mostly late marriage, European families were able to keep their sizes smaller than "naturally" possible. Smaller family size meant a smaller population overall, leaving greater surpluses in the hands of families to invest in improving agricultural and industrial productivity. Fewer people working harder to make their investable surpluses grow—an "industrious revolution," it is said—grew inexorably into the Industrial Revolution.[16]

The market-driven story line of industrialization suggests that the establishment and growth of markets for commodities, land, labor, and capital in Europe enabled European producers to be much more efficient and hence to accumulate sufficient capital to invest in improving agricultural and industrial productivity. Also necessary for the success of markets was a state that protected (or at least respected) private property rights. This combination likewise, according to the Eurocentric version of the origins of the modern world, grew more or less naturally into the Industrial Revolution.

Of course, the population- and market-driven story lines of industrialization are not incompatible, and many historians have melded them together in explaining why Europeans were uniquely capable of launching an industrial revolution. As proof, they often point to China as a counterexample. China, it is alleged, had "a preindustrial demographic regime," in which nothing was done to keep birthrates down. Hence, population surged, eating up any surplus above subsistence and rendering the investments necessary for an industrial revolution impossible.[17] Similarly, it is alleged, China was "despotic": it had a state that meddled in private affairs, property rights were not respected, and markets could not operate efficiently. Hence, it is concluded, there was no possibility for an industrial revolution.[18]

There is only one thing wrong with these assumptions about what "went wrong" in China: they are wrong. As I will show below, Chinese families in fact had numerous ways—albeit different from Europeans—of limiting their size and hence keeping the overall Chinese population above subsistence levels. Also, Chinese markets of all kinds not only existed but arguably functioned better and more efficiently than those in Europe. If both of those are true for China, then their value as "explanations" for why the Industrial Revolution occurred in Europe is questionable. To see why, we must take a closer look at China.

As mentioned earlier in this chapter, agriculture in China (as well as in India and numerous other parts of Asia) was highly productive, harvesting twenty bushels of rice for every one sown. Rice has the unique capability of gaining nutrients not directly from the soil, but from the water (and so it is grown in "paddies"), eliminating the need for the land to lie fallow, as was the custom in Europe, to regain its fertility. Additionally, Chinese farmers had learned how to prepare the soil, to irrigate, to fertilize, and to control insect pests in order to maximize the harvest yield. Moreover, farmers in the southern half of China could get two or sometimes three harvests per year from the same plot of land, drawing the amazement of early-eighteenth-century European travelers to China. "By what art can the earth produce subsistence for such numbers [of people]?" asked the Frenchman Pierre Poivre in the 1720s.

> Do the Chinese possess any secret arts of multiplying grain and provisions necessary for the nourishment of mankind? To solve my doubts I traversed the fields, I introduced myself among the laborers, who are in general easy, polite, and knowledgeable of the world. I examine, and pursue them through all their operations, and observe that their secret consists simply in manuring the fields judiciously, ploughing them to a considerable depth, sowing them in the proper season, turning to advantage every inch of ground which can produce the most considerable crop, and preferring to every other species of culture that of grain, as by far the most important.[19]

Such an impressively productive agriculture certainly allowed the Chinese population to grow, from 140 million in 1650, to 225 million in 1750, and then to 380–400 million by 1850. Numbers like these also convinced European observers, in particular Adam Smith and Thomas Malthus, whose ideas about markets and population have so shaped Eurocentric views of the modern world, that the Chinese just could not control their population growth. Malthus believed that populations like the Chinese who could not control their growth would overshoot the capability of the land to support their numbers until "negative" population checks, such as famines or wars, reduced the population size. Malthus also believed that Europeans avoided those fates by having "preventative" checks on population growth.

Where Malthus certainly was right about Europeans, he was wrong about the Chinese. The fact is, they could—and did—control their family size, although in ways quite different from the Europeans. Although almost all Chinese women married and married early, Chinese families developed many methods for controlling the number of children. Abstention from having sexual relations, especially early in the marriage, was a preferred mechanism and was enforced by married couples living with their parents. Infanticide, especially of daughters, was another means to limit family size, leading as well to a gender-unbalanced population of more men than women, and hence of forced celibacy for many poorer men. As James Lee and Wang Feng summarize the Chinese demographic system:

> In contrast to the European system, in which marriage was the only volitional check on population growth, the Chinese demographic system had multiple conscious checks, and was therefore far more complex and calculating than Malthus

or his successors thought. As a result . . . population never pushed the economy to subsistence levels.[20]

Nevertheless, because of the productivity of agriculture and the ability of the Chinese economy to produce more than enough food for its population, the population did in fact grow, and as mentioned above, it grew rapidly from 1750 to 1850.[21] In the densely populated core areas of the Pearl River delta in south China, along the southeast coast, and in the Yangzi River delta, populations did reach the size where people started migrating out into less-populated areas. Sometimes these regions had exceptionally fertile soil that could be brought into production by clearing the land, as in Hunan up the Yangzi River from Shanghai, or in the West River valley in Guangxi province; or sometimes the land that was brought into production was more marginal and less fertile, as in the Jiangxi highlands on the southern bank of the Yangzi River.[22]

Wherever new land was being brought into agricultural production, especially by 1800 when it was land that was not as fertile or productive as land in the densely populated core regions, that was an indication that the limits of growth within the biological old regime were being reached. That does not mean that a Malthusian disaster was imminent—the Chinese were in fact very much in control of their reproductive capabilities—but that good agricultural land was becoming in short supply. The reason for this is that the four necessities of life—food, clothing, shelter, and fuel—all came from the land and hence were in competition. Clearing land for food decreased the amount of wood available for fuel, either to cook and heat homes or to make charcoal for industrial purposes. Switching land from cotton to rice production also put pressure on the supply of the raw material for clothing, while doing the opposite would decrease the amount of food available. There just was not much room for maneuvering when the limits of the biological old regime were being reached, as they were in China in the late eighteenth century,[23] and, as we will see, in Britain too.

It was not just that meeting the needs for sustained population growth meant increasing pressure on the land and decreasing other things at the expense of food, but to keep food production increasing while at the same time keeping supplies available for clothing, shelter, and fuel meant that greater and greater amounts of labor and capital had to be expended in agriculture just to keep pace. For instance, clearing land was expensive, and so was building irrigation works or terracing fields from hills, all of which improved the output of Chinese agriculture in the eighteenth and nine-teenth centuries. Allocating more labor also could increase output, and Chinese farming families did that too: planting rice in nurseries and then transplanting it to the fields or picking insects off rice plants by hand, for instance, also increased agricultural yields and sustained a growing population. So too did capturing and recycling nitrogen from human and animal waste; Asian farmers were biological-old-regime champions in maintaining or even increasing the fertility of their fields.

Markets

Another way the Chinese economy improved both overall production levels and productivity was by the use of markets, especially for agricultural commodities. It used to be thought that markets were first and most highly developed in Europe (reading backward from the Industrial Revolution to find reasons why it happened there first). But in the past thirty years, historians of China have shown how fully developed and efficient markets were in eighteenth- and nineteenth-century China.[24] Peasant farmers in the Pearl River and Yangzi River deltas, for instance, came to specialize in sericulture (that is, the whole process of producing silk), raising silkworms and growing the mulberry trees with which to feed the silkworms, boiling the cocoons to obtain the silk threads, then spinning, weaving, and dyeing the silk. Other areas might specialize in cotton, sugarcane, or other nonfood agricultural crops.

Such specialization meant that those peasant producers had to obtain their food from other sources, usually places upriver that came to specialize in rice and could easily export it on boats to the more densely populated core regions. Massive investments in canals by both private parties and the state vastly extended and improved the Chinese inland water transportation system, linking China from Tianjin in the north to Guangzhou in the south by water. Efficient water transportation facilitated the movement of grain throughout the Chinese empire and the growth of markets and provided the material foundations for maintaining some of the world's largest cities.

Initially, the Chinese state intervened in the food markets quite regularly to ensure that peasant producers and urban consumers alike would be ensured adequate food supplies,[25] but by the mid-eighteenth century the Chinese state was increasingly willing to allow markets and merchants to handle the movement of grain across huge distances—up to a thousand miles—from where it was produced to where it was consumed. Measures of the efficiency of these markets show that they were more efficient than contemporary markets in France, England, or the United States.[26] Additionally, Chinese markets for land, labor, and capital all functioned well and arguably more efficiently than comparable markets in European countries.[27]

In short, eighteenth-century China was as "developed" as any other developed part of the world, if not more so, whether measured by levels of agricultural productivity, sophistication of manufactures and markets, or levels of consumption. Chinese families regulated their size and were responsive to changing economic opportunities, limiting their size when those opportunities diminished in order to maintain consumption above subsistence levels; specialization of function gave rise to markets and a highly commercialized economy; and an extensive water-based transportation system allowed the efficient movement of goods and people throughout the empire.

Not only did the Chinese have markets for commodities, land, labor, and capital, but in at least two parts of China, stock and futures markets also developed. As China's population increased during the eighteenth century, the demand for timber and wood rapidly grew, contributing to the deforestation already caused by the expansion of farmland. In a mountainous region of Anhui province with water transport and market connections with the thriving urban centers in the Yangzi River delta region, lineage leaders converted rice paddies to tree plantations to meet the downriver demand for timber. Tree plantations also developed another thousand miles upriver in Guizhou province for much the same reason. The problem in both places was that unlike farm crops, trees take twenty to thirty years to be harvestable. Landowners and tree planters then began dividing their standing trees into "shares" that could be bought and sold before the tree was harvested. A market for those shares soon developed, and what was created was a futures market, a very sophisticated financial instrument thought to have been invented first and only in the early stages of capitalist development in western Europe. But here they were in eighteenth-century rural China.[28]

Yet China's highly developed market economy did not lead to an industrial breakthrough.[29] Instead, by the nineteenth century, there were plenty of indicators that China was pushing up against ecological constraints imposed by the biological old regime. In several areas, fuel became in short supply in the early 1800s, with peasant families turning to rice straw and chaff for heating and cooking rather than wood. Moreover, some market exchanges between densely populated core regions and developing peripheral areas also served to slow Chinese economic growth.

One of the advantages of markets and a good transportation network is that they allow some areas to specialize in what their natural resources make most profitable and to exchange that produce with others, enabling both to be more productive and allowing everyone's income to rise. At least that is the theory, and to a point that is the way markets functioned in China. However, the exchanges began to break down regarding the trade of raw cotton from cotton-producing regions in return for manufactured goods—cotton textiles in particular—from the highly developed core regions in the lower Yangzi and Pearl River deltas.

Throughout China, rural families were free to decide what and how much to grow and how to allocate family labor on the farm. To this extent, they differed markedly from African slaves in the New World or serfs in eastern Europe, both of whom had their freedom curtailed and production decisions made by their owners or overseers. By contrast, Chinese peasants who migrated to more peripheral areas, like their counterparts in the more developed cores, were free to make their own decisions. Increasingly, what they decided was that it was in their interest to spin and weave their own cotton textiles for their own use and for local exchange, rather than concentrating on rice or raw cotton and importing the finished goods. In effect, large parts of rural China underwent a process of "import substitution," producing their own textiles. Not only did they reduce the amount of raw cotton sold to the textile-producing centers, but they also increased the area given over to cotton and hence decreased the amount of rice they were willing to export as well.[30]

The freedom of Chinese peasant families thus may have spurred what might be called "self-sufficient proto-industrialization" in peripheral areas, but that acted as a constraint on the growth of an industrial cotton textile industry in China's core regions. Contributing to the willingness of Chinese peasant families in peripheral areas to spin and weave their own textiles may have been the long-standing norm that "men plow, women weave." It was not just that "women weave," but that they weave in the household. Chinese families thus placed a high value on mothers and daughters staying at home to do the weaving, rather than leaving home to work in a factory, as English and Japanese girls did.[31] Paradoxically, the freedom of peasant farmers throughout China's core and peripheral regions, when compared with the limited freedoms of slaves and serfs in the European system, constrained China's ability to continue developing a textile industry in its most highly developed core regions. Efficient markets and personal freedom—often embedded in explanations for why industrial development sprouted first and only in northwestern Europe—led China down a different path: toward a more efficient exploitation of natural resources within the confines of the biological old regime. In fact, as we will see later in this chapter, the most economically advanced parts of the world were all heading into an ecological cul-de-sac with no way out. That makes what happened in a part of England so interesting and such a critical part of understanding the origins of the Industrial Revolution there.

In summary, China had a highly developed market economy within the constraints of the biological old regime. Nonetheless, that regime placed ecological limits upon growth, and the freedom of Chinese peasants coupled with practices governing the sexual division of labor, all combined, meant that China was bumping up against the limits of growth by the mid-1800s. Food, clothing, shelter, and fuel competed for land, and to get more from the land, Chinese farmers lavished increasing amounts of labor on agriculture. The dynamics of specialization, increased market exchanges, and improved transportation in the context of the biological old regime and the particularities of China's situation were pushing it toward an increasingly labor-intensive agriculture and the depletion of land resources, rather than toward an industrial revolution. As fuel supplies from wood declined, the Chinese turned again, where they could, to coal. Coal was available and used in North China, parts of Central China, and in South China too, where it was used in the iron foundries of Foshan town near the major city of Guangzhou. Nevertheless, this availability of coal in China did not lead to an industrial revolution there, or elsewhere in Eurasia for that matter. Particular circumstances came together in one place, England, that did create the right conditions for the leap into the fossil-fueled industrial age that became the modern world.

Exhausting the Earth[32]
Indeed, over the period from 1400 to 1800, the dynamics of the biological old regime, especially in those areas most densely populated and even with the institutions of private property, markets, and effective states, were leading not to a breakthrough to a "modern world" of fossil-fuel energy and electrified industry and homes, but to an increasingly intensive using up of natural resources. In part, this outcome was driven by a significant worldwide population increase, rising from 380 to 950 million people, most of that coming in the century following the depths of the seventeenth-century global crisis, which drove the removal of forests for more farmland (and food for people).[33] Interestingly, climatologists now think that this expansion of

farmland contributed significant amounts of global warming gases to the atmosphere, warming the climate and improving agricultural yields.[34]

Throughout northern Europe, signs of overexploitation of land in Denmark, France, England, Sweden, and central Europe were noted—"the landscape showed signs of erosion."[35] In China, despite its extraordinarily productive agriculture and efficient markets, New World food crops had made possible the farming of previously marginal land in hills, mountains, and sandy areas.[36] Japan had already exhausted its forests by the seventeenth century, but in an exceptional situation, its government implemented a series of measures to halt and then reverse the deforestation of Japan's islands, transforming Japan into a "green archipelago."[37] Another exception to the environmental exhaustion was India, which continued to have ample forests and hence access to wood for fuel well into the nineteenth century.[38] Elsewhere, a biological-old-regime energy crisis was looming as resources that people had gleaned from nature for millennia dwindled.

We might think of this moment in world history around the beginning of the nineteenth century as the early Anthropocene, when humans became aware not only that natural resources of all kinds were becoming scarce because of human action, but also that humans were partially responsible for driving animal species to extinction. This awareness appeared independently about the same time in both China and Europe. Russians seeking the furs of North Pacific sea animals killed the last of a species known as Stellar's Sea Cow in 1768, and that fact was reported in an English-language publication in 1802. In an 1811 Chinese publication, an official in South China noted the absence of several species that had been mentioned in ancient texts and bemoaned the fact that the clearance of land for farming had driven them to extinction. And the English geologist Charles Lyell too noted that the extension of arable land had driven species to extinction. The indelible impact of humans on changing nature forever—extinction is forever—dawned just as the Industrial Revolution was to give humans even more power over the forces of nature, ushering in the first phases of the Anthropocene.[39]

England, Redux

The mounting energy crisis included England, and Londoners increasingly turned to coal to heat their homes and cook their meals. By 1700, London had grown to a population of about half a million, and its consumption of coal accounted for more than half of England's production. The Netherlands too had an energy crisis because of a wood shortage, but it had only peat available for heating, not coal. Increasingly in England in the eighteenth century, coal was used for industrial purposes, especially lime burning (for producing a fertilizer for farming), brewing, glassmaking, and boiling seawater for salt. By the early nineteenth century, iron manufacturers began to use coal instead of increasingly scarce charcoal. The steam engine and "the use of coal in manufacturing were the two key elements in [the] new energy complex."[40] And this combination put England on the verge of the leap into the industrial age, eventually carrying the rest of the world with it. But why?

Surprisingly, a Chinese-like agrarian fate may well have awaited England and the other developed parts of Europe as well. Instead, England underwent an industrial revolution that changed everything, not just for England but also for the world. Part of the reason is that Britain had a "peculiar" periphery in the New World: slavery, mercantilist colonial legislation, and then the expansion of cotton plantations in the American South after independence created a very large market for British cotton textiles, thereby stimulating and sustaining the growth of the cotton textile industry in Lancashire. Paradoxically, greater freedom for China's peasant families in China's periphery and an efficient market system meant that they could choose not to buy cotton textiles imported from urban textile centers, but instead produce them themselves. And that fact meant that the demand within China for cotton textiles was high and might have sustained a factory system, but why would China's rural farmers buy cotton textiles from the city when they could spin and weave their own? By contrast, New World slavery not only kept demand for British cotton textiles high (slaves could not make their own clothing), it also supplied the raw cotton cheaply. Additionally, Britain's wars with France from 1689 to 1815 "virtually eliminated all rivals from the non-European world, except to some extent the young United States."[41]

British colonies and textiles went together. By 1840, Britain was exporting 200 million yards of cotton textiles to other European countries, but 529 million yards to Asia, Africa, and the Americas (excluding the United States). Between 1820 and 1840, the tables turned in terms of Britain's relationship with Indian cotton textiles. Whereas England had imported so much Indian cotton cloth in the early 1700s that its government had to ban imports, in the 1800s Britain began exporting cotton textiles to its new colonial possession: only eleven million yards in 1820, but 145 million by 1840. England's Lancashire textile mills began applying steam power to the production process, greatly increasing output, lowering costs, and outcompeting Indian cottons in the world market. In the process, India's great cotton textile industry declined, leading to what some historians call "the de-industrialization of India."[42]

Britain's North American colonies were important in another regard too—supplying Britain with foodstuffs and natural resources that otherwise would have to have been produced in England. Raw cotton from the slave plantations of the American South obviously fed the textile machines of Lancashire. But timbers from North America's forests provided masts, staves, decking, and hulls for the Royal Navy. The bountiful fisheries off New England yielded so much cod that it was cheap enough to become a staple food of both England's working poor and slaves on the cotton plantations. From its Caribbean colonies came sugar and via trade with South America, coffee and chocolate too.[43] One historian dubs this natural bounty produce from England's "ghost acres." If England had been forced to provide these natural products from its own land, it would have had to switch it from other purposes, say wheat or sheep pasture, which would have been insufficient either to sustain its growing population or to provide resources for industry.[44] In other words, England's industrialization would not have taken off. In this sense, that major development in world history was contingent upon numerous factors, its American colonies included.

But so too was the development of the new energy and industrial complex of coal, iron, and steam. To make the initial beginnings of that combination take off required a set of additional factors, especially those that created a demand for iron and utilized steam power in ways beyond simply pumping water out of coal mines.

Coal, Iron, and Steam

Despite the impressive growth of Britain's cotton textile industry, textiles alone would not have led to an industrial revolution. True, Britain's cotton textile industry accounted for nearly all economic growth there until the 1830s. Cotton textiles also called into existence a new class of urban industrial worker and created the "factories" and horrendous injustices captured by Charles Dickens in his various novels, and by the end of the nineteenth century, the textile industry had become the largest user of steam power in England.[45] But all of these could not initially transform the British economy from one that was mired in the biological old regime to one that was freed from those constraints. For that to happen, a whole new source of power was needed: coal-fired steam power.[46]

Unlike the story of cotton textiles, the story of how a coal and steam industry developed in England is mostly unique to England, and it shows how close England was to following in China's footsteps toward labor-intensive agriculture. For like China, as we have seen, population growth and agricultural development put pressure on the land resources of England. Indeed, by 1600 much of southern England had already been deforested, largely to meet the needs of the growing city of London for fuel for heating and cooking, which had turned increasingly to coal for those purposes. In contrast to China, where timber shortages led to tree plantations, marketable timber, and futures markets, the easy availability of coal provided England with another route around its environmental limitations.

By 1800, Britain was mining ten million tons of coal, or as much as 90 percent of the world's output.[47] Deforestation in China led to the consumption of much coal for cooking and heating, and in Japan—which was being reforested—restrictions on the use of wood contributed to a demand for coal there too. But demand for coal in those economies fed existing needs. In England, 70 percent of the coal went to heat London, while the remainder went into industry, including bricks and beer. Increasingly, the expanding use of iron led to increased demand for coal and for solutions to increasing coal output.[48]

The problem of getting water out of England's coal mines led Thomas Savery to patent the first steam engine that worked as a suction pump to get water out of the mines. Shortly after that in 1712, Thomas Newcomen improved upon that primitive contraption by adding a piston to pump the water, and James Watt further improved the design in the 1760s, although even these improved designs were still so inefficient that the cost of fuel would have rendered them useless except that at the mine head, coal was in effect free. Newcomen's (and later Watt's) inefficient steam engines thus could be used there. Between 1712 and 1800, there were 2,500 of the contraptions built, almost all of which were used at coal mines. But even that does not yet explain the Industrial Revolution, because the demand for coal (and hence steam engines) was fairly limited until new applications were devised. The one that proved most important was the idea of using the steam engine not just to draw water out of coal mines but to move vehicles above ground.

The real breakthrough thus came with the building of the first steam engine railway. Along with digging deeper, coal miners had to go farther from London to find coal deposits and thus had higher expenses for transporting the coal overland from the pithead to water. Fixed steam engines were being used to haul coal out of the mines and to pull trams short distances. But at a mine in Durham in the north of England, the idea of putting the steam engine on the tram carriage and running it on iron rails became a reality in 1825 with a seven-mile line connecting the mine directly to the coast. The first railroad was born.

Where in 1830 there were a few dozen miles of track in England, by 1840 there were over 4,500 miles, and by 1850 over 23,000 miles. The progeny of the coal mine, the railroad fueled a demand for more coal, more steam engines, and more iron and steel: each mile of railroad used 300 tons of iron just for the track. Between 1830 and 1850, the output of iron in Britain rose from 680,000 to 2,250,000 tons, and coal output trebled from fifteen million to forty-nine million tons.[49]

Steam engines also transformed the cotton textile industry, vastly increasing output. The spinning of yarn was first to be "industrialized" using water power; in 1790 Samuel Crompton's "mule" was adapted for steam power, resulting in a hundredfold increase in thread output over a worker on a manual spinning wheel, as was still in use in India and China. So much thread was produced that weavers could not keep up, leading to innovations in that part of the industry, including the use of steam to power the looms, so much so that by the 1820s there were few hand weavers left. So large was Britain's textile industry that of the twelve million men, women, and children in England in 1830, a half million—mostly women and children—were employed in the textile mills.

Recap: Without Colonies, Coal, or State Support

The Industrial Revolution is usually portrayed as the story of the invention and use of laborsaving devices that so dramatically increased the ability of people to produce that human society was placed upon a path of ever-increasing productivity, overall societal wealth, and higher standards of living. To a certain extent, that is true enough, in particular when thinking about the cotton textile industry. There, British producers—faced with competition from low-priced Indian products and their own high-wage labor force—had to find ways of lowering their costs of production, and hence they turned to mechanization.[50] However, without steam power, that process might well have played itself out as England used up all available locations for water-powered mills. For without coal and steam, cotton textiles alone could not transform the British economy from one limited by the biomass constraints of the biological old regime to one liberated from it by the new sources of stored fossil-fuel energy. Indeed, if there is any image that portrays "industrial revolution," it is that of smokestacks rising above a factory.

But as Kenneth Pomeranz has persuasively argued in *The Great Divergence*, a better way to think about the Industrial Revolution is that it proceeded by finding *land*-saving mechanisms. For throughout the Old World, from China in the east to England in the west, shortages of land to produce the necessities of life were putting limits on any further growth at all, let alone allowing a leap into a different kind of economic future. This understanding of the ecological limits of the biological old regime opens a new window onto the explanation of how and why the Industrial Revolution occurred first in England.

Steam could have been produced using wood or charcoal, but that would have required vast forests, and by the end of the eighteenth century, forest covered but 5 to 10 percent of Britain. Under the best of circumstances, using charcoal to produce iron in 1815 would have yielded but 100,000 tons or so, a far cry from the 400,000 tons actually produced and the millions soon needed for railroads. Tens of millions of additional acres of woodland would have been needed to continue to produce iron and steel.[51] That might have been feasible, but converting land from agricultural purposes back to forest would have had other rather dire consequences for England's food supply. Thus, without coal, and the historical accident that it was easily found and transported in England, steam and iron and steel production would have been severely curtailed.

Similarly, Britain's New World colonies provided additional "ghost acres" that allowed the first part of the story of industrialization, that of cotton textiles, to unfold. To feed its textile mills, in the early 1800s Britain was importing hundreds of thousands of pounds of raw cotton from the New World, mostly from its former colonies in the new United States, but also from its Caribbean holdings. If the British had been forced to continue to clothe themselves with wool, linen, or hemp cloth produced from within their own borders, it would have required over twenty million acres. Similarly, Britain's sugar imports from its colonies provided substantial calories to its working population, all of which would have required more millions of acres.[52] The point is this: without coal or colonies, the dynamics of the biological old regime would have forced Britons to devote more and more of their land and labor to food production, further constraining resources for industrial production and snuffing out any hope for an industrial revolution, much as had happened to China in the nineteenth century.

To these factors that go into understanding how the Industrial Revolution took off first in England, we need to add some global comparisons that additionally highlight the role of the state. What we have seen is that global competitive pressures induced English cotton textile manufacturers to seek state protection of their industry from Indian competition, and that environmental conditions forced the English to turn to coal for heating. Similar environmental constraints had pushed China in a similar direction, although we can wonder if the supplies of coal there would ever have been sufficient to meet the needs of its population, which at about 400 million in 1800 was at least forty times as great as England's twenty-five million.

Moreover, as Prasannan Parthasarathi has shown, a critically important difference between China and England was that the "British state took a more active interest in coal, both directly and indirectly, than did the state in China." Coal was essential for London, and the British state put in place policies that encouraged the production and transport of coal to London, and then to Lancashire. Coal could also be easily taxed, and it was, and duties that discouraged export were put in place; the Royal Navy additionally protected coastal shipping from French privateers. And heavy tariffs on iron imports protected Britain's emerging iron industry.[53]

In contrast, "the Chinese state did much less." As we now know, it is not that the eighteenth-century Chinese state lacked the capacity to govern effectively. To the contrary, the Chinese state was highly effective in regulating those economic and social activities that it considered strategically important, in particular the storage and marketing of food grains through the state granary system to ensure food supplies and food security over its vast territory. Managing this huge enterprise was the Chinese state's major concern, and neither the coal nor iron industries were of much help in that endeavor, and so were pretty much off the radar of the Chinese state. Different global and ecological circumstances, though, had made both of those industries of strategic interest to the British state.[54]

Science and Technology

Eurocentric explanations of the Industrial Revolution typically invoke the "scientific revolution," the immensely interesting and ultimately very important development beginning in the sixteenth century, whereby some Europeans began to think of nature as a separate entity that could be understood, modeled mathematically, and in principle "controlled." Although it is quite true that science has come to be an integral part of the world, and while it has come to play a leading role in conjunction with universities, corpora-tions, and the state from the late 1800s on in developing new chemical and other science-based industries, there is little evidence to tie European sci-ence to the beginnings of the Industrial Revolution or to the technologies that fueled it. The reasons are several.[55]

Let us start by defining science as the intellectual enterprise of under-standing the natural universe by using mathematics and the "scientific method" for replicating findings, and technology as the means by which humans gain mastery over natural processes for their own productive or reproductive ends. As long as the Industrial Revolution was believed to have been spurred by the search for laborsaving devices, it might have made sense to see the development of technology as critically important. But as discussed above, the critical shortage was land, not labor, and hence it was coal and colonies that eased that shortage and allowed Britain to industrialize first. In fact, the principles of technologies used in the Industrial Revolution were well known in China; what explains their development in England and not China, as suggested above, were the particular circumstances in England that made the fuel for the first, extremely inefficient steam engines effectively free. China did not have that good fortune.

Even if we grant new technologies—in particular steam engines and iron and then steel—an important role in the Industrial Revolution, there is little evidence that the mechanics and tinkerers who developed those machines were "scientists" or even had any scientific training at all; recent theoretical work posits instead the mutual interactions between mental and manual labor—the "mindful hand" as two historians of science phrase it.[56] Indeed, seventeenth- and eighteenth-century theoretical science had been most use-ful as a political tool wielded against the twin pillars of the old regime in Europe—monarchs and the Catholic Church. Finally, there is little reason to think of "science" as specifically or uniquely European; rather, scientific ideas flowed across the Eurasian continent, especially between China and Persia, and the European Renaissance itself progressed in large part by redis-covering Greek texts preserved in Arab libraries.[57]

Industrialization in Britain thus was contingent upon a host of factors, although the scientific revolution was not one of them. In the New World, the Great Dying created a demand for labor that was ultimately satisfied by African slaves, creating both a peculiar institution and a peculiar periphery that produced agricultural products for export (especially sugar and cotton) but needed to import food and clothing. In Europe, the sixteenth-century failure of the Spanish to create a continental empire led to a state system

marked by interstate conflict, competition, and warfare that produced win-
ners and losers, with Britain and France emerging in the eighteenth century
as the primary players. In Britain, deforestation to heat the growing city of
London produced a demand for coal, which the accidents of geography
placed within easy reach. In Asia, the decline of the Mughal empire in the
early 1700s allowed the British, Dutch, and French East India Companies to
compete for access to Asian products, and the victory of the British in the
Seven Years' War led to the exclusion of France from both the New World
and India. And finally, China's demand for silver and the fortuitous New
World supply of it provided Europeans with a means by which to buy spices
and industrial goods produced in Asia. To conclude this chapter, we thus
return to the China story.

Tea, Silver, Opium, Iron, and Steam

The 1760 British victory over the French in India, the subsequent growth of
a British colony there, and the defeat of the British by their American colonists in the War of Independence focused British attention once again on
Asia and trade there. Despite the mechanization of Britain's textile industry
and the sale of vast amounts of cotton textiles to India, Britain still could
not find any way to sell much of anything to the Chinese. To make matters
worse, the British had developed a taste for tea, and they began buying large
amounts of it from China. Fortunately, the British had access to lots of New
World silver: one of the terms of the 1713 Peace of Utrecht gave Britain the
right of *asiento*, that is, to provide slaves to Spain's New World colonies,
receiving in return New World silver. And that American silver was used to
buy Chinese tea—lots of it.[58]

Tea

The Chinese had been producing tea from the leaves of a particular ever-
green bush for over a thousand years and had perfected the process of selecting, drying, and brewing the leaves into a mildly stimulating hot beverage
(tea contains caffeine). The British East India Company discovered that
there was a market for tea in England, and soon it began importing chests of
it back home. At first tea was drunk mostly by the upper classes (which
remains with us in the practice of "high tea") because it was relatively pricey,
but as the EIC increased the amounts it bought for the English market, its
price declined to the point that common people could also afford it. Workers

especially came to appreciate its stimulating effect, and when textile factories and coal mines increased both the numbers of workers and the length of the workday, workers increased their consumption of tea. Fortified with sugar from the colonies and milk from local dairies, tea also became a major source of calories and caffeine to sustain the growing British industrial workforce. Where Britain imported five million pounds of tea in 1760, by 1800—when the textile mills were growing rapidly—they imported more than twenty million pounds, maybe twice that if smuggled tea is included.[59] By 1800, textile workers and coal miners were spending 5 percent of their income just on tea (10 percent if sugar is added).[60]

With British merchants sailing up and down the Chinese coast trying to find cheaper sources of tea than that available through official channels, and periodically insulting Chinese sensibilities and practices, in 1760—the same year that the British were defeating the French and consolidating their empire around the world through the Seven Years' War—China's rulers restricted all foreign trade, especially that conducted by the British, to the single south China port of Guangzhou. For the next eighty years, the "Guangzhou system," established by China and conducted by the rules it alone set, governed trade between England and China.

The British periodically tried to negotiate their way out of what to them was a restrictive arrangement, but to no avail. The largest and most famous of these missions came in 1793 when Britain sent Sir George Macartney to China to try to open regular diplomatic relations and to gain more open access to Chinese markets. After being shown the imperial splendors of Beijing and the summer palaces of the Chinese emperor, Macartney was sent packing. China's emperor Qianlong then sent a letter to King George III. Dismissing British pleas for more trade, the emperor told King George that "Our Celestial Empire possesses all things in prolific abundance and lacks no product within its borders," and ordered the British to obey the laws and customs of the Chinese empire.[61] Although his view of China's economy and its place in the world is belied by its need for imports of silver and exports of tea, silk, and porcelain, it did reflect the emperor's assessment of the relative strength of China vis-á-vis Britain. For despite their growing industrial power, the British still were no match for the Chinese in Asia. But that would change over the next forty years.

Silver

As tea consumption in England increased, and as the ability of the British to command New World silver shrank, in part because of the American Revolution, mercantilist fears of what the continued outflow of silver to China would mean for British power prompted the British to find substitutes for silver that the Chinese would accept for the tea. Pianos and clocks held limited interest in China, and there was not a demand for woolens or beaver pelts in south China. Unlike the rest of the world, the Chinese also had no need for Indian cotton textiles, since they had their own advanced cotton textile industry. By the late eighteenth century, about the only commodity the British East India Company could take to China in lieu of silver was raw cotton from its colony in India. But still that was not enough, and silver continued flowing into China, leaving the EIC and the British government with problems arising from the outflow of silver.[62] As it turned out, the British colonialists in India were able to produce another commodity for which there was a suitable demand in China to finance British purchases of tea: the addictive drug opium.

Opium

Many societies, China included, had long used opium for medicinal purposes, and so there was a small market there. In 1773, the British governor-general of India established an opium monopoly in Bengal, charged with increasing production of the drug there and pushing its sale in China. Finding some success even though the Chinese had prohibited opium smoking, the British expanded their market in China by distributing free pipes and selling the drug to new users at very low prices. Sales leapt in 1815 after a general lowering of opium prices, again in 1830 when Indian opium from another area was allowed into the EIC pipeline, and yet again in 1834 after the British government, now favoring "free trade," abolished the EIC monopoly on trade with Asia and private traders leapt into the business. Americans too had been bringing opium from Turkey to China, adding yet another source of supply.

Huge numbers of Chinese became addicted to the drug: up to 100,000 in the city of Suzhou, and hundreds of thousands more in the port city of Guangzhou. As tens of thousands of chests, each containing about 154 pounds of opium, flowed into China, silver began flowing out, reaching thirty-four million ounces per year during the 1830s. The Chinese state recognized it had a serious drug problem, and the court debated how to handle it. One side argued that the drug should be legalized, its trade and distribution regulated by the state, and treatment centers established to wean the addicts from the drug. The other side argued that the drug trade was both immoral and illegal, and that it should be stopped by halting its import and punishing the foreign merchants who trafficked in it. In the late 1830s, the latter argument won out, with the emperor appointing Lin Zexu a special commissioner with the power to do whatever it took to end the opium traffic.

Commissioner Lin proceeded to Guangzhou, investigated the situation, and, appalled at what he believed to be the immorality of the British and American drug dealers, composed a letter to Britain's Queen Victoria asking that she control her countrymen. Entrusted to English merchants, the letter was never delivered. He also decided to blockade the foreigners in their warehouses on an island in the river next to Guangzhou, insisting that they would be allowed to leave only if they turned over their stocks of opium and pledged never to traffic in the drugs again. After gaining their acquiescence on the first count, in June 1839 Commissioner Lin dissolved 21,000 chests of opium in irrigation ditches, and, before opening them to be washed into the sea, said a prayer asking the creatures of the sea to forgive him and to move away from the coast for a while.

That was, unfortunately, not the end of the matter. Further clashes between Chinese and British forces near the island of Hong Kong, continued Chinese blockade of the foreign trading warehouses in Guangzhou, and agitation within Britain by moneyed interests representing both the China traders and the cotton textile manufacturers of Lancashire to open China's markets to British goods ("400 million customers will keep the mills of Manchester running forever!") led to the British decision to send a naval expeditionary force to China.

Iron and Steam

Thus was launched the Opium War of 1839–42 between Great Britain and China. Although the details of this war are interesting, for our purposes two are worth discussing in a bit more depth. The first has to do with the British use against China of a new kind of warship, the first of which was called the *Nemesis*.

The *Nemesis* was the first steam-powered all-iron gunboat designed specifically for fighting in the rivers of Asia, although it turned out that it was the private British East India Company, not the British navy, that commissioned it. The British Admiralty preferred wooden sailing (and some steampowered) ships as the mainstay of the navy, which had already come to "rule the waves," as the British described their dominance of the Atlantic and Indian Oceans. The admirals were not convinced that smaller, steampropelled iron ships would be of much use to them in their defense of the high seas from other Europeans, so it was the East India Company that contracted secretly with the Birkenhead Iron Works of Liverpool to build the

Figure 4.1.　The *Nemesis*

new ships. Compared with other warships, these were relatively small: 184 feet long by 29 feet wide, only 11 feet deep and drawing but 5 feet of water. Powered by a 120-horsepower steam engine, the novelty of the ship is that it was completely made of iron—no wood whatsoever.

The East India Company was very interested in developing river gunboats by which to extend its colonial holdings in India and elsewhere in Asia. According to an account of the *Nemesis* published in 1844, the outbreak of war with China "was considered an extremely favourable opportunity for testing the advantages or otherwise of iron steam-vessels; and the numerous rivers along the coast of China, hitherto very imperfectly known, and almost totally unsurveyed, presented an admirable field for these requirements."[63] The EIC was also interested in demonstrating the speed by which it could convey goods, people, and mail from India around the Cape of Good Hope to England. And finally, the owner of the ironworks was interested in demonstrating the viability of his iron warships to the admiralty in order to secure future contracts.

The *Nemesis* was built in three months and arrived off the coast of China in late 1840. It soon saw action in operations in the Pearl River, destroying several Chinese war junks because of its ability to maneuver against the current and wind and its shallow draft (see the painting of the *Nemesis* in action in figure 4.1), and it played a major role in 1842 in blockading the intersection of the Yangzi River and Grand Canal, which carried much of the waterborne commerce of the empire in central and north China, and then in threatening to bombard China's southern capital at Nanjing. Effectively defeated and knowing that they were, China's rulers sued for peace. The Treaty of Nanjing, signed in 1842 between China and Great Britain, ended the Opium War, but it signified the beginning of a century of Western aggression against China.

By its terms, this treaty was the first of what came to be known as the "unequal treaties" by which Western powers (including the United States) over the next sixty years extracted concessions from China, curtailing both the sovereignty of China's government and its ability to raise tariffs to protect its own industries. Instead, China ceded territory to the British (Hong Kong), paid a twenty-one-million-dollar indemnity in Mexican silver to cover the losses of the British drug traffickers, and opened more ports to Western commerce. The opium traffic was not legalized as a result of the first Opium War, but it was after the next war in 1858–60.

Although the use of the Nemesis was not the only reason the British were able to defeat China in the first Opium War, the Nemesis did symbolize the immense changes that had occurred in Britain in the forty years since Lord Macartney had been sent packing in 1793. Quite forcefully, of course, the Nemesis represented the application of the tools of the Industrial Revolution—iron and steam—to the tools of war in general, but specifically to the Europeans' colonial ventures in Asia and later Africa. Indeed, much of the history of European advances against Asian and African governments and peoples for the remainder of the nineteenth century was a variation on that theme,[64] as was the use of ironclads and all-iron warships in the American Civil War (1860–65).[65]

But the interests of Britain's iron and steam producers were not the only ones served by going to war with China, for the British colonial government in India and the EIC depended on opium for revenue. Also, European governments (and mostly their militaries) were quite interested in developing and testing new technologies in war, and certainly that was the case with the Opium War. But Britain's cotton textile manufacturers also clamored for war, hoping to open the Chinese market to their exports. With the entire industry now mechanized and powered by steam engines, the Lancashire cotton manufacturers were confident they could undersell anybody on the planet, and so they agitated for "free trade" to prove it. Finally, Britain's colonial government in India was interested in the outcome of the war. Two-thirds of the "British" troops used in the Opium War were Indians from the

British colonies in Madras and Bengal, proving that native troops could be used to fight under British command. Indeed, as a French historian remarked: "It was as if the British had subjugated the Indian peninsula simply in order to use its resources against China."[66]

Conclusion: Into the Anthropocene

In the course of human history, the Industrial Revolution equals or surpasses that of the agricultural revolution in importance. Where agriculture allowed people to capture the annual energy flows of the sun, allowing human populations to rise and civilizations to flourish, albeit within the limits of the biological old regime, over time the Industrial Revolution enabled human society to escape from the constraints of the biological old regime and to build whole new economies and ways of organizing human life on the basis of stored sources of mineral energy, in particular coal and oil. As we will see in coming chapters, the lifestyle in the world we inhabit is made possible by the immense increase in material production spawned by the Industrial Revolution.

Where we have thousands of years of perspective on the results and consequences of the rise of agriculture, the industrial world is barely two hundred years old, but it is becoming clear that it has ushered in a new epoch in which the actions of humans have had such huge environmental impacts that the very relationship between humans and the global environment has changed—we have entered the Anthropocene, where the actions of humans have come to overwhelm the forces of nature.[67] That story line becomes especially noteworthy in the twentieth century, the focus of chapter 6.

Of course, it is only in hindsight that we now know that the development of coal-fired steam power set in motion forces that we now call the "Industrial Revolution," and it is important to remember that this was not inevitable. Indeed, similar developments elsewhere and at other times promised a transition to industry and self-sustaining economic growth, but those flames flickered out or were extinguished.[68] So the Industrial Revolution that "succeeded" and with the nation-state (see chapter 4) ushered in a modern world was both contingent and located in a global conjuncture. How the world got to that point is important to understand.

Globally, European textile manufacturers in the seventeenth and eighteenth centuries were at a disadvantage to Indian and Chinese competitors, whose calicoes and silks were of higher quality and much cheaper than anything they could produce. Support from a government willing to use force and arms to protect its domestic manufacturers, coupled with colonial legislation in the New World, enabled British cotton manufacturers to exclude Indian cotton textiles and to gain a market for their own goods and a source of cheap raw materials.

Ecologically, Old World (and biological-old-regime) economies from China to England alike were beginning to experience shortages of land because of the clearance of forests to make way for farms and to use as fuel for heating. Indeed, those actions led to extinction of some species even then. Increased market size and division of labor allowed China and England alike, for instance, to wring greater efficiencies out of the biological-old-regime (i.e., mostly agrarian) economy, but supplying the necessities of life required land. Without coal or colonies, the Chinese were forced to expend greater amounts of labor and capital on improving output from land, where the British were released from that constraint by New World resources and the ready availability of coal.

To be sure, British manufacturers and inventors rose to the challenges they faced, especially with regard to coal mining and the development of the steam engine, and the British state supported those efforts. But there is no reason to think that the Chinese or Indians (or other people with advanced old-regime economies, like the Japanese, for instance), facing similar global and ecological challenges, would not also have been able to solve those problems in similar ways. They and their states didn't face the same challenges, and they didn't have colonies or easily accessible supplies of coal—the British did, and that made all the difference.[69]

However, these first steps into the industrial world did not leave many traces in Earth's atmosphere. We now know that burning fossil fuels over the past two hundred years has unleashed vast quantities of global-warming gases, in particular carbon dioxide (CO_2) and methane (CH_4), into the atmosphere. Most of that increase comes from the late nineteenth century on, when global competitive pressures prompted some parts of the world to industrialize and get rich, while simultaneously creating the conditions for a huge gap whereby others fell progressively behind and became increasingly poor.

CHAPTER FIVE

The Gap

In the eighteenth century, China, India, and Europe were broadly comparable in terms of their level of economic development, standard of living, and people's life expectancies. As can be seen in figure 5.1, India, China, and Europe each claimed the same share—about 23 percent—of the total gross domestic production (GDP)[1] of the world. Together, those three parts of the world thus accounted for 70 percent of the globe's economic activity in 1700. A similar story can be seen in figure 5.2. In 1750, China produced about 33 percent of all the manufactured goods in the world, with India and Europe each contributing about 23 percent, totaling almost 80 percent of world industrial output. By 1800, the story is much the same, although India's share begins to decline while that of Europe begins to climb.

By the early 1800s, though, figures 5.1 and 5.2 chart a different story, as the share of global GDP and manufacturing output claimed by Europe begins to rise rapidly, while that of China stalls and then falls rapidly by 1900, as does that of India. By 1900, India accounts for barely 2 percent of world manufacturing output, China about 7 percent, while Europe alone claims 60 percent and the United States 20 percent, or 80 percent of the world total.

Figures 5.1 and 5.2 thus chart the course of a great reversal in world history. Where India and China accounted for a little over half of the wealth in the world in the eighteenth century, by 1900 they had become among the least industrialized and the poorest. Their shares of world GDP did not fall as far as their shares of world manufacturing output, though, largely because their populations continued to grow. Indeed, as figure 5.3 shows, from 1750 to 1850, China's population shot ahead of both India and Europe, where they had been broadly comparable since 1400. With growing populations and less wealth being created, Chinese and Indians became relatively poorer over the course of the nineteenth century, as Europeans and Americans became wealthier. Moreover, since neither China nor India was industrializing, as we will see, cities there could not accommodate those larger populations, thereby intensifying rural poverty.

Figures 5.1 and 5.2 thus show the emergence during the nineteenth century of a large and growing gap between the West and the rest of the world, here epitomized by India and China. "To explain this gap, which was to grow wider over the years," the eminent historian Fernand Braudel once said, "is to tackle the essential problem of the history of the modern world."[2] Braudel himself was quite modest about his own ability to explain "the gap," recognizing that when he wrote (in the late 1970s) more was known about the history of Europe than about India, China, or the rest of what became known as the "underdeveloped" or "third" world. One thing, though, did seem clear to him: "[T]he gap between the West and the other continents appeared *late in time*, and to attribute it simply to the rationalization of the market economy, as too many of our contemporaries are still inclined to do, is obviously oversimplifying."[3]

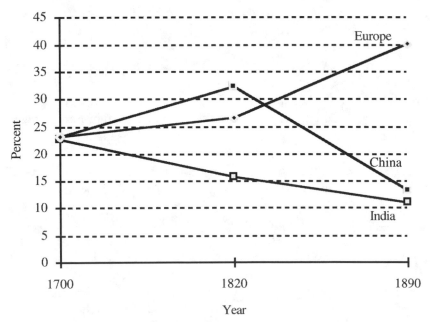

Figure 5.1. Share of World GDP, 1700–1890

Source: Mike Davis, *Late Victorian Holocausts* (London: Verso, 2001), 293.

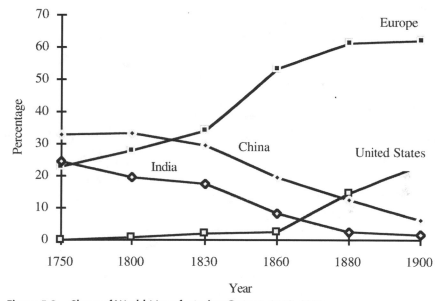

Figure 5.2. Share of World Manufacturing Output, 1750–1900

Source: Data derived from Paul Kennedy, *The Rise and Fall of Great Powers* (New York: Vintage Press, 1989), 149.

By that, Braudel was indicating his dissatisfaction with the various Eurocentric explanations of "the gap" previewed in the introduction. Most particularly, he thought that explanations that looked just at the emergence and "rationalization" of a market economy in Europe were too simplistic. Indeed, as pointed out in the previous chapter, China had a very well-developed market economy by the eighteenth century, and yet it came out on the losing end of the growing gap. This chapter examines the reasons why not only China and India, but much of the rest of Asia, Africa, and Latin America, became increasingly poor relative to Europe and the United States during the course of the nineteenth century.

In this chapter we will see how opium, guns, El Niño famines, and new industrial technologies corresponded to Europeans' colonial ventures, especially railroads, the telegraph, and quinine. What I will not resort to are the various Eurocentric explanations for Europe's increasing wealth and power vis-á-vis the rest of the world. There just is no evidence that Europeans were smarter, had a superior culture (that is, one that sustained if not created an industrial economy), or were better managers of natural and human resources than Chinese, Indians, or New Guineans for that matter. Instead, Europeans

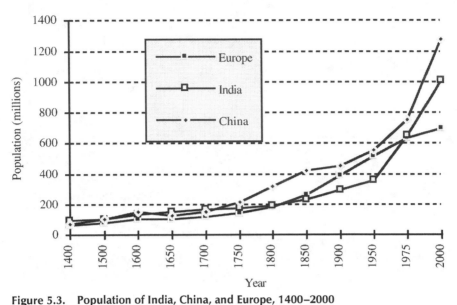

Figure 5.3. Population of India, China, and Europe, 1400–2000

Source: Colin McEvedy and Richard Jones, *Atlas of World Population History* (New York: Viking Penguin, 1978); United Nations, 2000 Revision of the World Population Estimates and Projections.

had colonies that supplied them with huge amounts of "free" energy (sugar, cotton, timber, codfish), and in the case of the British in particular, the good fortune to have coal deposits lying close to the surface and to the centers of population and manufacturing that needed new sources of energy when their forests were used up.

The story of the nineteenth century largely concerns the process by which the world became divided into the colonized and the colonizers, the developed and the underdeveloped, the rich and the poor, the industrialized and the "third" world, more recently called the "Global South."[4] Of course, from the environmental perspective used in this book, the gap also reflects the division of the world into those parts that remained within the biological old regime (which became increasingly poor) and those parts that began to escape the limits the biological old regime placed on material production (both industrial and agricultural). Moreover, the gap that emerged in the nineteenth century was not just between different parts of the world, but also within the societies we have been discussing. Industry produced not just wealth and power for some nations, but especially for some people within those countries—those who owned the new means of production. On the other hand, for those who worked in the mines and the factories, industry produced not only new jobs but also new forms of work, urban experiences, and understandings of poverty. And industry created huge environmental problems and challenges.

Opium and Global Capitalism

This narrative of the origins of the modern world started in the early 1400s with China's demand for silver to use in its economy, which, together with that of India, constituted the major source of wealth and industrial production in the early modern world. China's demand for silver set into motion a series of developments that led, willy-nilly, to most of the major events discussed so far in this book. Without China's demand for silver, it seems fair to say, the European role in the world economy would have been greatly diminished. As it was, China's demand for, and New World supplies of, silver enabled Europeans to enrich themselves by gaining access to Asian commodities and trade networks.

Similarly, Chinese demand in the nineteenth century for another commodity—this time the addictive drug opium—also played a major role in structuring the world economy. To be sure, the importation and consumption of opium did not have the positive effects on China's economy that silver imports had had four hundred years earlier. Furthermore, the demand for opium was driven by the needs of forty million addicted consumers, rather than state needs for its economy. Nonetheless, Chinese demand for opium in the 1800s did stimulate worldwide economic activity.

Despite Britain's defeat of China in the first Opium War (1839–42), Britain had not forced China to legalize the sale and distribution of opium. Nonetheless, the new British colonial possession of Hong Kong provided a convenient base of operations free from Chinese harassment. For the next twenty years, Hong Kong was the hub of the British drug trade. British trading companies imported about 50,000 chests of opium annually (6.5 million pounds) for sale to Chinese customers.

As opium flowed into China, silver flowed out to pay for it, and great fortunes were built, not just in England but in the United States as well. With American independence, U.S. merchant ships immediately started competing with British merchants in Asian waters; the first U.S. ship arrived in China in 1784, one year after independence. By the early 1800s, Americans were intimately involved with the opium trade, particularly the Russell Company, with American sources of opium located in Turkey, while the British maintained their monopoly on Indian opium. Profits from the American opium trade added to the endowments of prominent East Coast universities, padded the fortunes of the Peabody family in Boston (and hence the Peabody Museum) and the Roosevelt family in New York, and provided capital for Alexander Graham Bell's development of the telephone.

After a second war with China (the so-called Arrow War of 1858–60, named after a British vessel), the British forced China to legalize the sale of opium. Although this opened up more markets in China for the drug, the centrality of Hong Kong in the trade declined as British and American ships called directly at more Chinese ports opened to trade. As new sources of opium in India were developed and the markets there opened up, Persian, Indian, and Chinese merchants entered the trade. By the 1870s, Chinese farmers too began poppy cultivation and opium manufacturing, especially in the interior provinces previously little connected with the booming coastal trade.[5] Perversely, this "import substitution" occurred in many of the same places where Chinese peasant farmers earlier had exercised their freedom in choosing to plant cotton. In many of these places, cash cropping of poppies thus expanded at the expense of crop farmland, giving peasant farmers greater cash income but heightening their risks if the harvest failed.

By the late 1800s, so much opium was entering China or being produced there that 10 percent of China's population, or forty million people, were users, with as many as half of those "heavy smokers." At the turn of the twentieth century, China was consuming 95 percent of the world's opium supply, with predictable social, economic, and political effects.[6] Nearly every city had its opium dens, and the sale and use of opium had entered the fabric of Chinese life. Where opium smoking had started as an elite habit, it became an item of mass consumption. Indeed, even into the twentieth century, poppy cultivation and opium manufacturing in China provided China's governments with revenue and peasant farmers with cash income.[7]

After we take a look at what happened in India and then examine the process of industrialization in Europe, I will return to a consideration of how very important China's consumption of opium was to the world economy in the late nineteenth century. For now, suffice it to note that while the Chinese bore some responsibility for bringing the drug plague on themselves, British guns had forced open the door in the first place, and then China and India took particular (peculiar) roles in the global economy as producers and consumers of opium.

India

Most of the opium consumed in China initially came from India, where British colonial policies combined with Chinese demand for the drug created an agricultural export industry. Opium became one of India's major exports in the nineteenth century, and this is part of a larger story of the transformation of India from one of the world's greatest industrial centers in the seventeenth and eighteenth centuries to a primarily agricultural economy by the mid-1800s. Indeed, India's cotton textile industry was so thoroughly destroyed by the 1820s that historians have talked about the "deindustrialization" of India, even as they have continued to debate its causes.[8]

As we have had occasion to note in previous chapters, Indian cotton goods enjoyed a worldwide market, with Africans, Europeans, and American slaves all purchasing and wearing Indian textiles. In the early 1700s, as we have seen, the British erected trade barriers to keep Indian textiles out. Still, Indian textiles found other markets, and the textile districts in Bengal, Madras, and elsewhere were kept quite busy producing for the world market. Two things changed all that.

First, in 1757 the British East India Company (EIC) acquired its first colonial beachhead in Bengal, and in 1765 it gained the right to collect land taxes from much of Bengal. This windfall gave the private EIC the revenues both to increase its purchases of Indian textiles and, more ominously, to raise and pay for its own army of Sepoys, or Indians enlisted in an army commanded by British officers. The EIC then used that army to extend its control over other parts of India. The disarray of Indian political power, the jockeying for power among Indian princes, the uncertain but certainly declining power of the Mughal emperor, and the ambitions of Hindu warrior princes all created a climate in which the scheming of the EIC, backed by its army, resulted in the gradual extension of its control throughout most of India by the 1830s. Additional large-scale and costly wars brought EIC control over the Punjab and Sindh (areas that became Pakistan after 1947). By the mid-1800s, the British had colonized all of India.

Second, the Industrial Revolution resulted in greatly reduced costs for Britain's manufactured goods, cotton textiles in particular. Not only did British cotton textiles begin to win global market share from Indian textiles because of lower price, India itself became an important market for British cotton textiles. Where in the eighteenth century British tariffs had kept Indian textiles out of England, British colonial policy in India removed tariff barriers there to imports of British manufactured textiles. With lower prices, British manufactured textiles flooded the Indian market. Between 1800 and 1810, production and export of Indian cotton textiles continued to fall while the import of British manufactures into India continued to grow. By 1820, millions of Indian weavers had been thrown out of work, their looms stood still, and their houses empty: "By the year 1833, the process of 'deindustrialization' of Bengal . . . went quite far. India lost a great art and the artisans lost their employment. The housewife's spindle seldom now twirled on the cotton-floor."[9]

Instead of exporting finished goods, India then began to export raw cotton, first to China and then to England. Former Indian cotton weavers either emigrated or took up new occupations, many turning to farming. When they did, they had to farm something that could be sold, because the British East India Company collected taxes in money, not rice or cotton. Thus old and new Indian farmers turned to cash crops such as indigo, sugarcane, cotton, and the poppies from which opium is made. The "ruralization of India" had begun.

If this story of India's decline to what we would now call a third world country, or part of "the Global South"—one producing raw materials for export so it can import manufactured goods from the "developed" world, thereby becoming locked into "underdevelopment"—appears to be one merely of "economics," it was not. Rather, it was planned to work that way for the benefit of Britain, especially after the EIC monopoly on trade in Asia was abolished in favor of the free trade principles first championed by Adam Smith in 1776 in his famous book *The Wealth of Nations*.

Combined with David Ricardo's concept of "comparative advantage," free trade and minimal government intervention in the economy were intended to transform India into a producer of food and raw materials for export. Tariffs were to be abolished, the colonial government obviously would not move either to protect the cotton textile weavers or to promote a policy of industrialization (for that would be "redundant" and would compete with the British domestic industry), and "free" markets would ensure that food and raw materials moved out of India to Britain and that Indians purchased British industrial products. Indeed, from the mid-1800s on, India reliably consumed 25 to 35 percent of Britain's exports.[10] The principles of "free trade" enforced by the colonial government set India on the path to becoming a third world country. We will see later in this chapter how that, coupled with the effects of El Niño droughts, completed India's transition to a third world nation.

Suffice it to say here that the deindustrialization of India, coupled with China's demand for opium, provided the British and their global capitalist system with immense profits. So great were these opium profits that the entire structure of world trade patterns was reversed. From 1500 to 1800, Europeans had gained access to Asian trade with New World silver, and silver flowed in great quantities to India and China. Opium tipped that flow in the opposite direction, with silver flowing into British hands throughout the nineteenth century. Without opium, historian Carl Trocki argues, "there probably would have been no British Empire."[11]

Industrialization Elsewhere

As the first to industrialize and to apply the fruits of industrialization to its military, Britain established itself as the most powerful nation in the world, and as long as Britain maintained its industrial lead over all the others, its military power remained unchallenged as well. By 1830, Britain had a virtual monopoly on industrial production of iron, steam engines, and textiles, and it used that power to sell its products throughout the world and to build the world's largest empire, encompassing not just India but other parts of Asia as well. Its paramount position led to calls to lift tariff barriers on the import of food and other raw materials so it could expand its industrial system even faster. As we saw with India, global "free trade" became Britain's program for action. However, if Britain's imposition of the principles of "free trade" on India had contributed to its third-world-ization, Britain could not do so to several other European countries or to its former colony, the United States.

The European state system, defined as it was by the frequency of war among European states (and with independence, the United States too), created strong competitive pressures for others to follow Britain's lead, especially in the quest for new colonial possessions. As Britain's overseas empire grew, other European states tried desperately to improve their militaries to compete in Asia, Africa, and Latin America. Try as the British might to prevent the transfer or export of its industrial technologies, France, the United States, and Germany soon began to industrialize. And in the second half of the nineteenth century, two additional countries—Russia and Japan—began rapid industrialization, largely in order to maintain their independence from western European colonization. If industrialization in Britain had arisen from a conjuncture of forces that no one could have predicted or planned, after it happened its results could be replicated as the result of plans implemented by strong governments forced to compete with Britain and one another.

With few exceptions, then, industrialization elsewhere proceeded with a heavy role for the state.

France

Even in the early stages of British industrialization, the French government (and others) attempted to gain access to Britain's industrial know-how by stealing information, bribing manufacturers, or hiring British industrialists. France got its start in textiles and iron and steel this way, but it was seriously hobbled by a lack of large (and easily worked) coal deposits, periodic revolutionary upheavals and war (1789–1815, 1848–51, and 1870–71), and a relatively backward agriculture. Nevertheless, the decision of the French government in 1842 to build a national railroad system, completed in the 1860s, spurred France's industrialization. Unlike the private ownership of railroads in England, in France the government provided the capital to build them, then privatized them on ninety-nine-year leases. Stimulated by the national market made possible by the railroad, other parts of the French economy also industrialized, or at least standardized. Of all the European states, France appeared to be better poised than others to make the leap into the modern world. Goldstone argues that eighteenth-century France was the closest thing to a modern nation-state in Europe, with a strong central government and a people with a common language and culture.[12] Moreover, in Georges-Eugene Haussman, France had a visionary who drove Paris into modernity.[13] Nonetheless, France remained much less able to industrialize rapidly, in part because French peasants continued to hold on to the land holdings they had won in the French Revolution and remained on their farms, leaving France at a disadvantage both to Britain and to other countries as they industrialized.

The United States

Industrialization in the United States centered on the Northeast and the Ohio River valley, and, like Britain, relied mostly on private capital, not government initiative. Textiles were among the first industries to industrialize, and New England—with supplies of raw cotton from slave-worked plantations in the South—soon competed with British textiles in both the U.S. and world markets. The state used tariffs to protect the young American industry, and the Bank of the United States provided some capital for canals and railroads. Beginning in the 1830s, local rail lines were built, and by the 1870s the transcontinental railroad spanned the continent, providing a huge demand for iron, steel, and steam-powered locomotives. The Civil War

(1860–65) spurred Northern industrialization and, as we will see later in this chapter, contributed to the industrial production of guns and a more industrial way of warfare.

Concurrently with those developments, the United States expanded west across North America from its colonial bases along the eastern seaboard. Some of this expansion came through purchase (especially the Louisiana Purchase), some came through negotiation with other powers (Britain in particular for the border between the Oregon territory and Canada), but much came through wars, especially the U.S.-Mexican War of 1846–48 and wars against Indians. In North America during the first half of the nineteenth century, for example, Mexicans in their northern states conducted many wars against Kiowa Apaches and Comanches, who in turn fought and won many battles. These wars were so brutal that parts of northern Mexico were depopulated. These conflicts then got rolled into the U.S.-Mexican War in very complicated ways and may have contributed to the U.S. victory that led to the United States getting about half of Mexico's territory, adding parts of what are now California, Arizona, New Mexico, Nevada, Utah, and Wyoming to the United States.[14] Wars against American Indians continued through the nineteenth century, with those that removed Indians from California following its 1849 incorporation into the United States so exceptional for their overt racism, violence, and effect of removing Indians from California lands (except for reservations) that historian Benjamin Madley labels the episode "an American genocide."[15]

Americans also pioneered the application of industry to agriculture on these lands cleansed of Indians. Where the British allowed their agricultural sector to decline, preferring to import cheap food from eastern Europe, Ireland, and the United States, and where French peasants acquired a tenacious hold on their minuscule landholdings as a result of the Revolution of 1789, which hindered their ability to buy or use modern farm implements until well after the end of World War II in 1945, the United States had vast plains devoid of native peoples and little labor to work them. Horse-drawn and then later steam- and gasoline-powered harvesters and combines (built by the Chicago magnate Cyrus McCormick) produced such huge agricultural surpluses that the United States became (and remains to this day) a major exporter of food in global markets.

Germany
Unlike Britain, the United States, or France, Germany was not actually unified under a single state until 1870 but rather was divided among numerous

principalities, each with its own ruler but speaking a common language that ultimately provided a basis for national unity. This political disunity hampered German efforts to industrialize. Indeed, the lack of a single state meant that the German textile industry did not have tariff protection against British imports, leading to the destruction of German textile production by the 1830s. A customs union in the 1830s, followed by the abolition of serfdom in the 1840s and the building of railroads in the 1850s, provided sufficient unity for industrialization in some areas to begin, in particular the coal- and iron-rich Ruhr River valley.

Industrializing later than Britain, France, and the United States, Germany was at a competitive disadvantage and could not industrialize following the same route (i.e., textiles to iron and steel). Instead, after unification in 1870, Germany emphasized heavy industry (iron and steel) to sustain its national railroad program and to support the growth of its military. The development of the Bessemer process for making steel combined with innovations in large-scale business organization pioneered by the Krupp metallurgy and armament works spurred rapid German industrialization in the 1870s and 1880s. Germans also linked their universities to industrial research, leading to whole new chemical and electrical industries, and for the first time explicitly applying science to industrial development.

Russia

Of the European countries with the biggest obstacles to overcome in order to industrialize, Russia stands at the head of the list. In profoundly rural Russia, peasants had been enserfed to noble estate owners until their emancipation in the early 1860s, leading to yet another form of rural society with nobles still owning the land and former serfs renting it. For centuries, Russia had exported grain to western Europe and had imported fineries consumed by the nobility. Russia also had vast natural resources—forests, coal, iron ore—that attracted western European investors who extracted them and sold them to the industrializing countries. Despite having a large army and being considered one of the "powers" of Europe (mostly because of its size and population), Russia in the nineteenth century was beginning to take on third world characteristics: exporting food and raw materials, having little or no industry of its own, and relying on others for whatever manufactured goods it could afford to import.

All of this began to change in the 1880s when the Ministry of Finance, headed energetically after 1892 by Count Sergei Witte, launched a massive railroad-building program followed by heavy industry (coal, iron and steel, and oil). Where Russia had less than 700 miles of railroads in 1860, it had 21,000 by 1894 and 36,000 by 1900, the longest stretches reaching eastward into Siberia, thereby tying that vast region and its resources closer to the needs of the industrializing parts of Russia. Like Germany and France, the Russian government, rather than private capital, played a major role in these first stages of Russia's industrialization, creating banks, hiring foreign engineers, and erecting high tariff barriers to protect its new industries from foreign competition.

Count Witte was quite clear on the reasons for Russia's crash industrialization program: to escape colonial-like relations with western Europe.

> Russia remains even at the present essentially an agricultural country. It pays for all its obligations to foreigners by exporting raw materials, chiefly of an agricultural nature, principally grain. It meets its demand for finished goods by imports from abroad. The economic relations of Russia with western Europe are fully comparable to the relations of colonial countries with their metropolises. The latter consider their colonies as advantageous markets in which they can freely sell the products of their labor and of their industry and from which they can draw with a powerful hand the raw materials necessary for them.

But Russia would not become a semicolony, Witte argued, because "Russia is an independent and strong power. . . . She wants to be a metropolis [i.e., colonial power] herself."[16]

Japan

Unlike Russia, Japan had few of the natural resources that an industrial economy needed, in particular coking coal and iron ore. Moreover, in the mid-1800s it was still following a policy of "closed country" implemented two hundred years earlier. When U.S. Commodore Matthew Perry steamed into Edo [Tokyo] Bay in 1853 demanding that Japan open itself up to "normal" international commerce ("or else . . ."), it came as a huge shock to Japan's leaders. Knowing what had happened to China at the hands of the British in the Opium War, Japan's leaders decided to negotiate an opening to the West, leading both to increased trade and contact between Japanese and Westerners, but also to the collapse of the old regime in 1868.

The new regime that replaced it, called the Meiji era after the reign title of the new (and very young) emperor Meiji (r. 1868–1912), after some fits and starts, set about dismantling the old feudal system and establishing a strong, centralized state that took on the task of industrializing Japan when private capital failed to take up the challenge. However, with few natural resources and with tariffs limited by the treaties imposed on it by the United States, Japan's industrialization took a peculiar path. Having to first export in order to import industrial raw materials, Japan turned to its silk industry, standardizing and mechanizing as much as possible to sell in the world market, taking their market share from the Chinese and the French. In the 1880s and especially the 1890s, Japan developed a cotton textile industry, again designed for export in order to acquire the foreign exchange with which to purchase industrial raw materials—coking coal and iron ore—for a heavy industry strongly tied to the needs of its military. To compete in world textile markets, Japan kept its workers' wages very low, employing large numbers of girls and women and prohibiting the formation of labor unions.

This strategy paid off handsomely. Its military was strong enough to defeat China in an 1894–95 war and then a decade later to defeat Russia. Recognizing Japan's military might in 1902, the British concluded a military pact with Japan, and in 1911 the Western powers renounced the unequal treaties that had limited Japan's ability to control its own tariffs. By 1910, Japan had the industrial capacity and technological know-how to build the world's largest warship, the *Satsuma*. Even as China and India continued to decline relative to the West, Japan's industrialization by 1900 was an early indication that the West would not continue to dominate the world through a monopoly of industrial production, but that prior patterns of Asian vitality would begin to show through.

As this brief survey suggests, among the requirements for industrialization was a strong state determined to create the material prerequisites for powerful militaries. For differing reasons and at various times, France, Germany, Russia, and Japan were able to build strong states. Those parts of the world that had weak states (e.g., most of Latin America or the Ottoman empire), states that were becoming enfeebled (e.g., China), states that had been colonized (e.g., India, much of Southeast Asia, and, as we will see, Africa), or even stateless people within empires who wanted independence (as we will see below) were doomed to remain in the biological old regime, at best exporting raw materials or food to the industrialized world and getting progressively poorer relative to the industrialized world.

New Dynamics in the Industrial World

By 1900, 80 percent of world industrial output came from Europe and the United States, with Japan contributing another 10 percent; China contributed 7 percent and India 2 percent, totaling 99 percent of all industrial production. Thus the one hundred years from 1800 to 1900 saw a great reversal, with Europe and the United States taking the pride of place previously held by India and China. Part of the immense gap between the wealthiest and poorest parts of our world thus can be explained by industrialization and the escape by some parts of the world—Europe, the United States, and Japan—from the constraints of the biological old regime. Actually, of course, it is more correct to say that industrial output came from selected regions, not entire countries: parts of New England in the United States, Lancashire and other parts of northwestern England, the Rhineland in Germany, Milan in northern Italy, and so on. For even within those industrializing and increasingly rich countries, there remained impoverished regions.

In the biological old regime, the size and quality of agricultural harvests determined the economic health, wealth, and well-being of a society: the larger the harvest, the more food, the lower wages, the more competitive industry, and so on. Of course, the opposite was also true. Although climate and the vagaries of the weather certainly had a major impact on agriculture, people's ingenuity, social organization, and hard work could minimize adverse climatic effects. But still, the biological old regime set the tune by which agrarian economies danced.

That was (and is) not so with the new industrial economies. Having escaped from the limits of the biological old regime and its dynamics, the new industrial economies were entering into uncharted waters that became ever more uncertain as more of Europe industrialized. So, in the nineteenth century, the industrial world began to experience a new kind of regulator on economic activity: boom and then bust. As more and more factories were built to produce the same commodity, especially in different countries, global supply at times vastly outstripped demand, leading to falling prices to clear the inventory buildup. Competitors slashed prices by slashing wages, further depressing demand, at least for consumer goods, leading to a "recession" or, depending on how deep it was and how long it lasted, a "depression." The first multi-national recession occurred in 1857, and it was fairly short lived, followed by a resumption of the economic boom, which lasted until the early 1870s. But then in 1873 another recession began, which lasted, in some historians' views, until 1896; during those twenty years, prices in Britain fell by 40 percent. This pattern of economic "boom and bust" has persisted to the present.

Until the 1870s, most industrializing countries had followed Britain's lead in favoring international free trade, for all in one way or another had benefited. But the slump of 1873 changed that, with Germany and Italy raising tariffs to protect their textile industries, followed in the 1890s by France, the

United States, and, as we have already seen, Russia. Japan was forbidden by treaty from raising tariffs. Expectedly, as a result of the new tariffs, British exports to the United States and the industrializing parts of Europe dropped, creating a sizable balance-of-payments problem for Britain and fueling calls within Britain for protectionist tariffs. Had that happened, the industrializing world might have entered a period of sharp contraction into something like the exclusive trading blocs that arose in the 1930s in the wake of the Great Depression, followed by the horrors of World War II. Global capitalism may well have been strangled shortly after its birth.

Except that Britain's huge trade surpluses with Asia, India, and China in particular, made possible by the opium trade, kept the system from crashing. With these huge trade surpluses, Britain was able to settle its debts to the United States and Germany in particular, keeping capitalist development alive there (and elsewhere in Europe).[17] In a very real sense, opium—China's consumption and Britain's trafficking—is one of the factors that kept the capitalist world economy going through the recession of 1873–96.

Although the industrializing world did not then collapse into exclusive and warring economic trading blocs (as it would in the 1930s), the slump did sharpen competition and tension between industrializing countries in the late nineteenth century. As we will see later in this chapter, this contributed to the "New Imperialism" of the period, where European countries and the United States competed to grab large parts of the world to create, or add to, their colonial empires.

The Environmental Consequences of Industrialization

As most of us know from our daily experience, factories can expel significant amounts of waste that enters the air, water, and land, polluting the environment. The same was true with factories in the nineteenth century, only more so because controls on the amount of pollutants factories could release had yet to be enacted and enforced. Paintings and photographs of nineteenth-century textile mills and iron foundries belching huge amounts of black smoke from tall chimneys (designed to get the smoke high enough that the workers, managers, or owners at the factory itself wouldn't have to choke on the discharge) tell a significant part of the story (see figure 5.4).

Vignettes from three places can convey a sense of the levels of nineteenth-century industrial pollution.[18] In England's coal-mining districts, digging up the mineralized biomass spread coal waste everywhere. "Imagine black roads," a German visitor remarked, "winding through verdant fields, the long trains of wagons heavily laden with black treasures. . . . Burning

Figure 5.4. Factory Smokestacks, Nineteenth-Century England

mounds of coal scattered over the plain." In Manchester, "the cloud of coal vapor may be observed from afar. The houses are blackened by it. The river, which flows through Manchester, is so filled with waste dyestuffs that it resembles a dyer's vat." So much soot, fumes, and noxious gases were released into the air that it killed plants of all kinds, stained buildings, and caused all manner of lung diseases. When faced with complaints, mill owners and town fathers pointed out the jobs that had been created, took deep breaths of the acrid air, and said, "Ah, the smell of money!"

In North American textile mill towns that used waterpower to turn spindles and power looms, the building of dams "tamed" the wild Merrimac River and harnessed its power to the will of humans. After the textile mills turned to steam to power their factories, the Merrimac became "a sink" for industrial waste. Dyes from textiles, chemicals from tanneries, and waste from lumber mills clogged the Merrimac. "The poisonous dyes and mill refuse . . . find an outlet in the river. The disease-laden water flows only nine miles, and then the people of Lawrence drink it. No wonder that disease and death follow." The southwestern part of Pennsylvania around "Steel City," Pittsburgh, mined coal and made iron and steel. Hundreds of "beehive" ovens belched particulates and noxious gases into the air, and the whole surrounding area was covered in a dusting of ash, dust, and coal tar.

Such industrial pollution was mostly local, coming directly from the factories themselves or from the urban areas that sprang up where the hundreds of thousands of workers lived. The British manufacturing cities of Leeds, Sheffield, and Birmingham grew 40 percent in a decade (1821–31); Manchester, a leading textile mill town, grew from about 25,000 in 1772 to 367,232 in 1850. And like factories and people (and all other living things), cities had a metabolism: they took in food, water, fuel, and energy; used them; and then expelled wastes. Certainly, burning coal for heating and cooking added smoke to urban areas, making the air sometimes chokingly thick with black fumes. In addition to the pollution caused by industrialization, I want to explore another part of the environmental story line here, the place of nitrogen in human and urban waste cycles.

In chapter 1, I introduced the idea that nitrogen is essential for plant and animal life, that of humans included. Plants use nitrogen in the process of photosynthesis, and humans (and all animals) need nitrogen to form the amino acid building blocks of protein and hence of muscle. Without nitrogen, humans cannot exist, and so we ingest it by eating plants that have nitrogen or animals that already have produced proteins in their muscles. After converting the nitrogen we need into proteins, we then expel both excess nitrogen and that produced as human tissues break down in our solid and liquid waste (human feces and urine). Adults in North America with today's diets annually expel about four pounds (two kilos) of nitrogen in their bodily waste.

Several issues arise from these biological, material, and social facts of our existence. Nearly all of the food that humans consume in cities is produced on farms and then shipped, trucked, or carried into cities. The very act of growing food, as discussed earlier, takes nutrients from the soil. Selling food to urban consumers thus, in essence, transfers those nutrients from rural farms to urban cities, creating problems for both. Farmers have to figure out ways of getting nutrients back into their farmland, or else it will be quickly degraded and no longer productive. For several decades in the nineteenth century, one way farmers in the United States, Germany, England, and elsewhere in Europe replaced nitrogen in their fields was by drawing on the vast guano deposits on islands off Peru and mineral deposits of sodium nitrate from Peru's arid deserts.[19] Until they were depleted toward the end of the nineteenth century, these supplies of nitrogen pumped up farm yields, but in the meantime nitrogen continued to be removed from the soil and transferred to cities in the form of food. For cities, the major problem is how to dispose of all the human (and animal) waste that this process produces on a daily basis.

Some agricultural societies with cities addressed the problem by recycling human and other urban waste back to farms, where it was treated and used to fertilize fields. The two most extensive and long-standing of such systems operated in China and Japan, keeping cities clean and getting the nitrogen excreted in human waste back to farms.[20] Certainly, American and European cities too had systems whereby "night soil" was collected and returned to farms. But as industrial cities sprang up and populations swelled beyond the point where all human excrement could be retrieved and recycled, it flowed untreated into streams and rivers, not only polluting those water sources with human waste and the disease-carrying microbes it carried, but sending valuable nitrogen literally "down the tube." So much human waste was dumped into England's Thames River that in 1858 "The Great Stink" prompted London to build a sewer system that collected the waste and dumped it further downstream, where the stench didn't offend Londoners. The mined and quickly depleted Peruvian guano and sodium nitrate added little to the global flow of reactive nitrogen that bacteria fixed and denitrified on land each year. We will see in the next chapter how an industrial process shattered the limit on the natural supply of nitrogen in the world. In the meantime, because nitrogen was essential for farmers, it provided urban planners with an incentive to try to capture nitrogen from human waste and return it to farms—to recycle it.[21]

The first major industrial attempt to address these interrelated rural and urban waste problems came in the early years of the twentieth century in the American city of Milwaukee. Because of the bacteria in human waste and urban wastewater, it could not be applied directly to farmers' fields without first being treated in some way. Sanitary engineers worked on this problem, and by the mid-1890s they had worked out most of the issues by directing wastewater into settling tanks where sewage-digesting microbes turned the excrement into a sludge that could be discharged into drying fields. Once dry, it could then be cut or chopped up into nitrogen-rich material that could be sold and trucked back to farms and spread on fields. Over the next decades, engineers and politicians in the city of Milwaukee designed and built a wastewater treatment plant that came on line in 1925 to solve Milwaukee's human waste problem by turning human sewage into fertilizer. Milwaukee's success appeared to show the promise of a vast nitrogen recycling system that would simultaneously solve the problems rural farmers faced with the removal of nitrogen from their lands and those of cities trying to cope with all that human waste.[22] But as we will see in the next chapter, the development of an industrial system to produce nitrogenous fertilizer out of thin air killed this recycling process, leaving cities with the problem of what to do with their mounting piles of processed human waste. The problem remains with us today.

Sources of Global Warming Gases in the Nineteenth Century
Surprisingly, though, considering the visible local pollution of the atmosphere from industrialization in the nineteenth century, the footprint and effects of the release of the greenhouse gases carbon dioxide (CO_2) and methane (CH_4) were less noticeable in terms of the global climatic system. To be sure, the burning of increasingly large amounts of coal did release CO_2 and CH_4 into the atmosphere. But so too did land clearance for farming—probably more than industry in the nineteenth century. John L. Brooke cites evidence that methane from Chinese rice paddies and the vast clearance of land for farming in North America "were far and away the most potent sources of greenhouse gas emissions until the very end of the nineteenth century." On the other hand, the depopulation of West Africa because of the slave trade probably resulted in reforestation there, with those forests acting as carbon sinks as African slaves cleared American forests for plantations.[23] But by the twentieth century, as we will see in the next chapter, industry far exceeded agriculture as the most potent source of greenhouse gas emissions.

The Social Consequences of Industrialization
The Industrial Revolution transformed—and still is transforming—the patterns of life. Just as the Neolithic agricultural revolution 11,000 years earlier transformed the relationships of people to one another and the environment, so too did the Industrial Revolution. Work, families, cities, time, culture, values, and more changed with the industrial mode of production. Although the precise ways these changes worked themselves out varied from place to place, there were broad similarities. In the place of fields and farms, there were factories; in the place of seasons and annual festivals as the markers of time, there came the hour and the time clock; in the place of large families, there came small ones; in the place of stability, there came change. The social and economic changes extended far beyond the industrial cores in Europe and North America to those parts of the world that became incorporated into the global systems supplying labor and raw materials for industrial

production and the consequent accumulation of additional capital for investment and accumulation and concentration of wealth into the hands of wealthy elites. The labor coerced from Africans shackled, beaten, and horribly disfigured in the Belgian Congo in the 1870s and 1880s to produce rubber is an especially egregious and brutal episode.[24]

Factories and Work

Industrialization in the first instance called into being a large new working class mostly concentrated in growing cities. Indeed, a common measure of industrialization is the percentage of a country's population living in cities. For England, 50 percent lived in cities by 1850; in Germany that mark was reached by 1900, in the United States by 1920, and in Japan by 1930. For new workers, especially those fresh from the farms, factories imposed a new concept of work. Machines dictated the pace of work, supervisors set rules for eating and bodily functions, and owners set wage rates as low as possible to ensure high profits.

Factories were not pleasant places, and it is hard to imagine anyone actually choosing to work there rather than outdoors in the field. But, in England at least, prior changes in agriculture had pushed large numbers of peasants off the land *before* the Industrial Revolution. There were, therefore, lots of poor and barely employed people in London glad to take a job, even if the wages only met bare subsistence needs.

Because of the misery of working conditions, "disciplining" the labor force to the new rhythms of the workplace and ensuring that they returned day after day became the task of "management," which grew as a new occupation and formed the backbone of the new "middle class." Much of the early British workforce—especially in textiles but also in the mines—was composed of women and children, who could be more easily managed than men. Although that changed over time and more men than women composed the English working class by 1900, in Japan girls and young women too formed the backbone of the textile workforce. There, hard-pressed rural families "contracted" their daughters out to textile mills: the family patriarch got the pay (in annual installments), and the girls got work and the promise of life in safe dormitories until they were ready to marry.[25]

Women and Families

Industrialization remade the family. In agrarian societies, farming families were units of both production and consumption. Urban industrial life increasingly removed production from families, changing roles and relationships among men, women, and children. Where women and children initially worked in factories (giving us the horror-filled novels of Charles Dickens such as *David Copperfield* and *Oliver Twist*), legislation restricting children's and women's labor turned factories into workplaces for men. A woman's place was redefined as being in the home and taking care of domestic affairs, even while taking in laundry or other odd chores to help make ends meet. Prohibited from working until age twelve or thirteen, the task of children became (minimally) to master an elementary school education. As children came to be seen as causing family expenses and not contributing to family income, the number of children married couples were willing to have began to decline, especially in the period after 1870, and families got smaller.

Resistance and Revolution

Factories were battlefields for daily confrontations, sometimes small and sometimes large, between workers and factory owners or their representatives. Simply not returning to work was one form of resistance, but then one would forfeit what pay was owed. Working as slowly as possible was another response, as was sabotage of the machinery to stop it, if even only for a little while. With time, workers discovered that collective action could win them higher wages, better conditions, or shorter hours, but usually only after long, bitter, and often bloody strikes.[26]

It is little wonder that the new urban hellholes and factories produced not just commodities flooding world markets but organized resistance to factories and to the industrial system. Early opponents were simply repelled by the smoke-belching factories, the "unnatural" modes of work, and the impact they were having on family life, calling instead for more "natural" ways of organizing work. The most rigorous and long-lasting challenge to the capitalist mode of production, though, came from ideas propounded by Karl Marx and his lifelong collaborator, Friedrich Engels.

Publishing *The Communist Manifesto* in 1848, Marx and Engels (whose father owned a textile mill) tossed down the gauntlet:

> A specter is haunting Europe—the specter of communism. . . . The history of all hitherto existing society is the history of class struggles. . . . Our epoch . . . shows . . . this distinctive feature: it has simplified the class antagonisms. Society as a whole is more and more splitting into two great hostile camps, into two great classes directly facing each other: *bourgeoisie* [capitalist class] and *proletariat* [working class]. . . . What the bourgeoisie . . . produces, above all, is its own grave diggers. Its fall and the victory of the proletariat are equally inevitable.[27]

And for a few months in 1848, it looked like Marx's predictions might have been coming true. Throughout western Europe, revolts of the laboring poor toppled governments in France, the Italian states, the Habsburg empire, and Switzerland; threatened the established order in Spain and Denmark; and shook Ireland, Greece, and Britain. Although the political demands of the rebels mostly envisioned greatly extended democratic rights for working people, nonetheless, the more comfortable middle class and especially the factory-owning capitalist class felt threatened and so supported the suppression of the revolts. But the growing division of society into warring classes—even the threat that that would happen—presented a serious problem to the rulers of European states. And satisfying the demand for factory labor create a new challenge for states: controlling migration.

Industrialization and Migration

Industrialization created two kinds of mass migration.[28] The first was rural-to-urban migration within industrializing regions. Within Europe, migrants from Ireland traveled to England for work in factories, and others from southern and eastern Europe migrated to factory towns in northern Europe, especially France and Germany.[29] Japan too saw young women relocated from farms to urban textile mills. Within the United States, a mass migration of African Americans out of the former slave states came in the early twentieth century when many decided that the reign of terror and violence perpetrated on them following the end of the Civil War—sometimes euphemistically called "Jim Crow" but which was actually a segregated and unequal society enforced with beatings and terror at the hands of Ku Klux Klan—was intolerable. With the prospects for better lives working in the factories than remaining sharecroppers, between 1916 and 1940, six million African Americans joined "the Great Migration" to northern industrial cities.

The industrial development of the United States spurred a second kind of mass migration, the transatlantic flow of people from Europe to the United States, but that is not the whole story of migrations in the industrializing world. To be sure, tens of millions of people did migrate to the Americas with a huge surge toward the end of the nineteenth century and into the first decade of the twentieth. Nearly two-thirds of these went to the United States, with the rest divided among Canada, Argentina, and Brazil. In addition, the availability of farmland in the American Midwest and West, cleansed of native peoples murdered or herded into reservations, drew another ten million to western frontiers. To be sure, "Europeans fled grinding poverty, economic exploitation, and an untold number of hardships," yet the focus on the European migration experience neglects, in the words of Eliot Dickinson, an "African experience [that] was different in that it was indescribably violent and outright deadly."[30]

The story of migration to the United States is part of a much broader narrative of human experience that circled the globe. Like transoceanic migrations in the early modern world, the migration out of Europe and Asia also occurred in the context of transnational networks. Diasporas composed of ethnic networks of Armenian, Jewish, Chinese, and Indian merchants funneled labor and capital to distant outposts in Africa, South America, and Southeast Asia for the extraction of tropical raw materials. Families also remained at the center of decision making about migration. Relatives who had already migrated formed important nodes of information about when and where to migrate, and immigrant communities formed support networks for those who followed.

Work by historian Adam McKeown shows that long-distance migration flows from India and southern China to Southeast Asia and the Indian Ocean, and from Northeastern Asia and Russia to Siberia, Manchuria, Japan, and central Asia, were comparable in number—around 50 million from 1846 to 1940—to those from Europe to the Americas over the same period.[31] To be sure, industrialization of some parts of the world (see chapter 4) and not of others is the context for increased migration of settlers and workers to the industrial centers. Chinese migrated to California starting in the 1850s to work silver and gold mines there, but Chinese and Indians migrated as well to Southeast Asia to open up mines and rubber plantations. The same was true with developments elsewhere in Asia and Africa, as the compelling story of the young Ghanaian woman Abina powerfully illustrates.[32] McKeown's work is just the beginning of what he hopes will be much more scholarship on the global nature of migration rather than only the narrative of the Atlantic migration from Europe to the Americas. "The nearly contemporaneous rise of global migration suggests that non-Europeans were very much involved in the expansion and integration of the world economy, well beyond the direct intervention of Europe." European colonial empires structured their own migration flows of people from the colonies to the metropole—for example, with South Asian Indians moving to London or Algerians heading to Paris.

Second, the waves of mass migration from the 1870s on spawned regimes of regulation that established defined national borders for policing and attempts by various states "to encourage, restrict, select, protect, distribute, and monitor migration." Where China, Russia, and Italy encouraged migration to serve state purposes, others—especially the United States and Australia—sought to cut off immigration of "undesirables," in particular Chinese and other Asians. Following large inflows of Chinese miners into California and Australia, anti-Asian immigration laws after the 1880s "severely reduced migration to these destinations." Notably, the creation of borders and immigration rules and regulations for policing and regulating who would be allowed into countries coincided with and contributed to nineteenth-century nationalist movements and racist social Darwinist ideas about a hierarchy of races, topics of the next sections of this chapter.

Nations and Nationalism

States, or what we now more commonly refer to as "governments," have been around for a long time and have taken a number of forms. In this book, so far we have talked mostly about agrarian and conquest empires, especially in Asia and Mesoamerica, and about the various monarchies and principalities in Europe and their transformations into centralized states under the pressures of war. The process of European "state building," which was discussed in chapter 4, it might be remembered, resulted in fairly large territorial states that had both the population and the wealth to sustain competitive interstate pressures, with seventeenth- and eighteenth-century Britain and France building the most successful states.

In the nineteenth century, states underwent additional changes, becoming much closer in form and function to twentieth-century states, and they became linked with another force, that of nation building, or nationalism, giving us the modern nation-state. Where the modern state can be defined, the concept of nation is a little bit harder, since exceptions always seem to be found. But let us start by defining the modern state as a territory (usually contiguous) over whose inhabitants the government rules directly through salaried bureaucrats, not through intermediaries or agents such as aristocrats with their own power bases, enforcing uniform administrative and institutional arrangements and taking notice of its subjects or citizens, generally through representatives (elected or otherwise).[33] The French Revolution of 1789 and the extension of some of its ideas, especially that of people's right to be politically active "citizens" rather than merely the "subjects" of their sovereign, and that of universal administrative codes and direct contact between state and citizen to other parts of Europe by the French general/

emperor Napoleon in the early 1800s (the Napoleonic Code), were especially important in the genesis of the modern state.

The idea of "nations" and "nationalism," on the other hand, arose only after modern states and industrial society had emerged.[34] States were confronted with a dilemma, especially acute after the French Revolution called into question all the traditional sources of state legitimacy (divine ordination, dynastic succession, or historic right), of how to ensure loyalty to the state and the ruling system. This question became critical as industrialization created new social classes, especially the urban working class and the capitalist class, the revolts of the early 1800s culminating in the mass uprisings of 1848, and the vast flows of Asians, East Europeans, and other nonwhites into industrializing countries. To the rulers of nineteenth-century European states, huge schisms were appearing among their peoples and between the people and the state, threatening to bring the governments down.

Also, industrialization created new forms of communication, especially the railroad and the telegraph, which in turn spawned economic and emotional needs among people who seemed to share common bonds of language and culture but did not have a unified state—in particular the various German and Italian states. This gave rise to the idea that a "nation"—that is, a "people" sharing a common language and culture—ought to have a single, unified state, and it led to a new role for professional historians in writing nationalist histories.[35] This kind of European nationalism fueled many movements in Europe from 1830 to 1880 of state building on the basis of a "nation" and "national boundaries." This was most strikingly illustrated by the Italian nationalist Giuseppe Mazzini and his call for "every nation a state; only one state for the entire nation."

This idea then informed the rulers of states, who were feeling pressured by the revolutionary uprisings from below, and offered them a way to begin ensuring the loyalty of "their people." The problem these rulers faced, though, was twofold. The first aspect was how to get their people to identify themselves as a "nation," and then how to link that identity with the state. For this, public education (at first elementary but in the twentieth century increasingly secondary too) was especially useful, and so too were historians in constructing celebratory "national histories."[36]

Some territorial states, though, had been constructed with more than one "nation" in them. Great Britain was formed with the union of Scotland and England, but also included the Welsh and Irish. The Russian empire as it expanded in the eighteenth and nineteenth centuries came to be known as "the prison house of nationalities." The Balkans were an especially nettle-some place for the Ottoman empire, with Slavs, Serbs, Croats, Bosnians, Albanians, and Macedonians under the rule of Turks. One possible solution to this problem of multiple ethnicities, or nations, within one state was the French and American one of defining "the people" not in ethnic, religious, or even linguistic terms but in political terms: "Americans are those who wish to be [Americans]. . . . French nationality was French citizenship: eth-nicity, history, the language or patois spoken at home, were irrelevant to the definition of 'the nation.' "[37] For eighteenth- and nineteenth-century Ameri-cans, that formulation obviously applied only to free whites and excluded slaves and native Indians, the latter of whom were either removed from the land and rounded up into reservations or exterminated in genocidal wars, as mentioned earlier in this chapter.[38]

By the second half of the nineteenth century, European states (and the United States) found it more powerful to invent nationalist traditions and to inculcate those into their populations, creating an imagined but nonetheless real nationalism. On the other hand, people who considered themselves "nations" but without states—Zionists, Irish, Serbs—began agitating for their own states. In short, nationalism of an exclusive, ethnic, and cultural kind—one that says "my people are great"—began to shape Europe and the United States, contributing to the way Europeans related to the rest of the world, to the pressures leading to World War I in the early twentieth century, and to the modern nation-state, with all its contradictions, ambiguities, and power over people.

Nationalism, economic competition among European states, internal social tensions arising from industrialization, and strategic considerations led to several wars among European states in the nineteenth century and to wars of imperialist expansion against Asians and Africans in the last thirty years of the century. The largest inter-European war was the Crimean War of 1854–56, pitting Russia on one side against an alliance of Britain, France, and Turkey and resulting in the deaths of over 600,000 soldiers on all sides. Russia's loss contributed to its decision to eliminate serfdom and to industri-alize. The American Civil War (1860–65) killed additional hundreds of thousands of men. Finally, the nationalist unifications of Italy and Germany contributed to four more major European wars, culminating in the Franco-Prussian War of 1870–71. Nationalism thus was injected into the ongoing tensions among European states, helping recruit young men into their armies but also contributing to racist ideas about the superiority of Europeans and white Americans, and the inferiority of others, especially Africans and Asians.

The Scrambles for Africa and China

After the Franco-Prussian War, Europeans for the most part stopped warring against one another (at least until 1914 and the outbreak of World War I) and instead directed their military power against China, Southeast Asia, the Middle East, and Africa.[39] Competition among European powers thus was displaced into those parts of the world we now call the third world, contributing to their decline into that status.

Africa

For centuries, Europeans found penetration of Africa to be almost impossible: various diseases endemic to the tropical parts of the continent, especially malaria, restricted slave-trading Europeans to coastal enclaves free from disease. By the nineteenth century, steamships may have permitted access to the interior on Africa's various rivers, but malaria still killed most of the explorers. Although the cause of malaria was not discovered until 1880 and the means of transmission by mosquito was not uncovered until 1897, a process of trial and error led to the realization by the mid-nineteenth century that the bark of the cinchona tree native to South America contained quinine, a substance that prevented malaria. British military personnel then successfully planted cinchona seeds in India and by the 1870s had greatly increased the supply of quinine to their troops. The subsequent European "scramble for Africa" may have been initiated in the 1870s by French insecurities arising from their defeat by the Germans in 1871, by the bizarre and secretive scheming by Belgium's King Leopold II,[40] and by British determination to protect their colonial interests in India, but all of those motivations would have been irrelevant had it not been for the discovery that quinine prevented malaria, or for the development of steamboats that could open the rivers, or for new technology in guns that killed more efficiently. The new technologies mattered.

In earlier chapters we traced some of the developments in the technology of guns, which remained fairly stable from the early 1500s to the early 1800s and featured the muzzle-loading musket. Muskets took several minutes to load, made huge puffs of smoke when fired, and were barely accurate even within a few hundred yards. Military tactics took account of these shortcomings, but clearly more accurate guns with greater range and less evidence of having been shot (thereby concealing the soldier's position) would be vast improvements.

Those improvements came rapidly after 1850 with the "rifling" of the barrel to improve accuracy, the creation of paper and then copper cartridges ignited by smokeless powder and inserted by breech loading, and the invention of mechanisms for repeating fire. The American Civil War and a European arms race in the 1860s and 1870s revolutionized guns and vastly increased the ability of European soldiers to kill rapidly, from a distance of a couple of thousand yards, and in any weather. The pinnacle of perfection came in the 1880s with the invention of a reliable machine gun, named after its inventor, Hiram Maxim.

By the 1870s, Europeans thus had the "tools of empire" with which to engage and defeat Africans on African soil. Africans put up valiant and stiff resistance, but their technology was no match for the Maxim gun. The most famous and perhaps deadly instance was at the 1898 Battle of Omdurman, where British troops confronted the 40,000-man Sudanese Dervish army. As described by Winston Churchill, the future British prime minister, the Dervish attack was quickly repulsed by Maxim guns mounted on river gunboats: "The charging Dervishes sank down in tangled heaps. The masses in the rear paused, irresolute. It was too hot even for them." On shore, the British "infantry fired steadily and stolidly, without hurry or excitement, for the enemy were far away and the officers careful." To the Sudanese "on the other side bullets were shearing through flesh, smashing and splintering bone; blood spouted from terrible wounds; valiant men struggling on through a hell of whistling metal, exploding shells, and spurting dust—suffering, despairing, dying." After five hours, the British lost twenty soldiers; ten thousand Sudanese were killed.[41] As a saying had it:

> Whatever happens, we have got
> the Maxim gun, and they have not.[42]

The high tide of the New Imperialism and the "scramble for Africa" was keenly exemplified by the Berlin Conference of 1884–85. Fearful that competition among European powers might lead to armed conflict, Germany's Chancellor Otto von Bismarck invited representatives from thirteen European countries and the United States to Berlin to regulate the colonization of Africa, an event captured in figure 5.5 that shows the delegates seated at a large conference table dividing up Africa among them. Of the African states, only Ethiopia, under the extraordinary leadership of King Menelik, defeated the weakest European power, Italy, and thereby maintained its independence.[43] (See map 5.1.)

China

If visions of vast stores of raw materials fueled imperialist dreams of Africa, for China it was access to its market. As Britain's cotton textile industrialists dreamed, "if we could add but one inch to the shirt of every Chinese, we could keep the mills of Manchester running forever." Although the market for "400 hundred million customers" continually evaded Europeans, their quest to "open" China was pressed throughout the nineteenth century, culminating in the "scramble for concessions" at the end of the century.

Following the Opium War (1839–42), China was torn by a massive civil war, the Taiping Rebellion (1850–65). Fueled by impoverished peasants and displaced workers and led by a man who believed himself to be the younger brother of Jesus Christ with a mission to establish the Heavenly Kingdom on Earth, the Taipings nearly swept the Manchu rulers of the Chinese empire

Figure 5.5. The Berlin Conference of 1884–85

from the historical stage. Combining appeals for a new, just social order resting on land reform, equality among all peoples (both social classes and genders within China, and nations globally), and ousting China's Manchu rulers, the Taipings swept up from south China to capture the southern capital of Nanjing on the Yangzi River. But for squabbling, bizarre behavior, and some poor strategic decisions among the Taiping leadership, China's modern history might have been very different from how it turned out. As it was, conservative landowners created their own armed forces, defeated the Taipings, and saved the Manchu regime.

Enfeebled by the civil war (during which some twenty million may have died), hobbled by the treaties imposed by the British after the two Opium Wars, and now committed to reviving the old agrarian regime to satisfy the demands of the landowners who saved the dynasty, the Manchus began a program of limited military modernization called "Self-Strengthening" to protect themselves against foreign aggression. Although having some success at building what appeared to be a modern military, China nonetheless was subject to constant foreign pressure not just from the British but from the Russians, French, Germans, and, as they industrialized, the Japanese. The latter two were to be responsible for sparking the "scramble for concessions," which led to the partition of China among "the Powers" in 1900.

Industrializing late, Japan too harbored imperialist expansion plans, directing its attention to Korea and the island of Taiwan. Although China considered Korea to be part of its tributary system and thus subordinate to it, Korea nonetheless had its own internal politics. When those sharpened and resulted in various insurrections in the 1880s and 1890s, the Japanese took the opportunity to support the side opposed to the Chinese. When China intervened (as it thought it had the right to) in 1894, war between China and Japan broke out. Surprising most observers, Japan rather handily defeated the Chinese in a major naval battle, bringing the war to an end.

Determined to press its advantage over a weakened and demoralized opponent, Japan extracted numerous concessions from the Chinese, including a huge $300 million indemnity, the island of Taiwan and the Liaodong Peninsula in Manchuria, the "independence" of Korea (thereby allowing Japan to exercise its influence over it), and the right of Japanese nationals to open factories and own mines in China. Russia, which opposed Japan's interests in Manchuria (its expansion into Siberia created its own interest in Manchuria), then convinced the Germans and French to join with it to force Japan to return Manchuria to Chinese sovereignty.

Map 5.1. The World circa 1900

RUSSIAN EMPIRE

Trans-Siberian R.R.

Siberia

TANU TUVA

Russian Manchuria

KHIVA

MONGOLIA

BOKHARA

Beijing

KOREA (Jap.)

PERSIA

AFGHAN-ISTAN

CHINESE EMPIRE

JAPAN

NEPAL

Delhi

PACIFIC

OMAN

INDIA (British)

Arabian Sea

Mumbai

BURMA (Br.)

South China Sea

Taiwan (Japan)

FRENCH SOMALILAND

Madras

SIAM

FRENCH INDOCHINA

PHILIPPINES (U.S.)

OCEAN

BRITISH SOMALILAND

Strait of Melaka

CEYLON (Br.)

BRITISH MALAYA

ITALIAN SOMALILAND

GERMAN NEW GUINEA

BRITISH EAST AFRICA

INDIAN

Singapore (Br.)

INDONESIA (Dutch)

GERMAN EAST AFRICA

OCEAN

E. TIMOR (Port.)

BRITISH NEW GUINEA

AUSTRALIA (British)

NEW ZEALAND (British)

India

PUNJAB

BHUTAN

Delhi

NEPAL

SIND

Ganges

GUJARAT

BENGAL

BURMA (Br.)

Mumbai

INDIA (British)

Arabian Sea

Bay of Bengal

Madras

CEYLON (Br.)

Succeeding in doing so and humbling Japan, the Russians earned the gratitude of China's rulers, who in turn granted the Russians concessions to develop a railroad in Manchuria. The Germans, who wanted a naval port in China to equal the British, French, and Russians, asked China for a base as a reward for their role in turning back the Japanese but were rejected. But then, in 1898, using the murder of two German missionaries in China as a pretext, Germany seized a harbor on the Shandong peninsula and forced China to lease the harbor to it for ninety-nine years. This act unleashed "the scramble for concessions," in which all the other powers also extracted ninety-nine-year concessions from the Chinese government, "slicing China like a melon," as the phrase at the time had it. By 1900 it looked as if China too would be divided up into colonial possessions, as Africa had been.

But Britain needed "open trade" in China to keep its global empire working. Fortunately for the British, the United States had just acquired a colonial presence in the Philippines as a result of the 1898 war with Spain and was easily convinced to carry the torch for "open trade" for all powers in China. Expressed as the Open Door Notes of 1900, the United States articulated a policy, for various reasons and rather surprisingly accepted by the other powers, that kept China from being colonized and kept it open so it could be equally exploited by all the powers, Japan and the United States included.

El Niño Famines and the Making of the Third World

Although industrialization, improvements in military technology, strategic jockeying among "the powers," and the economic slump, which began in the 1870s, go a long way toward accounting for the dominance of Europeans, Americans, and Japanese over Africans, Asians, and Latin Americans, there was as well an environmental dimension to the making of the third world and the gap between the industrialized and unindustrialized parts of the world.

Where the very success of China's economy in the biological old regime had begun putting stress on its forest reserves by 1800, leading to serious deforestation by the middle of the nineteenth century, other parts of Asia and Latin America were deforested by other processes. In India, forests in the peninsula were cleared long before the population began to grow around the middle of the nineteenth century. Warring Indian princes cleared forests to deny their enemies cover, a policy of "ecological warfare" that the colonizing British also carried out with gusto. Additionally, dislocated peasant farmers cleared land, and there was some commercial logging in the north as well.

All of these contributed to the extensive deforestation of India by the late nineteenth century.[44]

In Latin America, different processes led to massive deforestation. There, colonial powers, intent upon extracting raw materials and transforming their Latin American holdings into sugar or coffee plantations, cleared forests. In Brazil, the great forests of the Atlantic seaboard were first cleared for sugar plantations. In the early 1800s, Brazilian landowners switched to coffee crops. As a tree (not native, but imported from Ethiopia), coffee presumably could have been planted and replanted on the same land, given adequate care to the fertility of the soil. But as it turned out, landowners preferred to deplete the soil and after thirty years or so clear another patch of virgin forest. "Thus coffee marched across the highlands, generation by generation, leaving nothing in its wake but denuded hills."[45] And on Caribbean islands, French and British colonists in the eighteenth century removed so much forest for sugar plantations that even then observers worried that it was causing the climate of the islands to change, getting drier and drier with every stand of forest cut down.[46]

By the last quarter of the nineteenth century, then, large parts of Asia and Latin America experienced significant environmental damage caused by deforestation and the depletion of soil fertility.[47] Of course, being agricultural societies, these changes put additional stresses on the biological old regime, making them even more susceptible to climatic shock and increasing the possibility of widespread famine.

Mostly, harvest failures were localized affairs. But in the late nineteenth century, a climatic phenomenon we now know as El Niño (or by its more scientific name, ENSO, for El Niño–Southern Oscillation) intensified to the greatest extent in perhaps five hundred years, affecting vast portions of the planet. Moreover, we are now beginning to understand that the increased greenhouse gases added to the atmosphere from both industrial and agricultural sources "played at least a small role in enhancing El Niño patterns that developed during the latter nineteenth century."[48] Where El Niño brings excessive rainfall to the wheat belt of North America and does not affect Europe at all, it means drought for vast portions of Asia, parts of northern and western Africa, and northeast Brazil and flooding for Argentina. Three times—in 1876–79, 1889–91, and 1896–1902—El Niño droughts afflicted the future third world. The particularities of how El Niño affects Asia, Africa, Latin America, and North America, coupled with the workings of a world economy designed to benefit the industrializing parts of Europe and North America, and the aggression of the "New Imperialism" against Asians and Africans combined in a historical conjuncture of global proportions to spell famine and death for millions of people.

In all, an estimated thirty to fifty million people died horribly in famines spread across Asia and parts of Africa and Latin America. But these deaths were not just caused by the natural effects of El Niño, no matter how powerful they were in the late nineteenth century. Rather, as historian Mike Davis shows, these massive global famines came about as a result of El Niños working in conjunction with the new European-dominated world economy to impoverish vast swaths of the world, turning much of Asia, Africa, and Latin America into the "third world." In Asia, governments were either unwilling or unable to act to relieve the disasters. The British colonial rulers of India were more intent on ensuring the smooth workings of the "free market" and their colonial revenues than on preventing famine and death by starvation or disease. There people died in sight of wheat being loaded onto railroads destined for consumption in Britain, and the colonial authorities spurned famine relief in the belief that it weakened "character" and promoted sloth and laziness. In China, the Manchu government, switching resources and attention from the interior to the coasts, where foreign pressure was greatest, had neither the ability nor the resources to move grain to the isolated inland province of Shanxi where the drought and famine was the most severe. Likewise, in Angola, Egypt, Algeria, Korea, Vietnam, Ethiopia, the Sudan, and Brazil, El Niño–induced drought contributed to famines that weakened those societies and their governments, inviting new waves of imperialist expansion and consolidation.[49] The gap between the industrialized and future third world had crystallized.

Although it may appear to have been a historical accident that those late-nineteenth-century El Niños hit Asians, Africans, and Latin Americans hard while improving harvest yields in the American Midwest and bypassing Europe altogether, the socioeconomic impact they had was the result of a conjuncture of the historical processes discussed in this and the previous chapter with the climate changes caused by the El Niños. All of the adversely affected regions either had weak states (largely weakened because of imperialist aggression) that could not act either to industrialize or to provide famine relief to their people, or they had colonial governments (especially the British in India) whose policies had the same results. Thus, at the beginning of the twentieth century, large parts of the world and its people were condemned to fend off the worst effects of the biological old regime, environmental degradation, and the effects of global warming as best they could. It is hardly surprising that the life expectancies and life chances of people there were much less than those in the industrialized parts of the world. "The gap" was—and remains—a life-and-death matter, and the analytic tools of historical accidents, contingencies, and conjunctures can help us understand how and why that is.

Social Darwinism and
Self-Congratulatory Eurocentrism

By 1900, Europeans and their North American descendants controlled, either directly through their colonies or indirectly through financial, military, or political dominion, most of the world. That fact did not escape their notice, and the British in particular celebrated it throughout their empire on the occasion of the fiftieth and sixtieth anniversaries of Queen Victoria's reign in 1887 and 1897, respectively—and in the midst of the late-nineteenth-century famines discussed above. With the advances of science since the middle of the nineteenth century, the ease with which the Maxim gun cut down Sudanese, and the famine deaths of millions of Asians, some Europeans now thought that they had a scientific explanation for the rise of the West and the "backwardness" of Asians, Africans, and Latin Americans: social Darwinism and eugenics, or scientific racism.

Charles Darwin had argued in his famous 1859 book *On the Origin of Species* that evolution and the development of new species occurred by the processes of natural selection and the survival of the fittest species. Darwin soon extended the argument to humans, tracing human origins to earlier hominids. Then, in the late nineteenth century, Darwin's ideas about evolution were applied to societies. "Social" Darwinism purported to explain why some people were wealthy and others poor (virtue versus sloth), and why some societies were "advanced" and others "backward."[50] With Africans appearing to fall down dead at the sight of Europeans, with Indians (both kinds, in India and in North America) and Chinese dying by the millions from disease or during the El Niño famines, the idea that evolution could be applied to human society and the relationship between different races was believed to be true by large numbers of Europeans and North Americans. Both the wealth of millionaires and the "superiority" of white northern Europeans, according to Herbert Spencer, the foremost champion of social Darwinism, can be explained by natural selection:

> The poverty of the incapable, the distresses that come upon the imprudent, the starvation of the idle, and those shoulderings aside of the weak by the strong which

leave so many in shallows and miseries are the decrees of a large, far-seeing benevolence.[51]

To social Darwinists, the poor, the Asians, the Africans, and the Native Americans thus all deserved their dismal fates—it was "natural." In a world in which the gap between the rich and the poor within European and American societies and between the wealthiest and poorest parts of the world had become glaring, social Darwinism was a comforting ideology for those on top of the world.

In Latin America, especially Mexico and Brazil, ruled by light-skinned descendants of Europeans, a further extension of the idea of social Darwinism proved attractive. Eugenics, originally the selective breeding of plants and animals to produce the best stock, came to be applied to the belief that the condition of humans could be improved *only* through genetic manipulation, by increasing valuable human traits associated with northern Europeans and eliminating those associated with the poor and the nonwhite. So, to "improve" the stock of their human populations, Mexican and Brazilian governments embarked on programs to encourage the migration of light-skinned Europeans to their countries so that their populations could be "lightened," just like adding a bit of milk to coffee. In Europe and the United States, eugenics contributed to racist ideas about the natural superiority of whites and the inferiority of southern and eastern Europeans, in addition to Asians, Africans, and Native Americans. And of course, this kind of pseudoscience turned into twentieth-century genocide in the hands of the Nazi leader Adolf Hitler.

Conclusion

And so we have come full circle, with the concoction at the beginning of the twentieth century of explanations for the rise of the West that now seem silly (and dangerous) but which were accepted as "true" by many people in the wealthiest and most powerful parts of the world. Of course, we can now see that these ideas (discussed in more detail in the introduction) are more ideology than historical truth. For "the rise of the West" is more the story of how some states and peoples benefited from historically contingent events, geography, and environmental conditions to be able, at a certain point in time (a historical conjuncture), to dominate others and to accumulate wealth and power. There is no more mystery in it than that, and by coming to grips with the contingent nature of the wealth, power, and privilege of the

West, those who have benefited should be humbled by the actual sources of their good fortune, and those who have not should take heart that in the future new contingencies may well favor them. Europe was not always dominant or even bound for that destiny, even though Eurocentric ideologies may have propounded that myth.[52]

CHAPTER SIX

The Great Departure

Introduction to the Twentieth Century and Beyond

By 1900, the major elements of the modern world had been created. Nation-states had become the most successful organization for controlling territory and had been adopted throughout much of Europe and the Americas. Some of these nation-states had industrialized (notably those in western Europe, the United States, and Japan) and had harnessed their newfound industrial power for imperialist military and economic purposes to colonize most of Africa and much of Asia. Europeans, Americans, and Japanese had developed racist ideas of their superiority—the European whites arising from a Christian "civilizing" mission coupled with social Darwinism, and the Japanese from their purported uniqueness in Asia—which contributed to their colonizing programs, and a belief that the world order was as it should be with them on top.[1] The burning of fossil fuels for industry was pumping greenhouse gases into the atmosphere, continuing the process of transforming that part of the biosphere into the "anthroposphere," where human actions began to have impacts equaling or surpassing natural processes.

The twentieth century and the first decades of the twenty-first were to bring remarkable change. To be sure, we still live in a world of nation-states, of industry, of a growing gap between the richest and poorest parts of the globe as well as within specific countries, and of mounting environmental challenges. But the early twenty-first century differs substantially from the early 1900s. During the last century, whole new industries developed, dramatically restructuring the industrial world—oil and the automobile; electricity and the telephone, radio, television, and computers; motors and the airplane, jet engines, and space travel as well as washing machines and vacuum cleaners; the germ theory of disease and inoculation against it; genetic

175

manipulation; and robotization and artificial intelligence, to mention just a few scientific advances that would transform lives throughout the world. The twentieth century saw additional waves of industrialization and its spread around the world. These clusters of innovations created consumption patterns that required energy from burning vast quantities of cheap fossil fuels, and the effects of spewing vast amounts of greenhouse gases into the atmosphere became increasingly documented in climate change and global warming.[2]

In addition to technological change and its economic and environmental consequences, by the middle of the twentieth century, western European states would be dislodged from dominance. World War I (1914–18) shook the imperialist order of the late nineteenth century to its foundations and had major consequences for the shape of the twentieth century as a century of war and violence. But it was World War II (1939–45) that destroyed not only the old European colonial order but also the new Japanese empire and gave rise to a bifurcated world dominated by two superpowers: the United States and the Soviet Union (the USSR, or Union of Soviet Socialist Republics). During the twentieth century, nearly two hundred million people were killed in war, revolution, genocide, and other human-caused mass deaths.[3] Two world wars, punctuated by a global economic breakdown known as the Great Depression, constituted thirty years of crisis from 1914 to 1945. That "Thirty-Year Crisis" of the modern world destroyed Europe's global dominance and Japan's Asian empire, made way for the rise of two new superpowers (the United States and the Soviet Union) and their "Cold War," and created a host of newly independent former colonies seeking to unlock the secrets of industrial development.

In two great waves of globalization, one following the end of the Second World War in 1945 and the other the end of the Cold War in 1991, the world became increasingly interconnected: ideas, capital, and labor moved with increasing rapidity and ease around the globe, by the end of the century spreading fears about what the ensuing "deterritorialization" meant for nations and identities. This round of globalization, largely under U.S. auspices and with the specific goal of spreading capitalism and the institutions that protect it around the world, has benefited some, but not most, contributing to a continued and deepening gap between the wealthy Global North and poor Global South countries of the world. Most recently, what some have called the U.S.-led "rules-based liberal world order" has come under attack by nationalist leaders in many countries. Indeed, the rise of nationalism is one reaction to the rapid movement of capital and labor around the world irrespective of national boundaries. Moreover, the main cleavages between the Global North and the Global South—"the Rio Grande separating the United States from Mexico, and the Mediterranean Sea separating the European and African continents"—are the locus of the most intense conflict over the flows of migrants and refugees from south to north.[4]

And yet these may not be considered the most important changes in the modern world in the twentieth and twenty-first centuries; perhaps the most significant in the long run will be the impact humans have had on the environment. In the pursuit of rapid economic development in the capitalist world, the socialist world, and the third world alike, the relationship of human beings to the natural environment has changed to the point where human activity now affects global environmental processes—we have now fully entered the Anthropocene. Just as the use of fossil fuels in the nineteenth century freed industrial production and economic growth from natural constraints, so too in the twentieth century did synthetic fertilizer increase food supplies, sending the world's human population soaring. The combination of both rapid industrial and population growth in the twentieth century and beyond marks a "great departure" of humans and our history from the rhythms and constraints of the biological old regime.

To help readers, this chapter is divided into four parts. Part I takes the story to the end of World War I; part II analyzes the post–World War II era from 1945 to 1991; part III looks at globalization and its opponents from 1991 to the present; and part IV considers the extent to which the world has entered a new epoch—the Anthropocene—in which the actions and activities of humans have begun to overwhelm the forces of nature and are pushing us into dangerous new territory in terms of our relationship with Earth's natural systems. The story starts with the invention of synthetic nitrogenous fertilizer.

Part I: Nitrogen, Wars, and the First Deglobalization, 1900–1945

At the dawn of the twentieth century, social Darwinism and racism blinded Europeans to two dangers. First, they could not believe that the "advanced, progressive, civilized" races of the world (i.e., the whites) could go to war among themselves; that myth would come crashing down in World War I, and with it the vision of the omnipotence of Europe. Second, they could not conceive that the poor, backward, black, brown, and yellow peoples would ever be able to militarily challenge their European masters. That myth began to crumble in 1905 when Japan defeated Russia, but it would take successful revolutions and wars against Europeans to finally dispel it and bring down the old colonial order. One of the main reasons twentieth-century wars were so destructive is that the machinery of death was industrialized.

The peculiar thing about the technologies of war that imperialist states wielded against Asians, Africans, and indigenous peoples of the Americas through the nineteenth century is that the manufacture of a crucial element—gunpowder—was dependent upon extremely slow processes of nature. For all the steel, steam, and guns that their factories could produce, Europeans could not manufacture nitrates, the stuff that made gunpowder explode—they had to find the raw materials in the natural world. The critical element in nitrates is nitrogen, and although European scientists had figured that out, they had difficulty discovering how to take nitrogen from the air and "fix" it into reactive nitrogen (N_r; see the discussions in chapters 1 and 5).[5] Paradoxically, coal, steam, iron, and steel had enabled the industrializing countries to escape some of the limitations of the biological old regime, but the gunpowder they used to dominate the rest of the world was still limited to naturally occurring sources of nitrogen.

As discussed in earlier chapters, nitrogen is crucial to the growth of plants and is essential to the creation of the amino acids that sustain animal, including human, life. Life on Earth is part of a global nitrogen cycle by which a small portion of the vast sources of nitrogen in the atmosphere becomes available to plants and, through them, to animals. Certain plants— legumes like beans, peanuts, and clover—fix nitrogen to the soil, and that helps fertilize fields and improve crop yields, making more food available to humans. Lightning strikes too can produce small amounts of nitrates. Among the largest sources of naturally occurring nitrates are human and animal waste. Farmers around the world, knowing that, have long applied animal manure to their fields. These naturally occurring but limited sources of nitrogen sustained life, but they also limited the size of the human population by limiting the amount of food that could be produced. As we will see later in this chapter, similar dynamics apply to phosphorus, another element essential to life, and in the form of phosphate, a crucial component in fertilizer. As long as humans depended upon nature to supply nitrogen, they remained constrained within the rhythms and processes of the biological old regime.

Ironically, that same substance—nitrates—was essential to improving agricultural yields *and* to making explosives.[6] Paradoxically then, both the size of the global human population and its ability to conduct modern warfare depended on, and were limited by, nature. That fact led to a global search for naturally occurring deposits of phosphates and nitrates, mostly in the form of bat and bird guano. Guano is excrement that under certain conditions—in particular, the absence of rain that would otherwise dissolve the droppings and their precious nitrogen—could accumulate over time. Caves were one place that bat guano could build up and then be extracted by guano miners to make fertilizer and, increasingly in the nineteenth century, gunpowder. But it turned out that the largest supplies of bird guano had accumulated over thousands, if not millions, of years on the arid Chincha Islands off the coast of Peru.

The first clump of Peruvian guano was brought to Europe in 1804 by the German naturalist and world explorer Alexander von Humboldt and was then extracted in ever greater amounts and exported by British merchants. By 1890, the supplies of Peruvian guano were mostly exhausted, but another natural source (sodium nitrate, or saltpeter) that could be mined was found in southern Peru; in 1879 Chile had gone to war with Peru to gain control of the sodium nitrate and exported it to the industrializing world, which used it to make both fertilizer and gunpowder. In 1900, for instance, the United States used about half of its imports of Chilean sodium nitrate to make explosives. Food or explosives?[7] For the imperialist powers of the world, that was a tough enough proposition, but it was exacerbated further by the fact that Chile had a monopoly on the largest naturally occurring source of sodium nitrate. Moreover, for the saltpeter to get from Chile to Europe or the United States, it had to be shipped. Sea power was thus crucial to maintaining supplies of sodium nitrate, and any imperialist power vulnerable to a maritime blockade would be severely weakened, its food production and munitions industries held hostage to Chilean sodium nitrate.[8] That was particularly true with Germany. And it was there that the most intense search for a way to produce nitrates industrially was under way by the turn of the twentieth century.

It was not that other nations' scientists were unaware of the importance of the problem, for they certainly were. For Germany, its lagging agricultural output and its limited access to ocean shipping lanes made the problem pressing. In 1909 a chemist named Fritz Haber synthesized ammonia (NH_3, which contains nitrogen that can be processed into nitrates) in his laboratory, and a year later the issues of industrial production were resolved by Carl Bosch of the German firm BASF. The process of taking nitrogen from the atmosphere by synthesizing ammonia, known as the Haber-Bosch process, shaped the subsequent course of world history by lifting the constraints that nature had placed on the availability of nitrogen for plant growth.

The synthesis of ammonia, from which nitrogenous fertilizer could be manufactured, made possible the explosive growth of the world's human population in the twentieth century. Coupled with the expansion of farmland, the fertilizers from guano and saltpeter had enabled the world population to increase from about one billion in 1800 to 1.6 billion by 1900. But by 1900, most of the good arable land in the world was already being farmed, so increased food production could come most readily from the application of additional fertilizer; but, as we have seen, most of the naturally occurring guano had already been used up, and global military competition ensured that substantial amounts of saltpeter went to various states' munitions industries. One expert has concluded that using the materials and techniques available in the biological old regime to improve agricultural output, the world's population might have topped out at 3.5 billion people.[9] The Haber-Bosch process for synthesizing ammonia made it possible to increase the food supply and support the world's population in 2000 of about 6.2 billion people (which increased by another billion in just one decade, to 7.3 billion in 2010). In other words, in the twentieth century, the population of the world increased from about 1.6 to 6.2 billion (or 4.6 billion more people, most of them since 1950) largely because of the Haber-Bosch process.[10] That increase in the human population alone makes the twentieth century unique in all of human history.[11] The synthesis of ammonia and the consequent industrial production of nitrogenous fertilizer freed human population growth from the natural limits of the biological old regime. By the early twenty-first century, industrial processes had come to add more reactive nitrogen to the world's landmass and waterways than all natural processes combined. More than that, the synthesis of ammonia also made possible large-scale industrial production of nitrate-based explosives, and because Germany was the first to use this new technology, it increased the confidence of its military leaders. And that was to be an important factor contributing to the outbreak of world war in 1914.

World War I and the Beginning of the Thirty-Year Crisis, 1914–45

By 1900, there was precious little of the world left to be dominated by the imperialist powers; the largest chunks of land that were not yet spoken for were the Chinese and Ottoman empires. As for China, the Open Door Notes of 1900 led the imperialist powers to conclude that a weak Chinese state would enable them to enjoy the benefits of their "spheres of influence" without any one of them actually having to conquer and govern China, a task made all the more difficult by the competing powers, including the United States and Japan, aspiring to dominate the region. Indeed, it was hoped that the acceptance of the Open Door Notes had cooled competition among the imperialist powers in Asia and removed an irritant and possible cause of war.

A general war among the European powers would indeed break out, but the spark was ignited not in Asia but in the Balkans in southeastern Europe. In July 1914, a Serbian nationalist assassinated the heir to the Austrian throne, Archduke Ferdinand, and his wife while they were visiting the city of Sarajevo, an administrative center in Bosnia that had recently been absorbed by the Austro-Hungarian empire. Supported by Germany and intending to cause a war and increase the size of its empire, Austria sent an ultimatum to Serbia, which in turn was supported by Russia.

What made this little confrontation in the Balkans so explosive was that in the previous years, imperialist rivalries and European power politics had led to a system of alliances, largely fueled by French and Russian fears of the rising economic and military power of Germany. In the early 1900s, Britain joined France and Russia to form the Triple Entente, while Germany and Austria-Hungary formed the Central Powers. Thus Austria counted on German support in attacking Serbia, while Russian support for Serbia soon brought France and Britain into the equation.

When Russian and German armies mobilized to support their allies, all of Europe soon was at war. Then Britain's new ally in Asia, Japan, declared war on the Central Powers, the Ottoman empire sided with Germany for fear of being partitioned by the Entente powers, Britain's dominions (Canada, Australia, New Zealand) mobilized, Britain and France mobilized armies and resources from their colonies, and soon the whole world outside of the Americas was warring or mobilized to support Europeans at war with each other. And by 1917, the United States too, previously insulated from self-destructive European wars by the Atlantic, entered the war in support of Britain and its allies. By the time an armistice was called on November 11, 1918, over ten million soldiers had been killed, and upward of twenty million had been maimed, blinded, or otherwise wounded. The First World War was a particularly intense expression of the transnational interactions that mark the processes of globalization.

It had been the bloodiest conflict the world had ever seen, in large part because industrialization had made war more destructive than ever. Not only did Fritz Haber's invention free the production of explosives from natural constraints,[12] but also Haber discovered how to manufacture various poisonous gases that then were used in the trench warfare of World War I, and later by Hitler's Nazi regime in the extermination camps. Tanks, submarines, and great battleships increased the carnage.

Viewed in long-term historical perspective, the "Great War," as World War I was then known, was the beginning of the end of the European-dominated world order, an end that ultimately would take the Great Depression and another world war to complete. However, as the First World War ended, that outcome was not yet clearly in sight.

The 1917 entry of the United States on the side of Britain and France ensured the defeat of Germany and Austria. America had troops, war materiel, and an awesomely productive industrial economy to throw into the war effort. It also cost the United States over one hundred thousand dead and two hundred thousand wounded, a small fraction of the casualties suffered by the main European contenders, but enough to guarantee a seat at the Versailles Peace Conference called to draw up the terms ending the war. Germany had not surrendered but had agreed to an armistice and thus hoped to have a voice in what would happen to it after the war; that was not to be, as the losers were treated as losers. The British and French colonial subjects who had fought for their colonial rulers in the war thought they would get enhanced treatment, especially when they heard about U.S. president Wilson's "Fourteen Points" that included a call for respecting nations' sovereign rights, but that was not to be either. The various Arab peoples who were encouraged to revolt against the Ottomans in return for British and French promises of independence were likewise disappointed. And China, which had joined on the side of Britain and France (sending young men to France to work at factory jobs) in the hopes of regaining control of German concessions in Shandong province, would get a different lesson.

Instead of a more equitable settlement implicit in all of these hopes and aspirations, Britain, France, and Japan acted as victorious imperialists whose main task was divvying up the spoils of war. France took back Alsace-Lorraine from Germany, Germany was forced to pay huge war reparations, the Austro-Hungarian empire was taken apart, with the new states of Czechoslovakia, Hungary, and Yugoslavia being formed, and Poland was reconstituted, also from parts of Germany. Instead of China recovering its own Shandong peninsula from a defeated Germany, control passed to Japan, which also had entered the war on the winning side.

After the League of Nations was formed, Britain and France used it to gain "mandates" to control the Middle Eastern remnants of the Ottoman empire: France got Syria, Britain carved out Iraq, and neither Arab Palestinians nor Jewish Zionists got Palestine, which became a British mandate. Vietnamese who had helped the French, and Indians who had supported the British, also were slapped down by their colonial masters. However, actions by the victorious imperialist powers at the end of World War I provoked reactions that could not be contained, as German resentment built and provided support for Adolf Hitler and his Nazi program, and as national independence movements spurred opposition to imperialism and colonialism.

Revolutions

Added to that, the 1917 communist-led Bolshevik Revolution in Russia challenged the capitalist world order itself. Under the leadership of V. I. Lenin, the Bolsheviks seized power in October 1917 after the czarist regime had collapsed amid disastrous defeats in World War I, and promptly signed a separate peace with Germany, taking Russia out of the war. Despite armed intervention and a civil war that followed, the Bolsheviks established the world's first communist-led state with the avowed intent of building socialism and seeing an end to the capitalist world. After Lenin died in 1924, Joseph Stalin consolidated power and led the Soviet Union on a crash industrialization project that he termed "socialism in one country," relying solely on Russian resources and having as little contact as possible with the capitalist world.

Revolution was shaking not just Russia but other parts of the world as well in the years before and after World War I. In Mexico, moderate reform in 1910 was followed by peasant rebellions led by Emiliano Zapata in the south and Pancho Villa in the north that fueled the Mexican Revolution (1910–20), ushering in land reform and limiting foreign ownership of Mexican natural resources. In China, revolutionaries toppled the Manchu dynasty in 1911, and after a decade of confusing warlord politics, two new political parties formed with explicitly nationalist goals. Cooperating in the 1920s to eliminate warlords, the revolutionaries threatened to break imperialist control of the modern sectors of China's economy. In Italy, a new movement—fascism—emerged that was both anti-communist and promised to avoid the miseries of capitalism by fostering national unity and the power of the state under a strong leader, Benito Mussolini.

Colonial Independence Movements

Post–World War I challenges to the imperialist world order came not just from revolutionary movements in Russia, China, Mexico, and Italy, but also from independence movements in Europe's colonies, most notably India. There, Mohandas Gandhi created a nonviolent independence movement stressing boycotts of British goods (especially cotton textiles) and salt. In the process, civil disobedience was born. Gandhi broke colonial laws and invited imprisonment for doing so, all in the name of Indian independence. A Hindu himself, Gandhi stressed the multiethnic scope of the anticolonial movement by insisting that his Congress Party include Muslims and Sikhs in leadership positions as well.

In the face of setbacks and divisions among the imperialist powers in World War I, nationalism fueled anti-imperialist and anticolonial independence movements not just in India and China, but in Egypt, Vietnam, and Palestine as well. Nationalism, which had developed in nineteenth-century Europe and Japan, in the twentieth century became a global force. Where in Europe nationalism was mostly a conservative force that emphasized cultural, linguistic, and religious commonalities to blunt the class conflicts that grew along with industrialization, in Asia and Africa nationalism would have an explicit anti-imperialist content, often fueling socially revolutionary movements.

Normalcy?

World War I had brought the capitalist world system to a point of crisis that was only postponed by the apparent "return to normalcy" of the 1920s in the industrialized world. Although Europe had been deeply shaken by the war and much of its productive capacity destroyed, loans from U.S. banks (in particular to Germany) kept sufficient liquidity for Europeans to buy American products, restoring prosperity to Europe and stimulating U.S. industry. U.S. capital was keeping the global system afloat, though few realized it at the time. After the conclusion of the Versailles Peace Conference ending World War I, President Woodrow Wilson's fond hope that the economic and political conditions causing war could be ameliorated through U.S. leadership of new international bodies such as the League of Nations was shattered when an isolationist Congress refused to approve U.S. participation.

There were other signs of serious problems in the industrialized world, especially in agriculture. Wartime demand and rising prices throughout Europe and the United States prompted farmers to increase production, while postwar inflation encouraged them to take loans to expand food production even more. By the early 1920s, there was serious overproduction of food (together with malnutrition and starvation in poor regions), a sharp decline in agricultural prices, and a spike in foreclosures as farmers had difficulty repaying loans. The increased supply of food on the world market came also from Australia and New Zealand, as well as the newly formed states of eastern Europe. To make matters worse, prices for coffee, sugar, and other agricultural and primary product exports that Latin American countries had relied upon also collapsed. By the late 1920s, few rural producers anywhere in the world could afford to buy manufactured goods.

The Great Depression of the 1930s

To protect their nation's manufactures, industrialized states began raising tariffs on imported goods, which further cut international trade in industrial goods. Loans that U.S. bankers had made to European countries were called in, and when that happened, investors panicked, leading to "Black Monday" in October 1929 when the U.S. stock market crashed. Wealth vanished overnight, banks failed, and the savings of millions evaporated. The world economy entered a vicious downward spiral in which factories laid off workers whose income and purchases shrank. Lower demand led to further cuts in production—the only thing that was rising in the 1930s was the unemployment rate. In the industrialized world, between 22 percent of the workers (in Sweden) and 44 percent (in Germany) lost their jobs. The U.S. unemployment rate reached 25 percent by 1933.

By 1913, the United States had become the largest economy on Earth, producing one-third of the world's output. World War I provided further stimulation, and by 1929 the U.S. economy had grown to an astounding 42 percent of world output. So, when the Great Depression hit America, it affected the entire world. U.S. imports crashed by 70 percent between 1929 and 1933, and its exports fell by half.[13]

The Great Depression thus was a global phenomenon. States in western Europe, Latin America, Asia, and Africa all suffered. Only the Soviet Union, which had cut itself off from the capitalist world and was trying, under Joseph Stalin, to build "socialism in one country," emerged unscathed. As the rest of the capitalist world was plunged into the Great Depression, the communist-led Soviet Union was experiencing rapid economic growth and touting that fact as proof that communism was superior to capitalism.

The Great Depression was a global crisis of capitalism, leading several states to abandon the pre–World War I model of unfettered markets, becoming increasingly isolationist and protectionist. Some states experimented with reforms to provide a social safety net for the workers and farmers who suffered mightily (e.g., U.S. president Franklin D. Roosevelt's "New Deal"). In Germany, the reparations issue and the loss of territory after World War I, coupled with the crisis of the Great Depression, laid the groundwork for the 1933 rise to power of Adolf Hitler and his "Nazi," or National Socialist, Party, which promised that a powerful state headed by a strong leader would get Germany out of the crisis it was in: by the mid-1930s, Germany's economy was indeed growing once again, and many Germans credited Hitler's national socialism with improving their lot. In Japan, where exports of silk to the United States shrank as women cut back on purchases of silk stockings, military leaders saw dependence on the world market as a strategic mistake and began to move more aggressively to a position of primacy among the powers in Asia, building on its formal colonies in Taiwan and Korea and extending its reach in 1932 with the creation of Manchukuo out of Manchuria, a region it took from China by military force. By the early 1930s, nationalistic, authoritarian, and militarily aggressive regimes had come to power in Germany and Japan.

By its actions toward China during World War I, Japan had signaled that it intended to be a major player among the imperialist powers in Asia. Although it was not strong enough in the 1920s to resist the combined power of Britain and the United States, when the world entered into the crisis decade of the 1930s, Japan extended its empire at China's expense and ultimately militarily confronted the United States for control of the Pacific. While Japan and the United States jockeyed for dominance in Asia, they overlooked the growing power and world-changing significance of the Chinese communist movement that would establish China's independence in the wake of World War II, setting the stage for its rise to global power in the late twentieth century.

During the Great Depression, the global trading and monetary systems came apart; instead of seeking to increase international trade as a way out of the depression, those states that could severed ties to the global system and instead sought to gain as much independence from it as possible—the goal was "autarky." In the early 1930s, Britain attempted to protect its economy by binding its colonies ever tighter to the home market and discouraging other nations from trading there. The United States took similar actions with regard to its Caribbean and Philippine colonies as well as in Latin American countries under its sway. The Soviet Union already had successfully broken away from the international system. After Japan added Manchukuo to its colonial empire, it continued to build its own "Greater East Asian Co-Prosperity Sphere." Italy expanded into North Africa, and Hitler's Nazi Germany looked to reconstitute an empire in central and eastern Europe, annexing Austria in 1938, dismembering Czechoslovakia in early 1938, and then taking the rest of it in early 1939. The world system disintegrated into competing and then warring blocs, and it might have solidified in that deglobalized form if not for a second world war.

World War II

Britain and France had given guarantees of protection to Poland, so when Nazi armies invaded in September 1939, Britain declared war. The still isolationist United States stayed out of the conflict, but when Japan attacked Pearl Harbor on December 7, 1941, it entered the war in both the Pacific and Europe. By then the Soviet Union too had become involved after Hitler broke a nonaggression treaty and attacked the USSR in 1941. The communist-led Soviet Union then made common cause with capitalist Britain and the United States against the immediate threat, the Axis powers of Nazi Germany and Fascist Italy, soon joined by Imperial Japan.

The Second World War was even more destructive than the first. Not only were the numbers of dead and injured soldiers vastly greater, but civilians mobilized for the war effort (nearly all industrial production in the contending states was geared toward war) and then became targets as well. By 1943, the Allies (Britain, France, the United States, and the Soviet Union) had determined that only total, unconditional defeat of the Axis powers was acceptable, and by 1944 U.S. resistance to using military force against civilians was overcome. U.S. warplanes joined the British in the firebombing of Dresden in Germany; then in Japan they firebombed Tokyo and sixty-three other cities, before dropping the first atomic bombs on Hiroshima and Nagasaki in August 1945.

If war was hell, "total war" was total hell. The Nazis, of course, had industrialized the death of six million Jews and other "undesirables," while the Japanese had conducted the "three all" (kill all, burn all, destroy all) campaigns against Chinese villagers, among other atrocities. More civilians and more troops died in the Second World War than in the First. The number is staggering. More than fifty million people around the world perished, with twenty million in the Soviet Union and ten million in China accounting for most of the war dead.

The Thirty-Year Crisis had a dramatic effect on the wealth accumulated by the richest countries of the world over the previous century through the industrialization of their economies and the colonization of much of the rest of the world. To be sure, the actual physical destruction of property in Europe through the two world wars was significant, as was the destruction of capital through the waves of bankruptcies during the Great Depression. But even greater effects upon the accumulated wealth of European countries (and Japan) came from the loss of their colonial empires either as a result of their defeat in the Second World War or through expropriations of their capital

investments through communist revolutions in Russia and China and decolonization movements elsewhere. Moreover, countries funded their massive
expenses for war by deficit spending financed by loans from their own citizens, drawing down private wealth and limiting the ability of even the richest
in those countries to save or invest much.[14] Paradoxically, as we will see later
in this chapter in the section "Inequality within Rich Countries," the
destruction of wealth as a result of the Thirty-Year Crisis provided a basis in
the post–World War II era for more income equality within the countries
of the industrialized world, especially when coupled with tax and wage policies that improved the lot of working people.

Part II: The Post–World War II and Cold War Worlds, 1945–91

The end of World War II in 1945 would be much different from the end of
World War I. There was no "armistice" or standing down of armies; total war
yielded total defeat—the unconditional surrender of Germany (in June
1945) and Japan (in September) to the victorious Allies. Perhaps most
important, European states (victors as well as vanquished) would not have
the ability to reconstitute their colonial empires—over the course of the
coming decades, Asian and African colonies would become independent
states. In Asia, Japan's colonial empire was also dismantled during the U.S.
occupation of Japan in the years from 1945 to 1952. A civil war in China
would bring the Chinese Communist Party to power in 1949. In short order,
the former colonial world and a communist-led China began aggressive pursuit of economic "development" with an emphasis on industrialization.

Hitler's national socialism, Italy's fascism, and Japan's statist development
models, while successful in getting those states out of the Great Depression
faster than European and American states, also led them to war and defeat.
Europe's colonial model also was discredited and destroyed. Left standing and
considerably strengthened by the end of World War II and the Thirty-Year
Crisis were the United States and the Soviet Union, the two rising powers
of the postwar world. Indeed, the defeat of Nazi Germany would not have
been possible without the Soviet Red Army, just as the United States was
primarily responsible for the defeat of Japan.

Rather than construct an American colonial empire from the ruins of its
defeated enemies, the United States hoped to reconstruct a world order that
avoided the mistakes and miscues that led to both World War I and the Great

Depression. Unrestrained nationalism and the hatreds it fostered were anath-ema, as were isolationism, trade protectionism, and autarky. U.S. leaders were convinced that a more globally interconnected world with trade and diplomacy regulated by international agreements and organizations would be the best possible world for all, and the United States believed it had the power and the support to realize its postwar vision. What it didn't count on was the challenge from the socialist visions of the Soviet Union, as we will see in the section on the Cold War later in this chapter.

In the meantime, the United States and the Soviet Union could agree upon opposition to colonialism. For the United States, this was somewhat surprising since it had spent much of the prior fifty years amassing and ruling an overseas empire. Many of its colonial holdings had come from Spain in the aftermath of the Spanish-American war of 1898, including Puerto Rico in the Caribbean and the Philippine Islands in the Pacific. By the end of World War II, having emerged victorious and the most economically and militarily powerful state in the world, the United States had its colonial pos-sessions intact and additionally occupied Japan and parts of Korea, Germany, and Austria, with a total occupied population exceeding that of the conti-nental United States.[15]

Instead of ruling much of the world as a colonial power (as Britain had done after World War I), the United States gave up most of these territories and distanced itself from colonialism. Historian Daniel Immerwahr notes that the largest U.S. colony became independent (the Philippines), another became a Commonwealth with the inhabitants ultimately given U.S. citizen-ship (Puerto Rico), and two became states (Alaska and Hawaii). Immerwahr asks the important question of why the United States took this unusual step. In part, he says that colonized peoples, especially in the Asian countries that had been part of the Japanese empire, resisted and prompted not just the United States but other colonial powers to grant independence. But more important, the war effort spawned technologies that made it possible for the United States to have a global-girdling empire without colonies: airplanes, radio, shipping, and innovations in chemistry and industrial engineering, among others, that produced synthetic rubber, plastics, and the multitude of products made from synthetics not dependent on tropical colonies.[16] But most important, "in just a few years the [U.S.] military built a world-spanning logistical network" that depended less on colonies than overseas military bases built with the cooperation of other governments, or on uninhabited islands that the United States kept. The United States has "roughly eight hundred overseas military bases around the world. . . . These . . . are the foundations of U.S. world power." In the postwar period, the United States has deployed its military power from these bases 211 times in 67 countries. "Call it peacekeeping if you want," Immerwahr says, "or call it imperialism. But clearly this is not a country that has kept its hands to itself."[17]

For different reasons, then, both the United States and the Soviet Union took anticolonial stances after World War II and were opposed to European states maintaining their colonies, and that fact contributed to the surge of postwar anticolonial movements. But they also had vastly different social and economic systems—one primarily free-market capitalism (the United States) and the other state-planned socialism (the Soviet Union)—that each sought to project as a global model. The United States wanted to end colonialism not simply because it believed in the inherent right of national independence, but because it could then get access to those markets and raw materials denied it by colonial preference systems. The Soviets believed that ending colonialism would further the likelihood of socialist transformations in the colonies, a necessary step on the way to a communist world.

Although both the United States and the Soviet Union were anticolonial, their very different visions of the place of newly independent colonies in the world led to tensions between the United States and the Soviet Union that would produce the Cold War, an arms race with horrifying new nuclear weapons that each side realized could never be used, but which could deter the other from attacking. MAD, it was called: "mutually assured destruction." So the military standoff between the United States and the USSR would not result in an actual "hot" war but a "cold" war, one that would provide the context for most of the post–World War II world until the collapse of the Soviet Union in 1991.

Decolonization

While it is true that most colonies became independent states only after World War II, the process had begun in the aftermath of World War I. The sense of betrayal after World War I, combined with the clear recognition of the vulnerability of the colonial powers, had fueled nationalist-inspired independence movements throughout Asia and Africa. By the time World War II broke out, some nationalist leaders, especially in Asia, began to break with their colonial masters by siding with Japan and their call of "Asia for Asians."[18]

The independence of the largest of all colonies, India, was on the agenda by the end of World War II, and after the war Britain quickly arranged the terms of its departure and the independence of the subcontinent. The tragedy of Indian independence, though, is the massive violence that attended the process. Where Gandhi and the Congress Party had intended to create a multiethnic, multi-religious democratic state, one part of India's Muslim leadership in the 1930s had begun agitating for the creation of a separate Muslim state to be called Pakistan. Hindu nationalists too wanted an India for Hindus, and it was an ultranationalist Hindu who assassinated fellow Hindu Gandhi for proposing a single, multiethnic state with protections for Hindus, Muslims, and other ethnic and religious groups. By 1947, independence meant the partition of the colony into the states of predominantly Hindu India, and predominantly Muslim Pakistan (the latter in two parts, east and west). The state of Kashmir, which had a predominantly Muslim population but had been ruled by a Hindu prince, was divided and remains a source of tension and conflict between Pakistan and India.[19]

With the withdrawal of the British, and Hindus' and Muslims' fears of each other fanned by nationalists on each side, Hindus in what was to become Pakistan fled toward India, and Muslims in India streamed toward Pakistan. In the course of this huge movement of people during "partition," as it came to be called, millions lost their property and homes and hundreds of thousands were killed. Not surprisingly, India and Pakistan ever since have been wary, and twice warring, neighbors, in addition to having numerous border skirmishes, struggling over control of Kashmir, and (since 1998) aiming nuclear weapons at each other.

Indian independence and partition point to two significant aspects of the postwar decolonization of Asia and Africa. First, European colonialists assumed that independence meant the independence of territorial states. Some parts of their colonial holdings certainly had had historical experience with states (especially in Asia and the Middle East), but much of Africa did not. The borders that Europeans drew there for newly independent African states were often quite arbitrary and did not take into consideration the peoples living there. Thus, just as the lines dividing India from Pakistan wrought havoc for the tens of millions of Muslims and Hindus inconveniently on the wrong side of a line, so too did line drawing in Africa and the Middle East create states with people of common languages and cultures across two (or more) borders. Important examples are the Kurds who now inhabit northern Iraq, western Iran, and eastern Turkey, and parts of Syria, and the Hutus and Tutsis in Rwanda and Congo.

Much of Asia and the Middle East decolonized by 1950, and most of Africa was composed of independent states by 1960. Smaller island territories in the Caribbean and Pacific attained independence in the 1960s. This spurt of decolonization created a host of newly independent states, boosting membership in the United Nations from fifty-one at its creation in 1945 to 127 by 1970. By 2015 UN membership had increased to 193, reflecting the establishment of greater numbers of increasingly smaller independent states.

Asian Revolutions

The global scale of World War II created the conditions not only for decolonization but also for revolutions, mostly led by communist or other leftist parties. In China, the Communist Party had been formed in 1921 in the aftermath of the Versailles Peace Conference and the Bolshevik Revolution in Russia. Rural poverty in China provided a vast reservoir of support for the communists, who delivered on rent and interest reduction promises and then targeted the landlords whose exploitation of the peasantry deepened rural misery. When Japan invaded China in 1937, the communists formed a "united front" with the ruling Guomindang party to resist Japan. The Japanese invasion forced the Guomindang to retreat to China's far west, while the communists organized guerrilla warfare behind Japanese lines, strengthening their military skills and expanding the territory they controlled. When Japan surrendered to the United States in 1945, civil war between the communists and their Guomindang foes led to communist victory and the establishment in 1949 of the People's Republic of China. The Chinese communists were determined to create a strong China that would never again be threatened by foreign powers. That resolve was tested in 1950 when communist China fought the United States to a draw in the Korean War (1950–53).

In French Indochina at the end of World War II, the Viet Minh under the leadership of Ho Chi Minh declared independence from France after having fought an anti-Japanese guerrilla war there and building up not just vast popular support but also a formidable military. The French, though, were not ready to give up their Asian colony (just as they wanted to retain their Algerian colony) and so sought to reestablish their power in Vietnam. In the war that followed, Ho Chi Minh's forces defeated the French forces in 1954. The United States then became involved, at first diplomatically and then militarily. Rather than national elections and unification, which had been promised for 1956, the United States decided to support a client regime in the south, and Vietnam remained divided between North and South Vietnam. When the U.S.-supported southern regime had difficulty governing itself and maintaining popular support against the northern and the southern Viet Minh guerrilla fighters, the United States sent first advisors and then in the mid-1960s large numbers of combat troops to support the south. After a decade of war, the United States and South Vietnam were defeated, and in 1976 Vietnam was formally reunited under communist leadership by the Socialist Republic of Vietnam.

Violence was also necessary to shake French control of Algeria, which finally became independent in 1962. The other colonial power to resist granting independence to its colonies was Portugal, which held on to Angola on the west coast of Africa until forced by armed rebels to give up control in 1975. The age of empire,[20] spawned by the European industrial revolution and military superiority, was over. In the decades after the Second World War, Asians, Africans, and Latin Americans were determined to use their newfound independence to improve the lot of their peoples by industrializing.

Development and Underdevelopment

There is no mystery as to why colonies had not industrialized: with the exception of Japan's Korean colony, policies of the colonizing country mostly forbade it, seeing colonies instead as sources of raw materials and markets for manufactured goods.[21] China had some modern industry, but much of it was owned by foreigners and limited to pockets of coastal cities. For the first half of the twentieth century, China remained rural and in the grip of landlords. The Chinese communist victory in 1949 changed all that by eliminating the landlord class, nationalizing foreign-owned businesses, and having the military power to back up their actions.

Post–World War II decolonization and revolution brought to power regimes committed to explicit policies of economic and social "development." Moreover, since most of those former colonies (to say nothing of China) had bitter experiences with the capitalist West, the models they chose for the most part were strongly influenced by socialist, communist, or other statist ideas. In the postwar world, much of the underdeveloped world was beginning to move toward some form of state-driven industrialization. That was a problem for the United States, which had a different global vision, one centered on private ownership of property and capital and on the principles of international free or otherwise regulated and agreed-upon trade.

If the first half of the twentieth century had been marked by processes leading to deglobalization (the Great Depression) and two world wars, the post–World War II era saw two more waves of renewed globalization. Even before the end of World War II, the United States actively planned to reconstitute the world on the basis of capitalist principles emphasizing free trade to prevent the world from sliding back into the autarkic (and then warring) blocs of the Great Depression, and to ensure sufficient global demand to fuel the United States economy. Abandoning its prewar "isolationism," the United States also took the lead in setting up the United Nations to resolve international conflict and creating new institutions to manage the postwar global economy, in particular the World Bank and the International Monetary Fund. A strong Soviet Union, the Chinese revolution, and the influence of socialism in the former colonies threatened both that free market vision and the global reach of the United States; the United States responded in part by building anti-Soviet military alliances around the world: NATO (the North Atlantic Treaty Organization), SEATO (the Southeast Asia Treaty Organization), and CENTO (the Central Treaty Organization). The United States had a separate bilateral military agreement with Japan.

With the Soviet occupation of much of Eastern Europe at the end of World War II and the creation of "satellite" states there as well as Soviet support for communist North Korea and Vietnam and the growing power of communists in China, U.S. leaders decided to revive the German and Japanese economies, creating them as the workshops of Europe and Asia and bulwarks against Communism in Europe and Asia. This "reverse course" with respect to Germany and Japan and the policy of "containment" toward the Soviet Union were in place by 1947. The United States would seek not to go to war to roll back the Bolshevik Revolution (in today's language, to seek "regime change") but to "contain" its power and influence in the world.

By 1947 the Cold War was on, and would last until 1991, defining much of the post–World War II world. As part of its policy of containing communism, the United States would go to war in Korea (1950–53), confronting not just North Korean but Chinese communist troops as well; get involved in Vietnam and then war there (1956–75); use covert operations to overthrow democratically elected, left-leaning governments in Latin America; support authoritarian regimes there and in the Middle East; and prop up undemocratic authoritarian but anticommunist regimes throughout the world, ironically all in the name of "freedom and democracy."

The Cold War had other consequences as well. The United States began the post–World War II era as the only nuclear power, but in 1949 the Soviets detonated their first atomic bomb and the nuclear arms race was on in earnest, leading not just to fleets of warplanes equipped to drop nuclear bombs, but more ominously to intercontinental ballistic missiles (ICBMs) capable of reaching their targets just minutes after launch. There was (and still is) no defense against these weapons of mass destruction other than the surety of a massive retaliation once missile launches have been detected. By the 1960s, with each side having thousands of ICBMs and nuclear warheads, a nuclear attack could have ended not just human civilization but quite possibly humans as a species.[22] As it was, although there were numerous threats of nuclear attack, the world came to "the brink" just once in the early 1960s, when the Soviet Union moved missiles to Cuba shortly after Fidel Castro came to power in 1959.

The Cold War also militarized much of the world and led, for the first time, to the full-time military mobilization of many states, in particular the United States and USSR and their respective allies. Unlike the periods following previous wars, the United States and its allies, as well as the Soviet Union and its allies, remained fully mobilized and ready to fight wars on several fronts, in Europe as well as Asia. The U.S. government thus devoted about one-third of its annual expenditures to the military (about 5 percent of GDP in 1985), while the Soviet Union spent even more proportionally (more than 10 percent of its GDP) on its military. The size and vitality of the competing economies thus became a crucial element in the ability of the two superpowers to build and maintain their military arsenals during the Cold War years. More than anything else, the Cold War was a battle of economies. Hence as the U.S. economy developed beyond the "smokestack" industries into advanced computer technologies in the 1980s, the gap between the productivity of the U.S. and Soviet economies grew.[23]

Consumerism versus Productionism

As mentioned above, the Soviet Union had a planned economy in which the central state made the decisions and choices about the allocation of resources. To that extent, its economy was quite immune from the "boom and bust" cycles inherent in a capitalist free market economy. That explains a lot about how and why the Soviet Union was able to industrialize rapidly during the Great Depression when the capitalist economies were shrinking disastrously. After World War II, the Soviet Union also gained access to the resources and productive capacity of the East European countries it dominated.

What kept the Soviet bloc economies growing was the state plan. Although it is arguable whether state-run economies had anything to do with "true" communism, it is true that the communist leaders of the Soviet Union were influenced by Marxist views of human beings. Karl Marx had argued that human beings naturally were productive beings, and that their essence was to labor and to enjoy the fruits of their labor. The problem with the capitalist system, according to Marx, was not that people had to work, but that they worked for wages and were "alienated" from the product of their labor, which the capitalist expropriated and sold. In the socialist future, Marx envisioned that people would continue to work, but would find self-realization in their labor because it would be theirs, not the capitalist's.

In the Soviet system, people certainly worked, but the fiction was that because the state represented the interests of the working people, work on behalf of the state was work on their own behalf. The Soviet model was a "productionist" one: the more that was produced, the better. The Soviet state plans thus called for significant industry and factories, but most of that industrial production was destined to create additional industry or to support the military. Production, especially of and for heavy industry (e.g., coal, iron, steel, electricity), became its own end. Managers were valued and rewarded on the basis of how much they produced, and measures of production sometimes became skewed so that it didn't matter so much whether the coal that was produced actually reached a power plant but that it had been put on a railroad car. Some railroad managers thus reportedly shipped the same coal back and forth to increase the production ratings of their unit. The state plan called for very little investment in consumer goods, although the state did make a commitment to providing minimal housing (in huge apartment blocks), health care, and education.

The Soviets also harnessed science to their system and invested heavily in scientific education and development of new technology, especially with regard to military applications and space exploration. Thus the Soviets beat the United States to space by launching *Sputnik* in 1957, and they sent the first man into Earth orbit shortly thereafter, spurring the "space race" with the United States and President Kennedy's 1960 pledge to put an American on the moon by the end of the decade, a goal reached in 1969.

The Chinese communists after their 1949 victory initially followed the Soviet model of development, and China's first Five-Year Plan (1953–57) achieved annual growth rates of 18 percent and succeeded in establishing foundations for a heavy industry base for the Chinese economy. But China's leader, Mao Zedong, who was wary of the unintended results of the Soviet model, especially the creation of privileged urban elites that began to look like a new ruling class, sought a more egalitarian way to develop. He believed he found a new model based upon the large-scale rural collective (communes) and the full employment of labor through rural industrialization, and in 1958 he called for a "Great Leap Forward," proclaiming that China would surpass the industrial output of Great Britain within fifteen years.

That experiment was to turn into a disaster, in part because of three years of bad weather (drought in the north and floods in the south), but mostly because communist leaders became obsessed with reports of higher and higher figures for agricultural production, even when such reports had no basis in reality. The Chinese state thus carted grain out of the villages in the mistaken belief that adequate supplies remained for people to eat. In the ensuing three-year famine (1959–62)—made worse by the natural disasters—an estimated 15 to 43 million people perished, destroying the faith of other leaders in Mao's abilities and raising questions in the minds of Soviet leaders about China's path. When Soviet leader Nikita Khrushchev refused to share nuclear weapon technology with China and Mao publicly criticized the Soviet Union, the Soviets withdrew their advisors and a split in the communist world became apparent to the Western world for the first time. Tensions between the Soviets and the Chinese continued to mount during the 1960s, leading to armed border clashes along the Amur River in 1969.

Despite the differences between the Soviet Union and China over the proper road to socialism and the way to combat the capitalist world, they did share a commitment to increasing economic production. The productionist biases of the Soviet and Chinese models of communism had horrific environmental consequences. In the Soviet Union, the formerly crystal-clear Lake Baikal in Siberia was clouded by industrial pollution; the Aral Sea dried up as nearby cotton fields received all its water; the air around most cities was among the foulest on Earth; and in 1986 the nuclear power plant at Chernobyl exploded. Stinking heaps of industrial waste polluted land, air, and water.[24] In China, the "war on nature"[25] led to steel complexes spewing pollutants that covered nearby vegetation with gray soot, rivers running black with industrial poisons, residents of Beijing bicycling to work in the winter with masks to keep charcoal dust out of their lungs, and so much water continuing to be taken from the Yellow River for irrigation that it seldom empties into the sea. Perversely, the last thirty-five years of accelerated growth on the basis of market reform and private enterprise in China, far from improving the situation, have exacerbated it: seven of the world's ten most polluted cities are in China, and the near-term outlook is for environmental degradation there to intensify, even as its leaders now talk about building "an ecological civilization."[26]

Consumerism

As both the acknowledged leader of the postwar capitalist world and its economic powerhouse, the United States was determined not to allow the post-

World War II world economy to slide into the overproduction and economic decline that plagued the world after World War I. Not only were reforms of the international trading system necessary to lower tariffs and increase global demand for America's industrial products, but changes to the domestic economy were needed too.

Like the rest of the industrialized world, much early industrialization had provided products to create additional factories and industries. To that extent, industry created more industry, which drew workers into ever-larger cities. Cities and their populations certainly provided the labor for factories, but they also created demand for consumption. Until the post–World War II era, that urban consumer demand mostly had been for the necessities of life—housing, food, and clothing. But a series of post–World War II developments in the United States soon spurred the growth of whole new sectors of the economy to provide consumer goods.[27]

Indeed, the United States had already pioneered the mass production of goods sold primarily to consumers, not to other businesses or factories. Prior to World War I, Henry Ford had invented the assembly line for automobiles, but he also recognized that workers would have to be paid adequate wages to be able to purchase the Model Ts his factories produced if the economy was to be sustainable. The Great Depression and then World War II dampened consumer demand for cars, but the end of the war and the need to convert factories from wartime to peacetime production provided an opportunity for American auto manufacturers. Starting in the late 1940s, U.S. auto production soared, and soon many American families owned a car or light truck, in part because strong labor unions won substantial wage gains for American workers. But once everyone had a car, demand would slacken, and industrial production of autos would grind to a halt.

To keep demand for cars up, new demand had to be created, and that was done by two means: planned obsolescence and advertising. In the 1950s, cars became obsolete not necessarily because they fell apart but because the styles changed. And as styles changed, consumers were enticed to want to buy that new car by slick and powerful advertising. Many families became convinced of the need to buy a new car every three years, if they had the resources, or to want to if they didn't.

Easier credit helped the automobile become a consumer commodity. Credit first became available for purchasing houses. Prior to World War II, mortgages were relatively short (from three to five years) and purchasers had to come up with half of the purchase price before banks would lend the money. That limited the number of people who could afford houses to about

40 percent of the population in 1940. After World War II, changes in banking rules encouraged banks to lower the down payment requirement and to extend the mortgage to twenty years. Two new federal agencies—the Veterans Administration and the Federal Housing Administration—made mortgages even more available by guaranteeing the loan. In a further expansion, credit soon came dispensed via "cards" issued first by department stores to customers and then, by the 1960s, by firms simply organizing and selling credit (Diners Club, American Express, MasterCard, Visa). The vast expansion of credit, especially to buy houses, contributed to the "Great Recession" of 2008 when the global banking system froze up, employers couldn't get credit to keep their businesses open, and millions of people lost their jobs and their homes.

The car and cheap housing combined to create vast swaths of suburbs around cities, the archetype being Los Angeles. With cars there making the commute possible, the dismantling of the "Red Car" trolley system, and the construction of "freeways," Los Angeles–area suburbanites could get to work in the city in the morning and be home by dinner. The postwar building boom created new suburbs where cow pastures or orchards had once dominated the landscape and extended new housing tracts around small farming towns. The automobile revolution in postwar Los Angeles contributed to the production of such high levels of ozone-dense smog that into the 1980s local governments issued warnings to people to stay indoors on especially bad days. Concrete to build roads and other structures, not just in L.A. but around the world, has also contributed to air pollution and global warming.[28]

One other development made the post–World War II consumer revolution possible. Electricity, which had first begun powering factories and lighting cities in the late nineteenth century, extended to urban households in the early twentieth century. Then the various public works projects of the 1930s electrified most of rural America by 1940. When small electrical motors began running all sorts of household products such as refrigerators and washing and sewing machines, whole new industries flourished. With electrical outlets in every house and increasing leisure time, televisions flooded American living rooms, and most households came to have a telephone as well.[29]

The mass-consumption culture thus was created in the United States from the 1930s to the 1950s and came to represent a growing portion of the U.S. economy. By the early twenty-first century, 70 percent of its domestic economy was devoted to producing consumer goods; only 30 percent provided producer goods. That was a reversal of the proportions at the beginning of the twentieth century. The postwar growth of the U.S. economy, the engine of the world economy through much of the twentieth century, was largely powered by the consumer revolution, at least until the ability of average Americans to consume began to wane beginning in the 1980s. Americans had come to equate consumer purchases with "freedom" and to condemn the Soviet Union for its absence. Indeed, one critic argued that in the 1950s the U.S. government required only two things of its citizens: to be anticommunist and to consume.[30] Among its consequences was the fact that the consumer revolution liberated women from onerous daily tasks, making possible both their greater participation in the worlds of work and politics and demands for equal treatment.

The consumer society was premised on cheap and available energy— gasoline to run the car culture and electricity to keep the lights burning and motors running at home. If the nineteenth century had been the "Coketown" age of coal, iron, and the railroad, the twentieth century was the "Motown" age of oil, steel, and the automobile.[31] Like coal, oil is distributed unevenly around the world, and the United States was fortunate to have significant fields in Texas and Southern California. Mexico, Venezuela, Nigeria, and Russia also have deposits, but by far the world's greatest concentration of oil is in the vicinity of the Persian Gulf, notably Saudi Arabia, followed by Iraq and Iran and Venezuela in South America, although the recent surge of hydraulic fracturing, or "fracking," has dramatically increased the production of natural gas and oil in the United States. The automobile created the oil industry, and because U.S. consumption soon exceeded the capacity of its domestic wells, a global transport and financial system arose to move oil around the world. By the early 1970s, the United States was importing about one-third of the oil it needed for domestic consumption. That focused U.S. attention on the Middle East, but it also had deeper consequences: a technological "lock in" to a particular kind of global economy dependent on burning oil. The world is dependent not only on oil and natural gas for energy, but also on the particular social, economic, political, cultural, and military complexes that have arisen to control it.

In the 1950s, the consumer society spread to Britain and Canada, and in the 1960s to France, Italy, other West European societies, Japan, and pockets in Latin American cities, and with it the automobile and even greater demand for oil. By the 1970s, demand for consumer items such as refrigerators and TVs, if not the whole consumer society, spread to communist East Germany and Czechoslovakia as well.

Like the productionism of the Soviet and Chinese models, the consumer-ism of the West had significant environmental consequences. Not only did refining oil and burning gasoline pollute the air in virtually all major cities in the United States, Europe, and Japan, but extracting the oil and moving it around the world in tankers left spills on land and sea. Making cars also requires huge amounts of energy, creates nearly thirty tons of waste for every ton of car made, and uses charcoal burned from the Amazon rain forest, con-tributing directly to global warming and deforestation.[32] Fracking has sig-nificant impacts on water quality and probably seismic activity as well.

Third World Developmentalism

Decolonization and revolution after World War II created several score of new states, especially in Asia and Africa, but some in Latin America as well. Despite the friendliness of these new states to broadly statist and collectivist approaches associated with the Soviet model of socialism, many failed to emulate the Soviet Union, particularly following the Korean and Vietnam Wars, which showed graphically what could happen when the Cold War turned hot. As India's leader Nehru put it, when elephants fight, the grass gets trampled. So in the early 1950s leaders of several of these states, in par-ticular Indonesia, Egypt, Yugoslavia, and India, started a "nonaligned" move-ment to keep out of the Cold War alliance systems that the United States and the USSR were putting together. In 1949, the United States had created NATO (the North Atlantic Treaty Organization, essentially Western Europe and the United States and Canada) to confront the Soviets in Europe; the Soviet Union then responded with the Warsaw Pact, creating an economic and security bloc dominated by the Soviet Union. To "contain" the Soviet Union to its south in the Middle East, the United States got the conservative leaders of Iran, Turkey, and Iraq to form CENTO (the Central Treaty Orga-nization); Pakistan, Thailand, and the Philippines constituted the Southeast Asia Treaty Organization (SEATO). In response to these moves by the super-powers, "the nonaligned states" held their first conference in 1955 at Ban-dung in Indonesia. All those countries plus Latin American states soon became lumped together as "the third world," in contrast to the "first world" of the industrialized capitalist world and the "second world" of the commu-nist states.

Although there were many differences among third world states, they did share some common issues and problems, three of which stand out. First, their economies had been controlled either by their colonial masters or a regional hegemon (e.g., the United States in the case of Latin America), which had kept them largely rural and suppliers of food and raw materials. Even after gaining political independence, their economies remained "dependent." To break that dependency became a goal of "development." Second, because little industrial development and in some instances limited urbanization had occurred, third world states were predominantly rural peasant societies. Even today, with more than thirty years of rapid industrial development behind them, the world's two most populous countries—India and China—remain substantially rural societies, although they are rapidly urbanizing. And third, decolonization and revolution set the stage for the massive post–World War II population explosion in third world countries.

Rural societies typically have both high birthrates and high death rates (especially for infants). In the biological old regime, infectious disease and limited food supplies carried off as many as half of all children born. Ensuring adequate numbers of children to work the farms and provide brides for other families thus required many births—four to seven live births was not uncommon. Those high birthrates continued after World War II, but the death rates dropped precipitously because the newly independent states, with support from the WHO (World Health Organization, a UN organization), made modern drugs (e.g., antibiotics and immunizations) available to rural people. Infant mortality rates fell sharply (by as much as half) and populations exploded, in many countries doubling within thirty years. Increased food supplies sustained those growing populations. As a result, where in 1950 the population of the world was about 2.5 billion, by 1970 it was 4 billion, by 2000 it was 6 billion, and by 2010 the world's population was over 7 billion; most of those additional billions were born and live in third world (Global South) countries. That remains a compelling fact about the world in the early twenty-first century.

With growing populations, development first and foremost meant improving agriculture to increase the food supply. On the one hand, new land could be brought under the plow, but much of it was marginal, ecologically fragile land or forested land. Either way, trying to meet food demands by increasing the land under cultivation created environmental problems caused by deforestation and siltation. So to increase food production largely meant improving agricultural yields, and the quickest way to do that is to irrigate and apply synthetic fertilizer. As we saw at the beginning of this chapter, the industrial process for making ammonia-based nitrogenous fertilizer was invented at the beginning of the twentieth century and served to increase agricultural yields in Europe and the United States in the first half of the century. In the second half of the century, its use spread to the developing world, at least to those areas with farmers well-off enough to buy the artificial fertilizer. The combination of synthetic fertilizer with irrigation and the development of new high-yielding seeds in the 1960s came to be known as "the green revolution."

But even successfully implementing a green revolution would keep a third world country agricultural and poor—ever since the Great Depression of the 1930s, food and raw material prices relative to manufactured goods prices have been falling. To put it another way, an agricultural country would have to export increasing amounts of its products simply to buy the same amount of manufactured goods, *all while its population is increasing.* In other words, because of population increases and the relative price weakness of agricultural products, many people in much of the third world got poorer in the second half of the twentieth century and could not afford the industrially produced fertilizers that would increase their yields. The way out—for some countries at least—was industrialization.

Even in England in the decades around 1800 where industrialization began, a strong, well-organized, and efficient state with capable leaders pursued policies that nurtured industry.[33] Additional examples of strong, interventionist states include Japan and Germany in the late nineteenth century, Soviet Russia under Stalin in the 1930s, and China since 1949. In East Asia, some smaller states also vigorously pursued industrial policies in the late twentieth century, and all of them have had strong states to direct the process: South Korea, Taiwan, Singapore, and Hong Kong, the "four tigers" of Asia.[34] In Latin America, Brazil, Mexico, and Chile have established significant industrial sectors while maintaining large and poor rural sectors.

In part, those industrializing countries had strong states that took the lead in promoting industrialization, keeping in check the demands both of labor for unions and higher wages and of traditionalist religious leaders who felt their visions of the world threatened by the new ways of social organization represented by cities and factories. In addition, from the 1970s on, structural changes in the world economy provided opportunities that these states could benefit from. In particular, in a world of international trade and competition, improvements in global transportation and communications made it possible for first world manufacturers to relocate plants to lower-wage parts of the world, especially in Asia and Latin America. After the collapse of the Soviet Union in 1991, the former "Eastern bloc" also attracted factories from Western Europe. Powered largely by consumer demands in the wealthy countries, Nike shoes manufactured in Vietnam, T-shirts in Thailand, telephones, and a thousand other products from Asia and Latin America filled container ships heading for the ports of Long Beach, New Orleans, or New York and the nearest Walmart.

One part of the third world whose economy relied almost exclusively on the export of a single raw material—oil—until recently succeeded in significantly raising its international market price. Oil-producing countries (mostly in the Middle East, but including Nigeria in Africa and Mexico and Venezuela in Latin America) formed the Organization of Petroleum Exporting Countries (OPEC) in 1960, but OPEC had had little success in shoring up the price of oil; in 1970, oil sold for about $2.50 per barrel. But in 1973, in the midst of the second Arab-Israeli war, the Arab members of OPEC (with their separate Organization of Arab Petroleum Exporting Countries, or OAPEC) announced an embargo on their oil exports to the United States, the main supporter of Israel, and in its aftermath OPEC was able to pump up the price of oil to $40 per barrel by 1980. Dollars flowed into the oil-producing Arab sheikdoms, creating fabulously wealthy (if unindustrialized) societies.

Migration, Refugees, and States

Through the twentieth century to the present, global migration has been patterned by the territorial nation-state that became the near-universal form of political order and the continued industrialization of parts of the world.[35] As noted in the last chapter, states began the process of regulating and policing their borders to control foreign access to their nations. Globally, migration surged in the first four decades of the twentieth century; even as transatlantic migration shrunk, movement to Southeast Asia and North Asia continued the surge from the nineteenth century, and for the same reasons as discussed in chapter 5. Mostly the pattern of global migration was from the poorer parts of the world increasingly known as the Global South (mostly the formerly colonized or semi-colonized regions of Africa, Asia, Latin America, and the Middle East) to the industrialized core countries of the world known as the Global North, primarily Europe and North America. In the view of migration historian Eliot Dickinson, the attraction of the Global North is that "in comparative perspective, rich core countries offer job, educational opportunity, social mobility, stable government, and political freedoms."[36] As we will see in more detail later in this chapter, the "gap" between the richest and poorest parts of the world has not gone away, and in many ways has gotten worse for many people, pushing them to find ways to better their lives.

The twentieth century with its world wars and civil wars added another dynamic to global migration, with people fleeing war, destruction, persecution, and genocide in the context of nationalist and racist movements. Estimates vary, but interstate wars in the twentieth century account for between 125 and 175 million deaths, making that century the world's most violent.[37] Moreover, deliberate state actions in the Soviet Union in the 1930s and China in the late 1950s contributed directly or indirectly to famines that added another 60 to 80 million dead. Wars and political persecution also caused huge flows of people fleeing the violence; by the end of World War II Europe had 40 million refugees. In the wake of that war and with the establishment of the United Nations, the definition, status, and rights of refugees were codified in 1951 to include those who cross national boundaries to flee persecution and fear for their lives if they were to return, or otherwise cannot return to their country of origin. In the twentieth century, refugees comprised a growing proportion of migrants, a trend that has continued into the twenty-first century.

During the early years of World War I, the Ottoman state "relocated" Armenians to the southern boundaries of its empire, and during this process so many executions took place that the episode is known as the Armenian Genocide. In South Africa, black Africans were excluded from the political process, denied rights to reside in white areas, and were forcibly relocated to "townships" and kept there by the rules of "apartheid." The Nazi holocaust spurred many Jews to flee Europe to find safe haven elsewhere, including the United States, which in at least two instances refused Jewish refugees entry to the United States. The 1947 partition of India sent millions of Hindus fleeing south into what became India and Muslims fleeing north into what became Pakistan. In the process, hundreds of thousands were killed and most had their property and lands confiscated by others.

In the uneasy international peace accompanying the Cold War, civil wars often fought along national or racial bounds sent refugees fleeing to seek safety elsewhere. Civil wars in African countries in the 1970s and '80s contributed to streams of refugees flowing north to the Mediterranean and Europe, and civil wars in Central America sent refugees north to the United States, illegally crossing the U.S. southern border if necessary; these crossings took place despite the United States signing on to the 1951 UN Refugee Convention, which defined refugees as those outside their home country seeking protection from persecution there. It bound signatory states to abide by the Convention that obliges them to accept refugees. The vicious civil war in Syria, begun in 2011 and not over as of this writing, has resulted in the destruction of towns and cities of people opposing the Syrian government and being forced to flee: about a million have taken refuge in Turkey, and hundreds of thousands more trekked to Europe seeking asylum in countries there; most were accommodating, but at least one—Hungary—put up fences to keep all the refugees out. Another recent case is the flight of the largely Muslim Rohingya people within Myanmar to Bangladesh to escape persecution and death. The total number of refugees increased from over forty million in 2007 to nearly seventy million in 2017, many living in refugee camps with others distributed among the host country's population, as when Germany accepted about one million Syrian refugees in 2015.

With millions of refugees and people displaced within their own countries, the mass migrations continue for people seeking to better their and their family's material and political fortunes, migrating from Africa to Europe, Asia to North America, and Central America and Mexico to the United States. According to one calculation of global totals, where in 1910 countries had a total of 35.7 million foreign-born people among their population (or 2.0 percent of world population), by 2003 there were 175 million, or 2.8 percent of the world population.[38]

On the one hand, these cross-national movements of people, especially to urban areas, contribute to the creation of a vibrant cosmopolitan culture, where food, drink, art, music, ideas, and religion, among other cultural productions, add to and enrich the human experience of all the residents willing and open to the new. On the other hand, immigrants and their cultures can be experienced as a threat to the native (or nativistic) residents, either because there is the perception that the newcomers take jobs, or the racist assertion that the immigrants cannot and should not be accepted and assimilated because of the cultural and political changes that may follow in their wake. Over the past decade, many migrants have been from the poorest parts of the world—sub-Saharan Africa and Central America—looking for better life opportunities. That these migrants are arriving at the borders of European states and the United States has given rise to strong anti-immigration views and movements.[39]

Elsewhere, one of the largest mass migrations in all of history is underway in China, where in recent decades hundreds of millions have moved from the countryside to cities, and the Chinese state expects that by 2030 an additional 500 million people will migrate from rural areas to newly built cities and China will have at least two-thirds of its population living in cities of a million or more.[40]

The waves of globalization that were spawned in the second half of the twentieth century by numerous factors—industrialization; the movement of capital to regions of lower wages for manufacturing; the spread of global webs of supply chains to build everything from automobiles to smartphones; the impoverishment of large parts of the world; interstate and civil wars; and genocide—show no evidence of subsiding in the first decades of the twenty-first century. These challenges to the sovereignty of nation-states and the management of their borders—a process that some have called "deterritorialization"—in the context of the global Great Recession of 2008 have also created a political backlash that looks increasingly nativistic, nationalist, and potentially isolationist, trends to be discussed more in a later section of this chapter. Suffice it to say here that while the processes of globalization have led to the freer movement of goods, raw materials, and capital around the world, with barriers to all of those coming down, barriers to people moving across national boundaries have made the cross-national migrations of people in search of a better or safer life much more difficult.

Global Inequality
Despite the industrialization of some parts of the former third world, the luck of OPEC states, or the migration of millions to richer states, the gap between the richest and poorest parts of the world has not closed; indeed, it has increased. In 1990, the per capita income of the wealthiest countries was $18,280, or fifty-five times that of the poorest nations. Seen another way, from 1960 to 1995, the ratio of the income of the richest states in the world to the poorest increased from 30:1 to 80:1.[41] What is perhaps even more shocking is that the poorest people constitute *one-half* of the world's population.[42] Significant numbers of those are the rural poor in the world's two largest countries, China and India, even though they are rapidly developing, with millions more in Southeast Asia and the Caribbean island nation of Haiti. But the largest proportions are in Africa (see map 6.1).

Africa's poverty can be traced to several factors, including slavery, colonialism, postcolonial indebtedness, civil war, and debilitating disease. Decolonization left in its wake territorial states where none had existed. The new states constituted organizations that possessed the administrative and military power to extract and control resources, in the form of both taxes and raw materials. To fund "development," rulers of these new states sought loans from the World Bank, the International Monetary Fund, and the African Development Bank, but mostly such loans funded corruption. Controlling the state apparatus thus conferred wealth on leaders and desire for those

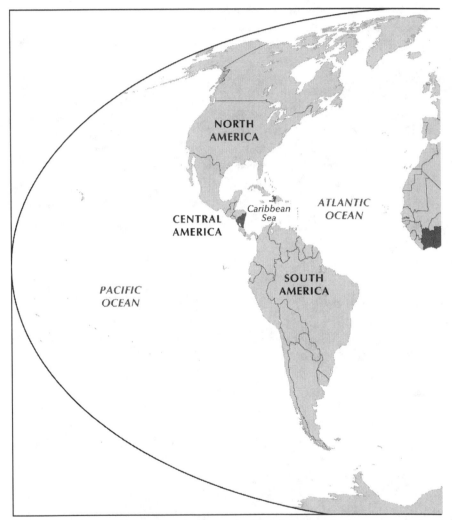

Map 6.1. The World's Poorest Countries by Region (defined as having a gross national income in 2017 of less than US$2,500, as indicated by darker shading)

Source: FocusEconomics, https://www.focus-economics.com/blog/the-poorest-countries-in-the-world.

outside the government to control wealth by gaining control of the state, mostly by violent means, thereby creating successive military regimes, armed opposition movements, and civil war. Often the contending parties belonged to different ethnic or linguistic groups who had been thrown together into the same state when colonial rule ended. Chronic diseases, in particular malaria, AIDS, and Ebola, sap energies and the ability of hundreds of millions to work in Sub-Saharan Africa.[43]

By the 1980s, much of Sub-Saharan Africa was so poor that it held little attraction to foreign investors, so little capital flowed into Africa; even Africans sent capital out of Africa for investment elsewhere. As a result, many African states became dependent on even more loans to keep afloat. So now, many African states are burdened by such crushing levels of debt on top of everything else that they have been labeled "Heavily Indebted Poor Countries," or HIPCs. Of the world's thirty-nine HIPCs in 2013, thirty-four were in Sub-Saharan Africa, three in Latin America, and one each in Asia and the Middle East.[44] The number of extremely poor people in Africa doubled from 1981 to 2001, and despite international goals to reduce African poverty, the poor there were expected to continue to increase, reaching 340 million by 2015.[45] Food security is a challenge, with over 40 percent of Africans unable to obtain food on a day-to-day basis, even from their own farms. Two-thirds of the soils in Sub-Saharan Africa are deficient in the critical nutrients of nitrogen and phosphorus, and farmers there cannot afford to apply chemical fertilizers; 30 percent of the population is undernourished.[46]

Perversely, policies of the industrialized world conspire to keep poor nations poor. The United States, Japan, and the European Union all subsidize their farmers and keep high tariffs on agricultural imports to protect their agricultural sectors. Their farmers are rich and can afford synthetic fertilizer, advanced seeds, and irrigation, all of which increase their agricultural output. Farmers in poor countries are disadvantaged enough, but the high tariffs on agricultural products make it almost impossible for them to compete in the international market: markets tend to work best for those with money. The demand for lowering rich country tariffs on agricultural products thus comes not from the industrialized world, but from the poor countries—to little response by the industrialized world.[47] The 2014 U.S. Africa Leaders Summit, hosted by U.S. president Obama, promised to focus on African development by increasing U.S. trade and investment.[48]

Inequality within Rich Countries[49]

Just as the post–World War II era has not seen a narrowing of the gap between the richest and poorest in the world—despite decolonization, some third world development, and the recent rise of China and India—so too has inequality within countries, especially the wealthiest, continued and in recent decades increased dramatically. This was not the case in the first three decades after World War II, when the lowest levels of inequality within the advanced industrial countries were reached. In the nineteenth century, industrialization, the accumulation of wealth, and the absence of taxes on income, capital gains, or corporate profits led to massive inequality in the richest countries (Europe and the United States for the most part), where the richest 10 percent of the population owned 80 to 90 percent of the wealth. The poorest 50 percent owned almost nothing, and the very small middle 40 percent owned 10 to 20 percent of the wealth.

As noted earlier, at the end of the section on the Thirty-Year Crisis of 1914–45, the shocks of two world wars and a global depression significantly brought down the shares of wealth owned by the top 10 percent, playing an "essential role in the compression of inequality," in economist Thomas Piketty's words. Income taxes, increasingly progressive taxes on capital gains and inherited wealth (estates) that had begun to be levied as early as 1913, and a rising minimum wage continued in the post–World War II era as the United States began building an economy based on consumption fueled by a rising middle class. The vast expansion of educational opportunities in colleges and universities also helped many families improve their economic position. By many measures, the thirty years from 1945 to 1975 saw the lowest levels ever of income inequality in the world's richest countries, a development that some economists wrongly attributed to the wonders of market capitalism.[50]

The relatively more equal condition of the postwar era began to fade by the early 1980s, to be replaced by an era of rising income inequality, to the point that the richest societies are now as unequal in their distribution of wealth as they were in 1913 on the eve of World War I, a period characterized by many as one of an extreme concentration of wealth (see figure 6.1). In nearly all societies now, the top 10 percent own 60 to 90 percent of all wealth, the least wealthy bottom 50 percent own less than 5 percent, and the remaining 40 percent (the "middle" class) own from 5 to 35 percent of a country's wealth (mostly from home ownership).

Figure 6.1. Income Inequality in the United States, 1910–2010

Source: Thomas Piketty, *Capital in the Twenty-First Century* (Cambridge, MA: Harvard University Press, 2014), technical online appendix (http://piketty.pse.ens.fr/en/capital21c2). Data points for 1911–16 inferred from chart I.1, p. 24.

There is little question that the world has returned to levels of inequality seen a century ago. Policy makers, economists, and historians among others are debating the causes and consequences of this rising inequality, especially in the wake of the global financial collapse of 2008 (often called the Great Recession) and its continuing effects. Inequality increased from the 1980s on as taxes on capital gains were dramatically reduced (especially in the United States and Britain during the Reagan and Thatcher administrations), and expensive wars in Afghanistan and Iraq (to be discussed in a coming section) were funded not with increased taxes on the wealthiest (as had been true of the two world wars) but by deficit spending. Since the 1980s, the share of income taken by the top 10 percent, and especially by the top 1 percent, has grown dramatically, while that of the remaining 90 percent has grown hardly at all. In other words, the vast majority of people in the wealthiest countries have seen stagnating incomes, while the rich have gotten richer. That trend will no doubt continue in the United States with massive tax cuts beginning in 2017 going to corporations and the wealthiest 1 percent of taxpayers. There is little evidence that the recent wave of globalization has benefited the vast majority of the world's people.

But so what? Doesn't income inequality create incentives for lower-income people to work harder and try to get ahead? To a certain extent, that may be true. But as a 2014 report by Standard & Poor's (a U.S. financial services company) points out, an unequal distribution of wealth hinders economic growth. That happens because the wealthiest actually have a lower propensity to consume than poorer or less wealthy people, who tend to spend more of their income than to save it. Thus, if overall national wealth increases, but those increases fall mostly to the wealthiest, overall consumption does not increase much. Demand for consumer goods does not grow, and the economy stagnates. That seems to be the situation the United States has been in recently,[51] and it seems to point to a serious problem for the functioning of a global economic order premised on mass consumption. With incomes stagnating, many people in the "lower" 90 percent could continue to consume only by taking on larger amounts of debt, and that system came tumbling down in the financial crisis of 2008, with millions of people losing their homes and then their jobs in the ensuing economic recession.

Part III: Globalization and Its Opponents, 1991–Present

The End of the Cold War

The 1973 "oil shock" caused by the OPEC oil embargo, designed to raise world oil prices, compounded global economic troubles first signaled in 1971 when the United States abandoned the gold standard and allowed the value of the dollar to "float," which it did—down (intentionally, to devalue the dollar and make it possible to pay for oil imports). The U.S. economy was thrown into the horrors of an unexplainable "stagflation," or economic stagnation *and* inflation, a combination that baffled economists. A stumbling U.S. economy drew the rest of the capitalist world economy down with it. Crisis? Slump? Recession? Historian Eric Hobsbawm sees 1973 as the end of a post–World War II "golden age" and the beginning of "the crisis decades."[52] Whatever the 1970s might have been called, it was a stressful time for the capitalist world.

But it was worse in the Soviet bloc. Economic growth had been slowing steadily since the 1950s, and it was not possible to supply the needs of the military, industry, *and* consumers. So consumers suffered, with long lines and waits at grocery stores for basic foodstuffs. Equally, if not more importantly, the "productionist" biases of the system were leading to huge environmental problems that could no longer be avoided. By the 1970s, it was clear that reforms were in order, but getting the huge and unwieldy Soviet bureaucracy to change was difficult, if not impossible, because the Communist Party cadre who staffed the state ministries benefited from their positions. Attempts at reform in other East European countries had been met with Soviet tanks (Hungary in 1956; Czechoslovakia in 1968). Keeping their East European satellites in orbit was getting increasingly expensive for the Soviet Union.

In these crisis years for both the United States and the USSR, two political leaders played significant roles in reducing and then ending the Cold War: Ronald Reagan (elected U.S. president in 1980) and Mikhail Gorbachev (selected to lead the USSR in 1985). In part to lift the U.S. economy out of the deep recession he had forced by sharply raising interest rates in 1981–82, President Reagan vastly increased military spending (and the U.S. deficit as well). Reagan hoped a renewed arms race would spend the Soviets into oblivion, and to a certain extent he was right. When Gorbachev came to power, he recognized the Soviet Union could not keep up with U.S. military spending and the threat of a U.S. space-based missile defense system and so sought not just nuclear arms control but arms reduction through agreements with the United States. He hoped his program of "glasnost," or openness to ideas and culture from the West, would breathe some life into the stale Soviet system, while "perestroika," or readjustment, would reform party, state, and economy. The Cold War was coming to an end, but so too was the Soviet system.

Simultaneously, communist power in East European states was being challenged, in part by labor leaders like Lech Walesa in Poland and in part by the Roman Catholic and Eastern Orthodox churches. Deep economic distress, political corruption, and weakening control from Moscow emboldened East European citizens to make public demonstrations that the state police and armies suddenly refused to suppress. From August 1989 to the end of the year, "people's power" peacefully drove communist regimes from power throughout Eastern Europe. Only in Romania was a Communist Party boss killed. The end of the Soviet Union too was at hand. As the nominally independent republics that constituted the Soviet Union became truly independent, the Soviet Union ceased to exist, rendering Gorbachev's position as head of that state irrelevant. In August 1991 some leaders of the Soviet military tried to use force to bring the "union" back together, but the leader of the Russian federation, Boris Yeltsin, stood up to them; the coup collapsed, and along with it the Soviet Union. By the end of 1991, the United States was the world's sole remaining superpower.

The immediate effect of the collapse of the Soviet Union was an increase in the number of nation-states in the world. Mostly, the process was peaceful, an outcome attributed to the cooperation of then American president George H. W. Bush and Mikhail Gorbachev. The former Soviet Union broke up into fifteen new states, the largest of which is Russia, which inherited much of the power, including nuclear weapons, of the former Soviet Union. In one case—Germany—the process yielded one fewer state when the former communist East Germany reunited with West Germany, which dominated the marriage. Czechoslovakia split into two states (the Czech Republic and Slovakia). In the former Yugoslavia, though, civil war, "ethnic cleansing," atrocities, war crimes, and ultimately military intervention by NATO and U.S. forces accompanied its breakup into six smaller states. In all, the number of territorial states increased to 191 members of the United Nations.

The End of History?

The demise of the Soviet Union and the end of the Cold War was greeted with relief, celebration, and caution: relief for those who had fretted that the Cold War might turn hot; celebration by those committed to the imminent global triumph of the values associated with capitalism and democracy; and caution by those wary of the intent and actions of a United States unburdened by the Soviet threat.

Indeed, the Soviet Union had been a defining feature of the twentieth century, from its origins in the wake of World War I as a challenger to capitalism, to its critical role in defeating Hitler in World War II, and then its contest with the United States for global leadership in the Cold War. With the Soviet Union gone and the Cold War ended, some believed that the causes of global conflict—and hence of "history"—had been eliminated for good and that the future would consist of the largely uneventful and peaceful unfolding of democratic institutions and free market economies.[53] Clearly, that has not been the course of history over the past thirty years.

To be sure, the end of the Soviet bloc meant the end of its form of "productionist" communism. Russia and most of the former Soviet and East European states have since legalized private ownership of property, established the rule of law to protect capital, welcomed foreign investment, and embraced free trade. In short, the part of the world open to capitalism greatly expanded in the 1990s; as a result, "globalization" entered the consciousness of many in the world.

Market reforms in communist China too added fuel to the expansion of free market capitalism and the intensification of global integration in the 1990s. Under the leadership of the Chinese Communist Party, in the early 1980s China began dismantling its state-owned and -controlled economy. That may seem strange, but concerned with spurring economic growth more than anything, China's leader Deng Xiaoping claimed he didn't care whether the cat was white or black, as long as it caught mice.

Beginning with the privatization of agriculture in the early 1980s and moving on to industry in the late 1980s and then opening China to foreign investment, by the early 1990s China's economy was basically capitalist, although the banking system and energy production remain state owned. Attracting foreign capital to build new factories (with the proviso that foreign firms do so through partnerships with Chinese firms and that the foreign companies transfer technology to their Chinese partners), China's strategy has focused on producing consumer goods for the export market. In the 1990s, so much Chinese-made stuff flooded the world market, especially the United States, that China each month exported about eighteen billion dollars more than it imported. As a result, China has a huge accumulation of dollars (about three trillion as of March 2019) with which it buys U.S. Treasury bonds and American companies (IBM's personal computer division—now Chinese-owned Lenovo—was a first notable instance). Since the 1980s, China's economy has been the fastest-growing in the world and, having surpassed Germany and Japan early in the twentieth century, recently exceeded that of the United States to become the world's largest (overall, but not per capita).

A Clash of Civilizations?
Some observers were not so sure that the end of the Cold War had banished conflict from the world, or that new forms of conflict would not emerge. One influential view was that the Cold War had merely served to cover up deeper "civilizational" differences that would emerge once again, in particular pitting "the West" against its historic challengers, the Islamic and Chinese civilizations. These theoreticians advised the United States to gear up for a coming "clash of civilizations."[54]

Numerous events since the end of the Cold War seemed to lend credence to that view, especially with regard to the Muslim world. In 1990, Iraq under Saddam Hussein invaded neighboring Kuwait, claiming that it was historically part of Iraq. The United States led a coalition of forces first condemning Iraq in the United Nations and then using military force in the first Gulf

War of 1991 to push Saddam's forces out of Kuwait. With U.S. forces then stationed in Saudi Arabia as a check on Iraq, Muslims who in the 1980s had fought against Soviet influence in the region turned their ire on the United States, attacking U.S. interests in Saudi Arabia (the Khobar Towers bombing in 1996), U.S. embassies in Kenya and Tanzania in 1998, and the U.S. destroyer *Cole* in Yemen in 2000. The Islamic group that carried out many of these attacks—al Qaeda, under the leadership of Osama bin Laden—then launched attacks on the World Trade Center and the Pentagon on September 11, 2001, in which 3,000 U.S. citizens were killed. This *casus belli* prompted the United States during the George W. Bush administration to go to war with Afghanistan in 2002, and then much more controversially in 2003 against Iraq, toppling Saddam Hussein, but finding none of the weapons of mass destruction he was supposed to have amassed as a threat to world peace.

The 9/11 attacks, Osama bin Laden's videotaped statement about it, the U.S.-built coalition against global terrorism,[55] and the subsequent U.S.-led wars in Afghanistan and Iraq all raise the question of whether or not the dynamics of the modern world have changed. The basic problem with both bin Laden's vision of a revived Islamic empire and the idea of "the clash of civilizations" between the Western and Islamic worlds is that they ignore the processes and forces that brought the modern world into being. While the gap between the richest and poorest in the world may well fuel resentment in the third world (among Palestinians, Afghans, or Pakistanis, for instance) against the United States, Europe, and Japan, there is little reason to think that bin Laden's dream of an Islamic empire approximating its eighth-century scope has any possibility of being erected over a framework of nation-states. To be sure, the civil war that began in Syria in 2012 provided an opening for the rise of a group called ISIS (Islamic State in Iraq and Syria) to seize territory in Syria and northern Iraq and to proclaim the establishment of an Islamic State (IS), but a de facto military coalition of Iraq, Turkey, Iran, and the United States, as well as stateless Kurds, evicted ISIS from its capital in Raqqa and Mosul in Iraq. As of early 2019, ISIS had been pushed into a few small pockets on the Syria-Iraq border with the coalition that formed to fight them committed to their destruction. The archaic vision of the future articulated by bin Laden and ISIS most likely has little possibility of coming to fruition in a world of national interests, even in Arabic-speaking lands where most people profess one version or another of Islam in the context of established nation-states. Palestinian hopes for the future, for instance, are rooted in their nationalism and prospects for a sovereign state, not a transnational Islamic empire. Neither is there any evidence that "civilizations" are actors on the global stage (even if they can be demonstrated to exist in the modern world). Divisions within Islam between Sunni and Shia, not to mention the rise of radical jihadist groups that challenge the interests of mainstream Sunni and Shia groups, for instance, appear so significant that it makes the idea of a single Islamic world or "civilization" irrelevant. In fact, the September 11 attacks are best construed as attacks not on Western civilization but on symbols of the building blocks of the modern world: global capitalism, represented by the World Trade Center, and the nation-state, represented by the Pentagon (or more pointedly, by the White House, if in fact it was a target).

In fact, what might appear to be a conflict between "the West" and Islam is mostly an accident of history. The United States became militarily engaged in the Islamic world not because of some civilizational crusade against Islam but because of an accident of geography: most of the world's supply of oil is to be found in the Persian Gulf region, the home of Islam. The United States would be involved in the Middle East regardless of who ruled the region or their religious beliefs. That the Persian Gulf is both the historic home of Islam and the depository of much of the world's supply of oil is coincidental.

Global Free Trade

Although not "the end of history" or "the clash of civilizations" following the end of the Cold War, the 1990s did in fact see the global spread of markets and capitalism. Indeed, the two major challengers to that way of organizing the world—the Soviet communist model (and its Chinese variant) and the statist German Nazi or Japanese imperial models—had been destroyed, leaving the United States as the sole superpower. Under its auspices, the global economic order has become much more uniform and much more globally integrated. Paradoxically, though, no state—no matter how powerful or rich, the United States included—can control the world economy.[56]

To be sure, the United States retains a powerful voice in the World Bank and the IMF as well as in the WTO, and the leaders of the industrialized "G7" countries meet every July to coordinate global economic policy. But the growth of the global market has rendered most governments quite powerless to control their own economic fate, placing all in ruthless competition, which thus far continues to be dominated by the rich, but not without challengers. Policies designed to ensure full employment or to control inflation (or deflation) have been shown to be useless in the face of international competition, which puts downward pressure on wages and benefits. In this highly integrated global economic environment, states that refuse to allow greater corporate profits by insisting on large payments of social security, unemployment, or health insurance face the prospect of companies closing their factories and moving elsewhere to more favorable sites. As a result, the costs of industrial production around the world fall, as well as prices for most agricultural and raw materials, not because of the results of "comparative advantage," as predicted by those championing international free trade, but because of declining living standards, not just in the poor, developing world but in rich countries like the United States as well.[57]

As the long-term linchpin of this global system of states and economies, the United States has been in a paradoxical position. On the one hand, it has the most powerful military on Earth; on the other, while economically powerful, its share of world production is falling while that of others, in particular China, has risen. It cannot control the world economy, but until recently has felt compelled to use its military power to channel global forces in ways that keep the international system well oiled (literally). Some see the United States as presiding over a new, global empire and "policing" the world for its interests,[58] although the Obama administration (2008–16) was very cautious about the use of American military power and was severely criticized by some for that stance. After his election as president of the United States in 2016, Donald Trump called for the withdrawal of American military forces from around the world,[59] but so far the global military reach of the United States seems to be unaltered.

Energy, Oil, and War

Human societies require energy. For most of our history on Earth, humans have relied on our own and animal muscles to do work, transforming calories from vegetable and animal matter into motion. The great fifteenth-century maritime explorations of Zheng He, Vasco da Gama, and Christopher Columbus began the age of sail, with humans capturing power generated by wind. The Industrial Revolution greatly expanded the sources of energy by tapping coal, and in the twentieth century other fossil fuels, in particular oil, have increased energy output and the mobility of energy-consuming machines such as automobiles and airplanes. Each of those ways of generating and using energy gives rise to technologies, social and economic relationships, and political interests that lock societies into those particular regimes.[60]

Societies that can mobilize sources of energy for industry, consumption, and armies are strong and powerful and use that power to ensure flows of energy from other parts of the world to themselves. Such power, like deposits of coal, oil, and natural gas, is distributed unevenly in the world, accentuating global differences in wealth and poverty: today, the consumer societies, with about 20 percent of the world's population, use about two-thirds of all the energy produced, nearly all of which comes from fossil fuels.

Additionally, the rapid development of China and India, including the advent of high-consuming "middle classes," has increased their demand for, and consumption of, oil, leading one analyst to see a "frenzied search" and "intensifying global struggle for energy," leading to competition and potential international conflict. China increasingly claims rights to large areas of the South China Sea where there are confirmed oil reserves, but the neighboring nations of Vietnam, the Philippines, and Indonesia have territorial claims there too, leading to international tensions. Increased global demand for limited supplies of oil certainly has led to increases in the price of oil, and with the technology of "fracking" (hydraulic fracturing) so much additional oil is being reclaimed from existing wells in the United States, along with a boom in natural gas production, that the United States may become self-sufficient in oil and gas.

Deterritorialization[61]

Opposition to globalization and its results over the past two decades has shifted from critics broadly on the progressive left to those on the right who are more nationalist or isolationist.[62]

Leftists began the opposition to globalization by pointing to the fact that the process was set up to reward first and foremost the owners of capital who could more freely move it around the world in the search for the greatest profits, regardless of the impact that had on people in states from which capital fled and on people and environments where new factories were established. International organizations such as the World Trade Organization and the International Monetary Fund, as well as the G7 (the "Group of 7" major industrial countries in the world), have pressed to loosen the regulations that kept financial capital from flowing via loans to developing countries by insisting on "structural readjustments" there to cut tariffs, social spending, and subsidies for farmers.[63] As the G7 statement from their 2001 meeting in Genoa, Italy, noted: "sustained economic growth worldwide requires a renewed commitment to [global] free trade. . . . Opening markets globally and strengthening the World Trade Organization (WTO) as the bedrock of multilateral trading is . . . an economic imperative."[64] In other words, parts of the world that had not been fully integrated into the global economy would be, thereby opening new areas for the expansion and growth of capital and profits at the expense of workers and the environment.

The first mass demonstration against contemporary globalization was at the 1999 WTO meeting in Seattle that became known as "the Battle in Seattle." Massive street demonstrations disrupted the meetings, while protestors dressed as sea turtles drew attention to the environmental impact that unrestrained capitalist development had. Annual protests followed the WTO or G7 meetings for several years—demonstrations at the 2001 G7 meeting were particularly bloody, with one protester being killed by riot police—until WTO and G7 organizers started holding their meetings in places like Doha that made mass-mobilization protests less likely or less effective (the 2015 G7 meeting was held in a remote and defensible Bavarian castle). More recently, though, the 2017 G20 meeting in Hamburg, Germany, was peaceful, in part because Chancellor Angela Merkel worked to include civil society representatives, and the main topic was global warming, high on many countries' agendas by that point.

In the meantime, the Great Recession of 2008 began to highlight to many unemployed and bankrupted homeowners, especially in the United States, the effects of globalized financial instruments known as CDOs (collateralized debt obligations) and the decision-making by global elites freed from national constraints or concerns. It became clear to many that these global elites and their organizations did not have the best interests of regular folk in mind. As historian Lynn Hunt puts it in summarizing one line of critique of globalization:

> Capital markets and with them financial speculation are no longer constrained by national borders or even by industrial productivity. Since global capital is not fixed anywhere, it is "deterritorializing" in its impact; transactions no longer occur in a particular place. This deterritorialization challenges the sovereignty of nation-states, which after all are built on the notion of control over territory.[65]

A glaring paradox of the second wave of globalization that began in the last decade of the twentieth century and continues to the present is that while capital and commodities could move much more freely across national borders—indeed, the further creation of wealth and accumulation of capital depended on it—at the same time the movement of people met with increasing border restrictions. With large numbers of migrants heading north from

Central America and Mexico to enter the United States, the charge that the southern border was open or porous and that U.S. citizens were having their jobs taken by immigrants, anti-immigrant feeling was building toward a moment when a political leader could tap into it and build a political movement. But these dynamics are felt much more widely throughout the world than just the United States. The economic uncertainties and fears generated by globalization have been accompanied by increased attention to national identity, race, and immigration, fueled by deepening political polarization between left and right.

Similar deterritorializing dynamics have affected the EU (European Union), and for similar reasons, although the explicit intent of the EU was to reduce the sovereignty of its member states with "the aim of ending the frequent and bloody wars between neighbours, which culminated in the Second World War," according to the EU's official website.[66] The EU was established by treaty in 1993 following decades of increasingly closer political and economic cooperation among European countries (e.g., the EEC—the European Economic Community—or "Common Market" formed in 1957). The union created a single market "without internal frontiers in which the free movement of goods, persons, services and capital is assured,"[67] eliminating all tariffs between member countries, creating a common currency (the Euro, adopted by most but not all EU members), and allowing citizens of member countries to travel freely to any other member county and to reside and work in any county. The attraction of membership was access to a large and growing common market, and so the Union has vetted and accepted new members, bringing the total to 28 members by 2013 with a population of over 500 million and a GDP of nearly $19 trillion, making it the second-largest economy on Earth, even if its member states have "deterritorialized" and many people within them chafe at their states having ceded sovereignty to what they see as EU bureaucrats residing in Brussels.

Member countries have ceded monetary policy to the European Central Bank in Frankfurt, and member countries are expected not to run unapproved deficits, a stricture that became difficult for several states when the global economy began tanking with the 2008 Great Recession. In return for loans to keep their governments solvent, Greece, Spain, and Italy all had to cut social spending and to run balanced budgets, creating economic and political problems for their citizens. The EU thus was already under stress when the Syrian civil war broke out in 2011, and soon waves of refugees started showing up at border states, especially Greece and Italy, looking for asylum. Germany's leader, Angela Merkel, allowed nearly one million refugees into Germany, while Poland and Hungary erected fences to keep the refugees out, sparking a fierce debate within the EU over migration policy and the impact of migrants on local economies and cultures.

Meanwhile in Britain, nationalist complaints about EU decision making in Brussels began to rankle some in the Conservative party who pressed for a referendum of the U.K. citizens about whether they wanted to remain in the EU or leave it. Those who thought that Britain should exit the EU—or "Brexit" as it became known—argued that control over its own borders and trade policies (the U.K. had kept its own currency, the pound sterling, and so had control over that already) would return national sovereignty to the U.K. Some in Britain also felt that there were too many migrants from other EU countries coming to Britain to work and taking British jobs. Brexiteers campaigned hard on leaving and made many dubious promises to Britons about the wonderful things that would happen to them upon leaving the EU. The Brexit referendum passed in June 2016, and the British government began negotiating the terms of its exit, a process that is not yet complete at the time of this writing.

But like the nationalist and anti-immigrant movement in the United States, Brexit too was spawned by opposition to the deterritorializing outcomes of the processes of globalization, leading to a focus on benefits of belonging to a sovereign territorial state. Similar nationalist leaders and governments have come to power in Hungary, Poland, and Brazil. Elsewhere within the EU, elections have been held in which more traditional leaders in Germany, France, and the Netherlands have beaten back anti-immigrant-fueled nationalist parties that remain active and continually point out the downsides of globalism and the necessity of asserting national sovereignty.

Does globalization thus mean the end of the territorial sovereign state, as many seem to fear? What is feared and opposed perhaps is less the process of globalization, and more specifically a kind of "globalism," which might be understood as the idea that decision making has been removed from nation-states and handed to transnational, unaccountable global elites who tend to make economic and political decisions based on global considerations, not based on national self-interest. In the minds of these critics, "nationalism" and nationalists are the antidote to globalism and globalists.

Angela Merkel, the chancellor of Germany, strongly disagrees and recently made it clear that addressing and solving global issues requires international cooperation. In a 2019 New Year's Eve speech, she said that when Germany takes on a two-year term on the UN Security Council,

Germany will press for "global solutions" to combating global warming, managing migration, and fighting terrorism. "We want to resolve all these questions in our own interest, and we can do that best if we consider the interests of others. That is the lesson from the two world wars of the last century. But this conviction is no longer shared by everyone today, and uncertainties of international cooperation are coming under pressure."[68] In her view, global cohesiveness is better than the alternative—global destabilization á la the Great Depression of the 1930s and the world wars that preceded and ended it.

Does History Repeat Itself?

The past may not change, but our understanding of it and of its significance in the present may lead us to reassess or reemphasize certain parts of our historical narrative to highlight contemporary issues that historical perspectives might help clarify or raise questions about. That is what the rise of nationalism and the potential breakdown of the post–World War II global economic system raise for us now: Is it likely that the world could return to the conditions and experiences of the "Thirty-Year Crisis" discussed earlier in this chapter?

To be sure, nationalism and nationalist leaders have taken power in many countries, including the rising powers Russia, China, and Iran, as well as the United States, Hungary, Poland, and Brazil. Sometimes nationalist leaders come to power by stoking anti-immigrant fears, or fears about global elites who are trying to undermine a country's national identity. And as the "Great Recession" of 2008 showed, a global economic crisis is indeed possible.

Are these countervailing trends enough to undo the seventy-year consensus of the post–World War II liberal order and change the course of history? That's the view of some. Historian Mitchell Learner says that in the United States Mr. Trump's actions "are not the simple mistake of an ill-informed leader but a blow at the very core of the modern world system." Kori Schake of London's International Institute for Strategic Studies says, "Decades from now, we may look back at . . . 2018 as a turning point in world history: the end of the liberal order."[69] If so, what happens to the globalized modern world? Another round of instability, deglobalization, and interstate war such as the world experienced during the Great Depression of the 1930s?

If the United States becomes increasingly isolationist, will some other country or countries step in to provide global leadership? At one point that looked like the most likely outcome, with China's leader Xi Jinping assuming that mantle at the 2017 Davos meeting; in addition he announced that

China would continue to push the world toward fulfilling the Paris Climate accords, and he launched a vast new infrastructure program called the "One Belt, One Road" initiative that lent billions of dollars to countries around the world to build airports, dams, roads, hydroelectric dams, and harbors from Southeast Asia to South America.[70] China has also launched its own multinational development bank that has the participation of Germany, France, Britain, and Australia. In addition, China has proposed that the International Monetary Fund add the Chinese currency, the yuan (or renminbi), to the U.S. dollar as the world's reserve currency. As James Dobbins, a former U.S. assistant secretary of state for Europe, concludes, "The real alternative to an American-led rules-based international order isn't successful (Trumpian) bilateralism. It's a Chinese-led order."[71] Another analyst alleges that this is China's "hundred-year marathon," a "secret strategy to replace America as the global superpower."[72]

An even somewhat more worrisome view puts the rise of nationalism into a longer-term historical perspective, looking back to the Thirty-Year Crisis of the twentieth century: two world wars and the Great Depression. How did the world get into that condition in the first place? Mostly the answer has to do with a conjuncture of the rise of virulent kinds of nationalism (especially in Germany and Japan), with a global economic crisis that led not just to the imposition of high tariffs and trade barriers that brought international trade almost to a standstill, but also to a breakdown of the international trading system itself. That contingent outcome is most clearly seen in the case of Japan in the 1930s and 1940s when its leaders understood that they could not rely on the global trading system to ensure them access to needed sources of raw materials for their manufactures and overseas markets for their goods, and concluded instead that the only secure sources of raw materials and markets were those that Japan controlled militarily. This calculation led Japan to invade Manchuria in 1931, China in 1937, Indochina and the Dutch East Indies in 1940, and to attack the United States in 1941. It claimed the part of the world it controlled as "The East Asian Greater Co-Prosperity Sphere," ruled by Japan and with Britain and the United States driven from the region. Germany was moving in similar directions, and the Soviet Union was already its own world with "socialism in one country."

So, the goal of the post–World War II U.S. planners was to forge a world that made it difficult if not impossible for nationalist hatreds and trade wars to lead to great power military conflict and another world war. That was the world they subsequently created, for good or ill, as the narrative in this chapter makes clear, and it is the world order that many in Europe and the United States think is endangered in one way or another, but is preferable.

We are now living through a great historical conjuncture. The post–World War II order is being challenged. The collapse of centrally planned economies in the former Soviet bloc and China opened the doors for the rapid movement of capital around the world looking for the greatest profits. As factories fled the industrialized Global North for less-expensive labor and fewer environmental protection regulations, unemployment and high incidences of drug use followed in their wake, especially in rural areas. Simultaneously, grinding poverty and violence in many parts of the Global South, also a consequence of globalization, have sent millions of people migrating in search of security and opportunity for themselves and their families. Except for the European Union, which eliminated barriers to the free flow of people among its member countries, globalization has made it safe and profitable for capital to flow across national borders, but many countries have thrown up barriers to people crossing borders. Adding to the stresses of these structural changes, the population of the world continues to climb, likely to reach over nine billion by 2050. And through the collective economic activity of humans, especially since the end of World War II, we are threatening the global environmental basis for a sustainable future for humans on Earth.

Part IV: The Great Departure: Into the Anthropocene[73]

The dependence of the modern world on fossil fuels is one reason a leading historian has argued that the twentieth century represents a major break with the past and the beginning of a vast, uncontrolled, and unprecedented experiment—a gamble that the fossil-fuel-consuming, twentieth-century way of organizing the globe will not undermine the ecological bases for life on Earth.[74] Twentieth-century American consumerism, Soviet productionism, and third world developmentalism, phenomena that have reverberated globally and shaped all societies in varying degrees, have placed a premium on industrialized economic growth, collectively creating an "anthroposphere" of such size and power as to rival, replace, and rechannel the natural processes of the biosphere. By the end of the twentieth century, humans were already taking 40 percent of the product of the natural process of photosynthesis.[75] We are living in a new epoch—the Anthropocene.[76]

In very rough terms, the size of the global economy at the beginning of the Industrial Revolution in 1800 was three times larger than it had been three hundred years earlier in 1500. Since then, economic growth has accelerated, tripling from 1800 to 1900. During the twentieth century, the world economy became fourteen times as large as it was in 1900, with most of that growth coming since the end of World War II, an era now dubbed "The Great Acceleration" of the Anthropocene.[77]

Economic growth is a rough indicator of our species' relationship with the environment because virtually anything that counts as "economic" results from a transformation of nature. Mining, manufacturing, and farming are all processes that change some part of nature into something usable or consumable by humans. The more economic development we have, the more we change nature. After World War II, consumerism, productionism, and developmentalism combined to push even more economic growth. The pursuit of economic development has dramatically altered not only global power relations but also the environment and global ecological processes. According to the Millennium Ecosystem Assessment, "over the past fifty years, humans have changed ecosystems more rapidly and extensively than in any comparable period of time in human history, largely to meet growing demands for food, fresh water, timber, fiber, and fuel. This has resulted in a substantial and largely irreversible loss in the diversity of life on Earth."[78]

Nitrogen-based chemical fertilizer, first manufactured in 1913 as a result of the Haber-Bosch process, now puts as much nitrogen into the environment as all global natural processes; during the course of the twentieth century, human action overtook the natural nitrogen cycle. By 1950, four million tons (Mt) of nitrogen fertilizer were used, mostly in advanced industrial countries. By 1970, thirty million tons were used; by 1985, that had increased to seventy million tons; and by 2000, it reached eighty million tons, with partial diversification to more countries beyond the industrial core. Significantly, 70 percent of that use is in just three countries: China (25 Mt), the United States (11 Mt), and India (10 Mt). Most of this fertilizer is used in agriculture, but a significant amount of it is for feed for animals that are raised for meat and dairy (cattle, milk cows, pigs, and chickens), and increasingly after World War II for suburban American lawns.

Not only does the amount of reactive nitrogen produced by humans in factories now exceed that produced by nature, it exceeds the amount that can be taken out of the biosphere by the action of denitrifying bacteria. What this has meant is that nitrate runoff gets into the water and air that humans and other animals need to live, and it can kill them if ingested in sufficient quantities, as happened on several farms in the United States and with "blue baby syndrome" when nitrates got into well water.

Like nitrogen, life on Earth requires another chemical element: phosphorus (P). The two strands of our DNA helix are held together by a phosphate ester bridge, without which life could not exist. Also like nitrogen, phosphorus is obtained by humans and other life forms by consuming what to us is food, in vegetable and meat form. Unlike nitrogen, however, phosphorous is mostly locked up in various rock strata in an exceptionally slow-moving natural global cycle that relies on the weathering of rock and the decomposition of organic materials to replenish phosphate to the soil.

Farming depletes phosphorus from the soil, and as food is shipped from rural farming areas to urban centers of consumption, the available supply of naturally occurring phosphorus declines. In the biological old regime, farmers solved this problem by recycling human and animal waste. Unlike nitrogen, though, phosphorus is mostly concentrated in urine rather than feces. Two biological-old-regime farming systems that successfully recycled phosphorus via captured human urine were in China and Japan. In Europe, the depletion of phosphorus from the soil was temporarily solved in the mid-nineteenth century with the application of guano mined from islands off Peru (see chapter 5 for that part of the story). When those sources dried up in the early twentieth century, mined phosphate rock became the major source of phosphorus for combination with nitrogen in manufactured fertilizer. Unlike nitrogen, though, phosphorus cannot be manufactured out of thin air. Its supply is limited to sources that can be mined in deposits that are unevenly spread around the Earth's surface, and there are fears that its production is not only limited but may have peaked and will begin declining by 2030, although that scenario is highly debated.[79]

Nitrates and phosphates have polluted streams, rivers, aquifers, and the ocean, leading to algae blooms in freshwater and "dead zones" in oceans in a process known as "eutrophication."[80] Nitrates also enter the air and are the cause of the smog in Los Angeles and other cities when inversions keep it trapped close to the ground and it gets baked by sunlight into the brown haze of nitrogen dioxide (NO_2). To deal with these environmental problems, the United States and state governments have enacted standards limiting the amount of nitrates allowed in drinking water and a tide of laws trying to limit the amount of nitrates that pollute the land, air, and water.[81]

Is it too late? The Stockholm Resilience Center has identified nitrogen and phosphorus loading into the environment as two of the "Nine Planetary Boundaries" that we on Earth have already moved beyond,[82] but there are actions that can be and are being taken to limit and then reduce the release of N and P into the environment.

The dual concerns of both the limited supplies of phosphorus and the environmental impact of their seepage into aquatic ecosystems has led even fertilizer industry groups to seek ways of recycling and reducing the use of phosphorus in chemical fertilizers to become more sustainable over the long term. Whether this succeeds or not remains to be seen, but there are experiments in the United States with collecting and recycling human urine on Vermont farms, with urine-diverting toilets in India and Sweden, and with treated urban wastewater that fertilizes 25 percent of the vegetables finding their way to urban tables in Pakistan.[83]

By contrast, almost no synthetic nitrogen or phosphorus fertilizer is used in Sub-Saharan Africa, the poorest place on Earth.[84] There and elsewhere, increasingly poor farmers with no money for artificial fertilizer, irrigation, or high-yielding seeds remain trapped within the biological old regime and increasingly use up natural resources to sustain their lives, further impoverishing their environment. Poor rural populations burn forests, grasses, or anything else for cooking, heating, and lighting—survival—further impoverishing both their environment and themselves. It's not just industry that transforms the global environment but rural poverty too.

Some suggest that new technologies such as biotechnology, computers, and the Internet might foster the needed economic growth that will break the grip of poverty, touting for example the liberating effects of the mobile smartphone, while reducing the impact on the environment. Manufacturing computer chips or manipulating genes uses very little raw material compared to, say, locomotives or ships. But without electricity, the computer and biotechnology worlds could not exist. Indeed, the world's energy use in the twentieth century parallels the century's economic and population explosions, with sixteen times as much energy being used in 1990 as in 1900. One analyst calculates that humans used more energy in the twentieth century than in all the ten thousand years from the agricultural revolution to the Industrial Revolution. Coal and steam fired early industry, but the twentieth century was the oil era, fueling the spread of both the automobile and power plants for electricity. Much electricity is generated by coal, and the combination of burning oil, gas, and coal—all nonrenewable "fossil fuels"—has led to global warming.

Global warming is caused by the release of greenhouse gases into the atmosphere, notably carbon dioxide from burning coal and gas, but also sulfur dioxide, from the industrial processes let loose by human action. Methane from irrigated rice paddies and animal herds also contributes to global warming.[85] Although dust in the atmosphere from volcanic eruptions, as well as sulfur dioxide, may have mitigated global warming in the nineteenth century

and the first half of the twentieth century, it is clear both that global temperatures have increased over the course of the twentieth century to the present
and that this rise in temperature has "tracked the dramatic rise in the volume
of greenhouse gases. . . . CO_2 had reached 295 ppm [parts per million] by the
1890s . . . and to 310 ppm as of World War II: since 1945, it has surged to
385 ppm, and shows no signs of slowing."[86] As noted in the introduction, it
has already passed 400 ppm.

To address the problem of global warming, over the past twenty-two years
the United Nations has convened several conferences to get the sovereign
states of the world to cooperate in setting limits to the emission of greenhouse gases, starting with the Kyoto Summit in 1997. Getting agreement
among the independent states has been difficult, at first because developing
countries led by China and India complained that limiting their use of fossil
fuels for energy production would hinder their economic development, and
because the U.S. Congress refused to ratify the Kyoto agreement. In 2015,
though, it appeared that a breakthrough had been achieved, preceded by a
prior bilateral agreement in 2014 between the presidents of the United
States, Barack Obama, and of China, Xi Jinping, to limit and then reduce
their greenhouse gas emissions by 2030.[87] With the leaders of the two countries responsible for 40 percent of the entire amount of carbon dioxide
released into the atmosphere, and hence for global warming, agreeing to sign
the Paris accords, 174 other countries (plus the European Union) signed
onto the agreement. At the December 2018 Katowice (Poland) Climate
Change Conference (also known as COP24), the participants agreed to a
range of matters necessary for implementing the Paris Agreement,[88] the one
that U.S. president Trump has pulled out of.

The effects of rising average global temperatures to date have been felt
mostly in polar or cold regions with melting glaciers and thawing permafrost.
A greater danger, though, is that it is not known how much more global
temperatures will rise and whether the rise at some point will have a sudden,
unexpected, and catastrophic consequence. That is why climatologists have
set 1.5° Celsius as the safe limit for an increase in global temperatures. Rising
ocean levels are already causing problems in Alaska, low-lying Pacific
Islands, and Bangladesh and threatening coastal areas everywhere, even Boca
Raton in Florida. Not everyone will be adversely affected by global warming.
Some parts of the world might see the growing season lengthened and
agricultural output grow, assuming rainfall patterns aren't also disrupted.
What the world has seen is increasingly variable weather patterns probably
caused by global warming: more intense rainstorms, tornadoes, typhoons,

and hurricanes, higher summer temperatures in many places, and colder lower winter temperatures, among other kinds of highly variable weather events.

Human activity in pursuit of economic growth and development has affected other natural processes as well. Besides disrupting the nitrogen cycle and global climate, humans have ripped up vast swaths of the Earth's surface for the coal, copper, gold, bauxite, and other natural resources that lie beneath. Cropland now takes up 20 percent of the Earth's total landmass, and nearly every river has been dammed, with humans controlling half of the world's freshwater drainage basins. Acid rain sterilizes lakes in the eastern United States, northeast China, and Japan. Lakes and oceans fill with nitrogen fertilizer runoff and bloom with algae, sucking oxygen from the water and creating dead zones. Additionally, expanding consumption of beef has increased the global cattle population to two billion eating, drinking, defecating, and gas-emitting animals that also contribute to global warming.

Forests in general and tropical forests in particular contain the most plant and animal species of any other ecosystem. The loss of forests thus correlates with the extinction of other species as well. In fact, since so much forest has been lost since the end of World War II, the world has also lost increasing numbers of other species in "the Great Acceleration" of the Anthropocene. Some biologists are now calling this spasm of anthropogenic species loss an "extinction crisis," with losses at hundreds of times the natural rate. Alarmingly, as many as 30 to 50 percent of all species may be heading toward extinction by the middle of the twenty-first century,[89] and the number of animals declined by 60 percent between 1970 and 2014.[90]

In addition to supporting a large number of plant and animal species, forests and forest soils are one of the great sinks for carbon, taking carbon dioxide out of the atmosphere and transforming it through photosynthesis into cellulose, a major component of wood. As forests disappear, so does one way natural processes remove carbon dioxide from the atmosphere, making our challenges in dealing with global warming all the more complicated. Moreover, scientists are beginning to understand that trees and forests are much more complex living things than previously thought, with relationships with other trees and species traced through root systems, and abilities to send signals (communicate) to other trees via scents and vibration.[91] We are beginning to see forests as living organisms,[92] the loss of which saddens humans as much as the extinction of snub-nosed monkeys or tigers.

Logging and farmland expansion denude vast rain forests in Africa, Asia, and Latin America, altering local climates and driving thousands of species to extinction. The chainsaw has become an exceptionally destructive force since the end of World War II. To be sure, people have been burning or cutting down trees since the end of the last Ice Age and the beginning of agriculture ten thousand years ago. Advanced biological-old-regime economies in China and England, for instance, had effectively deforested their lands by 1800. The pace quickened in the nineteenth century with the felling of North American, Russian, and Baltic forests, before slowing with war and the Great Depression in the first half of the twentieth century. But the fifty years after the end of World War II saw the most ferocious attacks on forests in human history. *Half* of all deforestation in human history has occurred in the last half century, prompting historian Michael Williams to call it "The Great Onslaught."[93] Nearly all of that recent deforestation has been in the tropical zones of Africa, Asia, and Latin America, where most of the world's poor live. With the loss of thousands of animal and plant species, natural ecosystems are being radically simplified and hence are becoming less diverse and resilient.

The result, in the words of climatologist William Ruddiman, is that "humans have now become the major environmental force on Earth."[94] Historian John L. Brooke agrees:

> The arc of history since the end of the Second World War constitutes a fundamental new departure in the human condition. . . . The Anthropocene has arrived . . . in the course of a single lifetime, since the end of World War II. The rapidity of this change is sobering, but its blinding speed may suggest that humanity can—and should—change course in yet another lifetime.[95]

The effect of human technologies reconfiguring the biosphere has had a massive effect on other species. Those selected by us multiply (e.g., beef cattle), while the populations of wildlife species have declined dramatically—there are now 50 percent fewer wild animals than there were in 1970[96]—and many have been driven to extinction. The role of human action in driving species extinction is now so great that it exceeds that of natural processes, leading many analysts to call the current situation "the sixth mass extinction," indicating that the rate of species extinctions now caused by humans is equivalent to the five previous natural episodes of mass species extinctions in Earth history.[97] The loss of biodiversity not only has adverse environmental effects: anthropogenic species extinction is arguably immoral.

Will it be our fate to poison our world with the unwanted pollutants of the industrial world? Will "island Earth" go the way of the Easter Islanders, who used up their natural resources and saw their population decline and descend into warring, cannibalistic groups huddling in cold, dark caves?[98] If the world we live in is contingent upon what has happened in the past and the choices that people have made, then so too is the future contingent upon choices and actions we make today. To be sure, the two major problems the world faces are daunting: on the one hand, providing a decent standard of living for a rapidly growing world population; and on the other, halting and then reversing the degradation of the environment caused by twentieth-century models of industrial development. Is the modern world, structured as it is, capable of addressing these global problems? Maybe.[99]

The fundamental problem is the prevailing view of the relationship of global economic growth to the environment.[100] Economic activity, which is essential for humans to exist, has always been dependent upon and hence part of natural processes. The major difference between the past century and all preceding human history is that the earlier human impact on the environment was so small or so local that modern economic theorists (beginning in the eighteenth century) developed models of how the world works that do not account for the uses or services to humans of the natural environment. In the twentieth century and to this very day, advocates of global free trade, developmentalism, consumerism, and (until recently) productionism assume that the global economic system is separate from the global ecological system.[101] That is proving to be a colossal mistake. The biosphere and the anthroposphere became inextricably linked during the twentieth century, with human activity increasingly driving biospheric changes in directions that can neither be known nor predicted. Albert Einstein once famously said that God does not play dice with the universe; apparently the same cannot be said about humans and the Earth.

Conclusion

The last century thus marks a major departure from the past in regard to the relationship of human beings to the global environment, and, relatedly, in terms of the number of humans on the planet. Neither of these were intended outcomes of the modern world, and we may well wonder whether the constituent elements of that system—sovereign territorial states linked globally by free markets that foster continued economic "growth" at the expense of protecting the environment—are capable of addressing the global issues that they raise for all of us.

The last century also marked a departure in the shift of the locus of global wealth and power from the West European core to the United States. Some have argued that the twentieth century thus was the American Century. To be sure, the United States had the largest and most productive economy at the beginning of the century, although few understood it at the time. It took the profound Thirty-Year Crisis of two world wars and the Great Depression to prepare the United States to step up to the leadership position in the capitalist world system. And when it finally did after World War II, challenging it was the Soviet Union, which like the United States had devoted massive resources to defeating Nazi Germany. Indeed, one could make the claim that the twentieth century was as much a Soviet Century as an American one, for without the Soviet Union, there is little about the course of the twentieth century that would have been the same.[102]

Moreover, labeling the twentieth century an American Century obscures the rise of East Asia over the past forty years. Japan's economic resurgence after World War II; the Chinese communist revolution, which led first to a powerful military and now to an industrial economy; and the industrialization of the "Four Tigers"—Taiwan, South Korea, Singapore, and Hong Kong (and the democratization of the first three), coupled with changes in India and Southeast Asia, have shifted the global center of both economic production and population back toward Asia. After the United States, the next two largest economies in the world are in East Asia—China and Japan.

Indeed, the rise of China's political, military, and economic power constitutes a challenge to U.S. interests and influence in Asia, and there seems to be little doubt that China intends to assert its historic weight in East Asia and increasingly elsewhere in the world.[103] That may make Japan, Korea, and Vietnam uneasy and prompt them to seek close ties to the United States, bringing rising tensions between the United States and China. But in contrast to the Cold War between the Soviet Union and the United States, where there was little trade between the two, each year China sells a hundred billion dollars' worth of manufactured goods to the United States, making it a major trade partner. And while the United States sells much less to China, it does invest there, and Chinese imports help to hold down the cost of living in the United States. The world may well be witnessing the beginning of an "Asian Century," although whether it will be one with Chinese or Indian characteristics remains to be seen. China is following the tried-and-true method of a strong state driving rapid economic growth for global strategic purposes and has little interest or desire in taking its citizens' views of the process into account. Indeed, China is so confident of its model of development that it is exporting it. In the words of Francis Fukuyama, "an historic contest is underway over competing development models—that is, strategies to promote economic growth—between China, on the one hand, and the US and other Western countries on the other. Although this contest has been largely hidden from public view, the outcome will determine the fate of much of Eurasia for decades to come."[104]

In India, on the other hand, a democratic state has opened its economy to global forces, and because it is democratic, the Indian government does listen to the voices of its rural population. As a result, there are now more well-to-do individuals living in India's 650,000 villages, and there is less pressure to migrate to the cities. So far, India's economic growth has been slower than China's, but its democratic institutions may make change deeper, better supported, and more widespread than is the case in China, where an authoritarian system suppresses the voices of the rural poor.

To the extent that the twenty-first century witnesses the "rise of Asia," world history may well revert to the previous pattern of the dominance of Asia from 1400 to 1800. But will it be the same Asia, appearing pentimento-like through the layers obscured by European and American dominance of the last two centuries? No. For just as the re-creation of an Islamic caliphate is not possible, the world also will not see Asian empires based on productive agricultures, as was the case in the early modern world (see chapter 2). The world has so changed that the secrets of wealth and power are unlocked by powerful states directing industrial economies. Whether China, India, and the rest of the developing world will be able to pursue the oil-dependent, car-and-consumer culture of the United States, though, is open to question given the increasingly obvious environmental costs of following that path.

In the long run, then, the question of who will "own" the twenty-first century may well shrink in importance as our changed relationship to the Earth's environment rises in significance. For it was not just the industrialization of the capitalist world that contributed to that "Great Departure"—so did the productionism of the communist model, the developmentalism of India and China, and the rural impoverishment of much of the third world. Intentionally or not, we are all exhausting the Earth.[105]

CONCLUSION

Changes, Continuities, and the Shape of the Future

This brief inquiry into the history of the modern world has synthesized the results of recent historical research into a global narrative. Unlike most world histories, which either chart the rise and fall of various high civilizations without exploring what connected them, or use Eurocentric glue to hold the pieces together, I have developed a global and environmental story line that shows how the modern world came to be while criticizing Eurocentric explanations. At times that may have seemed a paradoxical task, since I began by defining the modern world as industrial capitalism coupled with the system of nation-states and divided by a gap between the "haves" and the "have-nots," all of which highlight European or Western strengths and achievements.

What emerges as central to understanding the emergence of the modern world is a global and ecological point of view that is essential for understanding what happened in and to the various parts of the world. In fact, *interactions* among various parts of the world and between humans and the environment account for most of the story of the making of the modern world, not the cultural achievements of any one part. Indeed, those achievements are not understandable *except* in a global context. The whole—in this case the world and its modern history—thus is greater than the sum of its parts.

However influential Europeans and Americans may have been in the making of this modern world, they did not make it themselves, and the West certainly did not "rise" over other parts of the world because of cultural (or racial) superiority, just as China's recent "rise" cannot be attributed to its specific cultural traits. As this book has shown, Western superiority or pre-eminence has hardly been evident throughout much of human history over the past millennium, and the turn of the twenty-first century has witnessed the resurgence of China as a powerful challenge to European and American hegemony. Moreover, the history of the past century demonstrates the roles that Asians, Africans, and Latin Americans have played in shaping their own histories through revolutions, independence movements, and economic development.

A strong strain of post–World War II American political thought, rein-forced by scholars who paint a picture of American "exceptionalism" in world history, sees the United States as having attained a uniquely special place atop the global hierarchy. This dominant position, which actually materialized only in the specific circumstances of the Thirty-Year Crisis of 1914–45 and particularly since the end of the Cold War in the 1990s, is held by these proponents to be the end result of 2,000-plus years of Western development starting with Greek city-states and their form of democracy. The United States is, in this view, not merely the inheritor of the mantle of democracy and freedom from the British but its highest fulfillment. Not only is such a view the latest incarnation of a Eurocentrism that is blind to the actual ebbs and flows of world history, but it has informed the thinking of some American leaders who have attempted to impose those values on oth-ers, by force if necessary. Mr. Trump's actions as U.S. president, by contrast, seem poised to hand global leadership to China, which seems to want it. As historian Paul Kennedy has argued, the history of the past five centuries demonstrates that great powers not only rise—they also fall.[1] More recently, Graham Allison has shown that over those 500 years, all but four of the six-teen cases of rising powers challenging existing powers have involved war. "When the parties avoided war, it required huge, painful adjustments in atti-tudes and actions on the part not just of the challenger but also the chal-lenged."[2] Coupled with global warming, the world and its people clearly face important and urgent challenges. Historical understanding can help us peacefully navigate the way forward.

The Story Summarized

In this book's narrative, until very recently (about 1800 or so) nearly all of the world's inhabitants lived within the environmental constraints of the biological old regime. Within that world, agrarian empires proved to be suc-cessful states, developing high standards of living for their people, high cul-tural achievements, and substantial governmental power. The most highly developed economies and states of the Old World—especially in China, India, and western Europe—were broadly comparable, with well-developed market systems, institutional arrangements enabling people to squeeze the most from economies rooted in agriculture, and productive industries, albeit ones largely dependent on capturing annual flows of energy from the sun.

The ability of one part of the world—in this case western Europe, led by Britain—to escape the limitations of the biological old regime by tapping stored sources of energy (coal and then oil) was contingent and came about as a result of a global conjuncture. The first contingency was China deciding in the early 1400s to abandon its naval domination of the Indian Ocean, the crossroads where the wealth of Asia was traded for raw materials (including silver and gold) from the less-developed parts of the world, and to remonetize its economy using silver, creating a new, global demand for silver that would soon be met by New World supplies. For four centuries (from 1400 to 1800), the commercial and industrial prowess of China and India, both made possible by highly productive agricultures, enabled Asians to dominate the world economy and to attract the attention, and resources, of those elsewhere in the world who wished to gain access to the riches of Asia. The demand for silver in Asian economies thus set in motion several other world-changing processes.

The second significant contingency in our story thus was the accidental "discovery" of the New World and its stores of silver, the subsequent decimation of the native population by diseases carried by the conquerors, and the construction of an African slave-based plantation economy subordinate to European interests. Third, the failure of the Spanish in the sixteenth century to impose an empire upon the rest of Europe led to a system of competing European states locked in almost constant warfare, thus promoting rapid military innovation there.

In the eighteenth century, a vast conjuncture of forces enabled Britain—a small island off the westernmost edge of Eurasia—to begin breaking away from the pack. Wars between France and Britain, culminating in the Seven Years' War (1756–63), paved the way for Britain's dominance in Europe, North America, and India. Almost simultaneously, Mughal power in India began to crumble, largely for domestic reasons, providing an opening for British adventurers to gain a colonial toehold. China, though, was still too powerful for the British and so could define the terms of British participation in their East Asian world until the combination of opium from Britain's colony in India and their steam-powered gunboats led to China's defeat in the Opium War (1839–42). Coupled with China's internal difficulties, the

Opium War inaugurated a century of Western and Japanese aggression against China.

In retrospect, the tipping of the scales against China would not have happened had Britain not begun to industrialize and to apply the fruits of industry to its military. Moreover, industrialization there was contingent upon Britain having a peculiar kind of periphery in the New World, one that had the need for Britain's manufactured goods, especially cotton textiles, to clothe African slaves. Britain also had both the good fortune to be sitting on conveniently located coal deposits after Britons had deforested a good bit of the island to heat London, and a government willing and able to protect both its nascent textile industry and its strategically important coal industry. Thus, where Asia and Latin America by 1800 remained hemmed in by the ecological limits imposed by the biological old regime, Britain first, then other European countries (fearing the consequences of losing ground to Britain), began to escape by applying sources of stored energy (first coal and then oil) to industry and the military.

The resulting transformations changed economic dynamics and the relations of humans to the world's environment, resulting in the boom and bust of the business cycle, growing divisions between new social classes and between the people and the state, increased competition among European states for colonies that would be captive markets and guaranteed sources of raw materials, and scrambles for control of Africa and for concessions in China. Unfortunately for those parts of the world working within the constraints of the biological old regime, the most powerful El Niño conditions in five hundred years developed in the last quarter of the nineteenth century, with three strong El Niños (1876–79, 1889–91, and 1896–1902) killing tens of millions in drought-induced famines and driving much of Asia, Africa, and Latin America further into conditions we now associate with the third world or what is now more commonly referred to as the Global South.

As historian R. Bin Wong argued in *China Transformed*, in the nineteenth century two distinct ways of organizing human societies came to confront each other. One—agrarian empires with highly productive agricultural economies—had been the most successful for nearly a thousand years, as China and India demonstrated. Other peoples too (e.g., Aztecs and Incas in the Americas) had found ways to maximize the benefits of the biological old regime, but because their energy sources ultimately were based on tapping annual solar flows, the power of those states, the size of their populations, and the productivity of their economies were limited. The other, newer way—nation-states with economies harnessing energy from fossil fuels to dramatically increase industrial output and military power—developed first in western Europe during the nineteenth century. That new political economy gave Europeans the power to dominate 85 percent of the world by 1900. Dominance was not achieved because Europeans had a superior culture to others, despite attempts to contrast the "civilized" heirs of ancient Greece with the "barbarians" of Asia and Africa. The idea of cultural superiority is nonsense, but it can be dangerous when infused with nationalism, as the world found out earlier in the twentieth century and is dealing with again.[3] As we have seen, "the rise of the West," if we must use that term, has more to do with the Great Dying, sugar, African slavery, pilfered silver, coal, opium, guns, and war.

With those advantages, at the beginning of the twentieth century Europeans and Americans ruled or controlled much of Asia, Africa, and Latin America—the Global South. They were not so much interested in changing those agrarian regimes as tapping them for the natural resources that could not be manufactured but were necessary for modern industry. The lifting of third world countries from the limitations imposed by the biological old regime thus needed to await Asians, Africans, and Latin Americans creating and ruling their own states. How and why that happened through anti-imperialist independence movements and social revolution—that is, movements centered not in Europe but in Asia, Africa, and Latin America—is an integral part of the story of the twentieth century. Indeed, much about the modern world changed from the beginning of the twentieth century into the first decades of the twenty-first. Two world wars and the Great Depression destroyed the empires and power of the European and Japanese states, opening the way for the rise of the United States and the Soviet Union, and the Cold War between them. Simultaneously, the independence of the former colonies coupled with revolution in China gave those countries a stake in industrial development, leading to a massive increase in humanity's productive power and impact on the environment in the second half of the twentieth century.

That explosion in economic activity enlarged the size of the human footprint on the Earth, in many cases exceeding natural biospheric processes. By the early twenty-first century, human actions (both intentional and otherwise) resulted in the production of more reactive nitrogen than natural processes; we are affecting global climate processes by adding to the atmosphere the greenhouse gases carbon dioxide and methane to reach levels unseen in over a million years; through dams, we control the hydrology of over half of the fresh water on Earth; our machines move more earth than the natural processes of erosion by wind and water; and by all of these processes, humans are causing the sixth great extinction of life on the planet Earth. Humans have become so active that we rival, exceed, or displace global forces of Nature. While humans have been remaking nature in major ways since the development of agriculture, the biological old regime placed limits on the impact we could have on Nature. But that began to change rapidly in the nineteenth century with industrialization, and it has reached a tipping point since 1950. We now live more than ever in a human-created, but nonetheless unintentional, "anthroposphere," and we have entered a new epoch in terms of our relationship with Earth's natural environment—the Anthropocene. That is a "Great Departure" from past historical patterns.

But so what? Along our long evolutionary path as a species, humans have sought to please, placate, ameliorate, or channel the forces of Nature, and with the rise of modern science, to understand, use, and manipulate Nature as well. Some twentieth-century leaders even called for humans to dominate and train an unruly Nature.[4] But the impact that humans have now had has been unplanned and unintended, with unfolding consequences for us and planet Earth that we do not yet fully comprehend. But recognition of the fact that we live in a new epoch largely as a result of human actions (however shortsighted and unintended) is a precondition for figuring out how best to plot our way forward, as we must.[5] Most scientists and a significant number of people in the world and some of their leaders think that addressing the issue of global climate change is not just the first place to start, it is an urgent item on humanity's agenda.

In addition, humanity needs to begin addressing (and undoing or scaling back) several of the key features of the modern world. In the view of Crispin Tickell, "First we need to confront the effects of our own population proliferation in all its aspects; next to look again at economics and replace consumerism as a goal; then to work out new ways of generating energy; to manage and adapt to what is in effect climate destabilization; to give higher priority to conservation of the natural world; and last to create the necessary institutional means of coping with global problems in a world in which society is more integrated than ever before."[6] That calls for examining the roles of market economies, industrialism, and the nation-state, all building blocks of the modern world, in the search for a better relationship with the fragile natural world we all inhabit.

Globalization

The speed with which ideas, information, germs, people, plants, animals, and commodities now circulate around the world may make it appear as if globalization is a recent phenomenon. But if globalization is understood as the process by which markets, politics, values, and environmental change are integrated across the globe, then globalization has a long history that is intertwined with the story told here of the emergence of the modern world. Even prior to the Portuguese circumnavigation of the globe in 1521, Asians had created such dynamic economies that goods and ideas flowed around the Indian Ocean, linking China, Japan, and the "spice islands" with India, the Middle East, East Africa, and even northern Europe. Before that, in the thirteenth century the Mongols had created the largest land-based empire the world had ever seen. Among its consequences was enabling the plague to travel across Eurasia from China to Europe, with great devastation to human populations. And dar al-Islam, or "the abode of Islam," was a cultural and linguistic ecumene that by the thirteenth century stretched from Spain and Tunis in the west to Aceh in what is now Indonesia in the east.

Despite the size and significance of those Asian worlds, they did not encompass the entire globe. So, if the birth of globalization has a date, it is not 1492 but 1571, when Spain established its colony of Manila in the Philippine Islands.[7] Even though the globe had been circumnavigated earlier, and people, plants, and pathogens had begun their Columbian Exchange around the world on wooden sailing ships, there was not yet the regular exchange of people, commodities, plants, animals, pathogens, and genetic material around the world. Manila made that possible for the first time in human history, with New World silver not just traveling across the Atlantic but being loaded onto Spanish galleons in Acapulco and heading west across the Pacific. From 1571 on, global flows of silver found their way directly to Asia, and Asian goods streamed around the world to Europe and the Americas; riding on those ships as well were people with ideas and customs, plants and animals, and deadly diseases, all of which spread around the world. Driving that *first wave* of globalization, nonetheless, was the voracious appetite of China for silver.

The *second wave* of globalization began in the nineteenth century. First the British and then other western European states, the United States, and Japan harnessed the fruits of industrialization to military power and turned that new power to colonizing Asians and Africans. Imperialists established colonies, semi-colonies, and dependencies to provide secure markets for their industrial products and sources of supply for industrial raw materials such as rubber, gold, oil, and bauxite, among others. Even greater amounts of goods and ideas flowed around the world during the second globalization, including nationalism, which energized Asian and Arab dreams of independence from European colonial domination.

This second wave of globalization, often called the "New Imperialism" of the nineteenth century, did not lead immediately to a new phase of globalization but rather to its breakdown. World War I and then the Great Depression divided the world into more or less autonomous "autarkic" zones of imperial powers. These powers were trying to resolve the crisis of the depression on their own terms yet came into increasing conflict with each other, leading to World War II. The United States and the Soviet Union emerged from that war as global "superpowers," each with its own vision for structuring the world, leading to a *third wave* of globalization in a polarized world. Both the United States and the USSR created institutions designed to further their global objectives of creating, respectively, a capitalist or a socialist world. They shared, however, participation in the institution—the United Nations—founded at the end of World War II to prevent conflicts between states from escalating into global conflagrations. Decolonization created nearly a hundred new nation-states, so that by the 1970s nearly every human being on earth lived within the boundaries of states that claimed to rule over them, if not hold their active allegiance.

The *fourth and latest wave* of globalization began with the demise of the Soviet Union in 1991 and has proceeded since then largely under U.S. auspices. With the Soviet Union and eastern European socialism gone and China abandoning the socialist model, the goals pursued by the United States—global free trade, privatization of state-owned enterprises (e.g., land and factories) in all states, and more open ("transparent") political systems—have more closely integrated the former socialist world and the Global South into the rhythms and needs of the global capitalist world. In this latest round, globalization means the expansion—led by the United States—of capitalism into every nook and cranny of the world. Many observers see the United States, while powerful, in decline and perhaps China and/or India best poised to reap the fruits of the current wave.

If there is to be a fifth wave, it will probably be generated in Asia, just as the first was. China already has the largest (though not the richest, as measured by per capita GDP) economy on Earth, surpassing in size the United

States, Japan, and Germany. India is rapidly developing as well, and the successes of the "four tigers" of East Asia (South Korea, Taiwan, Hong Kong, and Singapore) have been touted for thirty years. The combination of China, Japan, and Southeast Asia—already a fairly well-defined economic unit with massive demands for raw materials (including oil) and exceptionally productive industries—with India could reorient the economic weight of the world back to Asia, just as it had been in the period from 1400 to 1800. That China has built its first aircraft carrier and with it the ability to project military power far from its shores, has opened its first naval base on the Red Sea in Djibouti, and is militarizing the South China Sea is seen by some as evidence that China intends to replace the United States at the top of the hierarchy in the global system.[8]

Into the Future

In the 1950s, a Chinese communist leader was asked what he thought of the French Revolution of 1789. "It's too soon to tell," Premier Zhou Enlai replied. What he meant was that processes set in motion by that event were still working themselves out, so its history was not yet complete. That being the case, Zhou thought it premature to pass judgment.

Similarly, we were born into the modern world—a world with its origins and development over the six hundred years of history introduced in this book, but one that has not yet run its course. To that extent we are all insiders with insiders' advantages, but also the disadvantage of not being able to see ourselves and our times as clearly as someone two hundred or three hundred years in the future might be able to. Nonetheless, a long-term historical perspective does enable us to draw some meaningful conclusions about the past and present and to make educated forecasts for the future, and to guide each of us as we make personal and political decisions about what kind of world we want for us now and for future generations.

Agrarian empires and the limitations of the biological old regime are gone, probably forever. To be sure, the world still depends on agriculture to feed its human population, but agricultural yields have been dramatically increased by the liberal application of chemical fertilizers produced in factories using electricity generated from fossil fuels. The population of the Earth thus continues to climb. Having reached the one billion mark in the early 1820s, the world's population doubled to two billion over the next one hundred years, and then doubled to four billion by the 1970s. It has reached over seven billion today and is projected to climb to over nine billion by 2050 and possibly ten billion by 2100.

The chances are fairly high that most of the additional three billion people will belong to the world's poor as population stabilizes or declines throughout the middle-income and richer societies. The poor, the disenfranchised, and the oppressed have little stake in the way the modern world works and provide a deep reservoir of support for opponents of the existing world order. Globalization and the modern world thus have their enemies. From the time the Tupi in coastal South America ran into the Brazilian forests to avoid being enslaved to work Portuguese sugar plantations, peoples have resisted the new forces infringing on their world. That Osama bin Laden and al Qaeda, and more recently other jihadist forces such as ISIS (the Islamic State in Iraq and Syria) find support among vast numbers of poor Muslims throughout the world who see them as "freedom fighters" should not surprise us, nor that some clearly identify the face of the fourth wave of globalization —the United States—as their foe.

Paradoxically, although the United States has defined al Qaeda and ISIS as "terrorists," or non-state actors who have attacked a state, the U.S. "war on terror" is waged through the system of sovereign states codified in 1648 with the Treaty of Westphalia. The United States attacked Afghanistan in 2002 not because its Taliban leaders were terrorists (the United States had earlier supported the Taliban as the best hope for ousting a pro-Soviet regime) but because the Taliban refused to control the actions of those within its sovereign borders—al Qaeda—and turn them over to the United States for prosecution. To justify its invasion of Iraq in 2003, the United States had to manufacture claims (later proven false) that Saddam Hussein possessed—and intended to use—weapons of mass destruction. Similarly, the United States was on shaky legal ground when it sent Seal Team Six into Pakistan on May 2, 2011, under cover of darkness and without Pakistan's permission to kill Osama bin Laden.

The nation-state and the state system, even as mediated through the United Nations and under severe strain by the deterritorializing tendencies of the processes of globalization, thus appear to remain the framework through which much global business is and will continue to be conducted (or forestalled) in the foreseeable future, although nonstate actors and their military forces—called "fighters" and not "soldiers" or "armies" to distinguish them from the militaries of states—pose real and continuing threats to states and their territorial rule throughout the world.

But the most important legacy of the modern world no doubt will be the changed relationship of humans to the natural environment. As we have seen in this book, the biological old regime placed limits on human societies and the size of human populations. The Industrial Revolution and the use of fossil fuels have relieved those limits, ushering in a period of unprecedented economic and population growth. But does the new regime—the world that we now live in—also have ecological limits? Mostly, we act as if there are none; fossil fuel use continues to climb both with the population and the rapid industrialization of China and India, probably with rather dire, but as yet unknown, environmental consequences.

Global warming surely is but one of many emerging signs that we are pressing the limits, just as such signs appeared in the biological old regime. Nineteenth-century Chinese, faced with limited land for agriculture and raw materials for industry, lavished more and more labor on small plots of land to grow food. Similarly, we now try to keep squeezing more and more drops out of limited oil, natural gas, and phosphate deposits, although a good argument can be made that now is the time to leave sources of atmospheric carbon dioxide buried where they lie. There is no guarantee that a new round of innovation comparable to the Industrial Revolution will loosen the energy constraints that are beginning to limit further extension or elaboration of the mass consumption/automobile/fossil-fuel economy that has been constructed over the past century. But just as what happened in the past was not inevitable, preordained, or written, so too is the future not predetermined by our present circumstances. But we need to understand our past and how we got here in order to envision a future that is not just a continuation of past patterns, especially with respect to humanity's relationship to our natural environment. "The longer you can look back the further you can look forward," Winston Churchill once said.[9] I hope that reflection on the historically contingent nature of the world we live in will enable us to make the choices—and take actions—that will ensure a sustainable future for all humanity.

Notes

Introduction: The Rise of the West?

1. IPCC (Intergovernmental Panel on Climate Change), *Special Report: Global Warming of 1.5C*, edited by Valerie Masson-Delmotte et al. (Switzerland, 2018), https://report.ipcc.ch/sr15/pdf/sr15_spm_final.pdf.

2. World Meteorological Association, "State of the Global Climate in 2018," http://ane4bf-datap1.s3-eu-west-1.amazonaws.com/wmocms/s3fs-public/ckeditor/files/Draft_Statement_26_11_2018_v12_approved_jk.pdf?

3. James Hansen et al., "Target Atmospheric CO_2: Where Should Humanity Aim?" *Open Atmosphere Scientific Journal* 2 (2008): 217–31. For a broader discussion of these and other issues regarding climate and human civilization, see William F. Ruddiman, *Plows, Plagues, and Petroleum: How Humans Took Control of Climate*, Princeton Science Library (Princeton, NJ: Princeton University Press, 2010).

4. *Fourth Annual Climate Report (2018)*, vol. 2, *Impacts, Risks, and Adaptation in the United States* (Washington, DC: U.S. Global Change Research Program, 2018); https://nca2018.globalchange.gov. For an overview of this 1,656-page report, see Brad Plumer and Henry Fountain, "What's New in the Latest U.S. Climate Assessment," *New York Times*, November 23, 2018, https://www.nytimes.com/2018/11/23/climate/highlights-climate-assessment.html.

5. Binyamin Appelbaum, "2018 Nobel in Economics Is Awarded to William Nordhaus and Paul Romer," *New York Times*, October 8, 2018, https://www.nytimes.com/2018/10/08/business/economic-science-nobel-prize.html.

6. For a discussion of the IPCC report and an interview with William Nordhaus, see Michael Barbaro, "A New Climate Tipping Point," *The Daily, New York Times* podcast, October 19, 2018.

7. "A Global School Walkout to Highlight Climate Change," *New York Times*, March 16, 2019, A9. See also Sarah Kaplan, "How a 7th-Grader's Strike against Climate Change Exploded into a Movement," *Washington Post*, February 16, 2019.

8. Jo Guldi and David Armitage, *The History Manifesto* (Cambridge, UK: Cambridge University Press, 2014).

9. Will Steffen, Jacques Grinevald, Paul Crutzen, and John McNeill, "The Anthropocene: Conceptual and Historical Perspectives," *Philosophical Transactions of the Royal Society A* 369 (2011): 842–67.

10. Karl Marx and Friedrich Engels, *The Communist Manifesto* (New York: Washington Square Press, 1964), 64–65.

11. Philip D. Curtin has sensibly defined "modernization" as the drive to achieve high economic productivity and high consumption levels, regardless of cultural differences. *The World and the West: The European Challenge and the Overseas Response in the Age of Empire* (Cambridge: Cambridge University Press, 2000), 110. However, post–World War II "modernization" theorists of the 1950s and 1960s developed a list of what it meant to be "modern" that looked very much like the United States.

12. The term is taken from a book by E. L. Jones, *The European Miracle* (Cambridge: Cambridge University Press, 1981).

13. Especially the British economic historian Patrick O'Brien. See his article "European Economic Development: The Contribution of the Periphery," *Economic History Review*, 2nd ser., 35 (1982): 1–18.

14. As examples of these various theses, see David S. Landes, *The Wealth and Poverty of Nations: Why Some Are So Rich and Some So Poor* (New York: W. W. Norton, 1998) and *The Unbound Prometheus: Technological Change and Industrial Development in Western Europe from 1750 to the Present* (Cambridge: Cambridge University Press, 1969); Lynn White Jr., *Medieval Religion and Technology: Collected Essays* (Berkeley: University of California Press, 1978); Alfred Crosby, *The Measure of Reality: Quantification and Western Society, 1250–1600* (Cambridge: Cambridge University Press, 1997); Geoffrey Parker, *The Military Revolution: Military Innovation and the Rise of the West 1500–1800*, 2nd ed. (Cambridge: Cambridge University Press, 1999).

15. For overviews, see J. Donald Hughes, *What Is Environmental History?* (Malden, MA: Polity Press, 2006); J. R. McNeill, "The State of the Field of Environmental History," *Annual Review of Environment and Resources* 35 (2010): 345–74; and J. R. McNeill and Alan Roe, "Editors' Introduction," *Global Environmental History: An Introductory Reader* (London: Routledge, 2013), xiii–xxvi.

16. For a thoughtful exploration of this idea and the urgent relevance of historical understanding to acting in our world today, see Jo Guldi and David Armitage, *The History Manifesto* (Cambridge, UK: Cambridge University Press, 2014).

17. As former U.S. president George W. Bush put it, international free trade is "a moral imperative" that will "build freedom in the world, progress in our hemisphere and enduring prosperity in the United States." Quoted in the *New York Times*, May 8, 2001, national edition, A7. He was expressing what scholars term the "neoliberal" conception

of the rules by which the world should work—deregulated trade within and between countries and minimal government regulation or funding of public goods or social services. That idea is not without its critics. See, for example, David Harvey, *A Brief History of Neoliberalism* (Oxford: Oxford University Press, 2007), and Naomi Klein, *This Changes Everything: Capitalism vs. the Climate* (New York: Simon & Schuster, 2014), 64–95.

18. Historian Paul Kennedy has made the point that the "rise" of great powers is always accompanied by their "fall." *The Rise and Fall of the Great Powers: Economic Change and Military Conflict from 1500 to 2000* (New York: Vintage Books, 1989).

19. For a review of three recent books on this topic, see David D. Buck, "Was It Pluck or Luck That Made the West Grow Rich?" *Journal of World History* 10, no. 2 (Fall 1999): 413–30.

20. J. M. Blaut, *The Colonizer's Model of the World: Geographic Diffusionism and Eurocentric History* (New York: Guilford Press, 1993), 1.

21. Samir Amin, *Eurocentrism* (New York: Monthly Review Press, 1989), vii.

22. Andre Gunder Frank, *ReOrient: Global Economy in the Asian Age* (Berkeley: University of California Press, 1998), 32.

23. Blaut, *Colonizer's Model of the World*, 8–9.

24. The idea of scientific paradigms and the exploration of the conditions under which they might change was first developed by Thomas Kuhn in a classic work, *The Structure of Scientific Revolutions*, 2nd ed. (Chicago: University of Chicago Press, 1970). Kuhn's primary example was the Copernican revolution, that is, the change from a view of the solar system with the earth at the center (the view then supported by the Catholic Church) to one with the sun at the center. Although Kuhn discussed "paradigms" and paradigm shifts only with respect to science, the idea has been extended to the way social science works too. Popular culture has taken up these ideas in films such as *The Matrix* and *The Truman Show*.

25. Some might object that even this approach remains mired in Eurocentrism because of several unexamined assumptions about the very concepts being used, the objects being identified as in need of explanation, and even history as a method, all of which some claim are implicitly Eurocentric. For example, some have questioned whether states and industrial capitalism are really all that important to explain, raising instead the possibility that other aspects of our world might be more important to explore, such as our very concepts of self, body, sexuality, place, causation, and story, and they have proposed new "postmodern" methodologies of "deconstruction" or "discourse communities" and their "privileged language," which confers "power," to explore them. This is an extremely complicated topic, but those wishing a sensible introduction might start with Joyce Appleby, Lynn Hunt, and Margaret Jacob, *Telling the Truth about History* (New York: W. W. Norton, 1994).

26. Not all stories are "true." Some are invented by the author: they are fiction (like Goldilocks and the Three Bears, or the Harry Potter books). While both history and fiction develop stories, what distinguishes history from fiction is that historical facts are true.

Historians have developed sophisticated tools and methods for writing historical narratives (i.e., stories that are "true"). As the following discussion of "master narrative" shows, though, the idea of historical truth is complex and cannot be reduced merely to what is true and false, but must include a consideration of how we determine the criteria for deciding what is true and what is not.

27. Appleby, Hunt, and Jacob, *Telling the Truth about History*, 232.

28. For a succinct discussion of determinism and chance in history, see E. H. Carr, *What Is History?* (New York: Vintage Books, 1961), chap. 4.

29. For an example of work that challenges the central claims of Kenneth Pomeranz's *The Great Divergence*, see Robert C. Allen, *The British Industrial Revolution in Global Perspective* (Cambridge, UK: Cambridge University Press, 2009).

30. George Huppert, *After the Black Death: A Social History of Modern Europe*, 2nd ed. (Bloomington: Indiana University Press, 1998), 13.

31. James Z. Lee and Wang Feng, *One Quarter of Humanity: Malthusian Myths and Chinese Realities* (Cambridge, MA: Harvard University Press, 1999).

32. See the works by Blaut, *Colonizer's Model of the World*; Jack Goody, *The East in the West* (Cambridge: Cambridge University Press, 1996); Frank, *ReOrient*; R. Bin Wong, *China Transformed: Historical Change and the Limits of European Experience* (Ithaca, NY: Cornell University Press, 1997); Kenneth Pomeranz, *The Great Divergence: China, Europe, and the Making of the Modern World Economy* (Princeton, NJ: Princeton University Press, 2000).

33. See Giovanni Arrighi, Takeshi Hamashita, and Mark Selden, eds., *The Resurgence of East Asia: 500, 150, and 50 Year Perspectives* (New York: Routledge, 2003).

34. Fernand Braudel (d. 1985) was a path-breaking historian who took a global approach to explain at least one part of the European miracle: capitalism. His three-volume *Civilization and Capitalism, 15th–18th Century* (New York: Harper and Row, 1979–84) is an intellectual tour de force in which he argues that while many parts of the world developed highly sophisticated market economies, few came close to developing real capitalism, and it only flourished in Europe. Braudel makes the interesting point that capitalists were not at all interested in free markets and open competition, but instead worked to obtain monopoly concessions from European monarchs: under those peculiar circumstances, capitalism grew rapidly in a European hothouse. We will have an opportunity in later chapters to examine Braudel's ideas in more detail.

35. See Pomeranz, *Great Divergence*, chap. 1. The question of whether the world was a single, integrated system and, if so, when it first became a single system is an interesting one that will be taken up more in the chapters to follow. Suffice it to say here that there are at least three basic positions. Like Karl Marx and Adam Smith, Immanuel Wallerstein (*The Modern World-System*, 3 vols. [New York: Academic Press, 1974–89]) and J. M. Blaut (*Colonizer's Model of the World*) take 1492–1500 as the time of the creation of a single world system; Janet Abu-Lughod (*Before European Hegemony: The World System A.D. 1250–1350* [New York: Oxford University Press, 1989]) has put forward strong evidence for a world system circa 1250–1350, which fell apart prior to the establishment of the

modern world system; and Andre Gunder Frank and Barry Gillis have argued for a 5,000-year history of a single world system ("The Five Thousand Year World System: An Introduction," *Humboldt Journal of Social Relations* 17, no. 1 [1992]: 1–79).

36. This model, it should be pointed out, is equally shared by Marxists and by champions of capitalism, so I am not proposing to develop a Marxist narrative of the making of the modern world as an alternative to a celebratory rise of the West; that has already been done, several times over. See, for example, Eric J. Hobsbawm, the four-volume set including *The Age of Revolution*, *The Age of Capital*, *The Age of Empire*, and *The Age of Extremes* (New York: Vintage, 1994–96) and the Marxism-influenced work of Wallerstein, *Modern World-System*.

Chapter One: The Material and Trading Worlds, circa 1400

1. For an overview, see Robert B. Marks, "'Exhausting the Earth': Environment and History in the Early Modern World," in *The Cambridge World History*, vol. 6, *The Construction of a Global World, 1400–1800 CE, Part 1: Foundations*, ed. Jerry H. Bentley, Sanjay Subrahmanyam, and Merry E. Wiesner-Hanks (Cambridge: Cambridge University Press, 2015), 29–53.

2. The phrase is from Fernand Braudel, *Civilization and Capitalism, 15th–18th Century*, vol. 1, *The Structures of Everyday Life*, trans. Sian Reynolds (New York: Harper and Row, 1981), chap. 1.

3. Because no one actually took a census, these population figures are reconstructions by historical demographers, and there is much discussion and debate about all matters having to do with the size, distribution, and dynamics of human populations in the period covered by this book. Braudel's discussion in the chapter mentioned above is as good a place as any to enter into the uncertainties about the size of premodern populations. See also Colin McEvedy and Richard Jones, *Atlas of World Population History* (New York: Penguin Books, 1978). For the latest global population estimates and trends in the period from 1400 to 1800, see the relevant chapters in Jerry H. Bentley, Sanjay Subrahmanyam, and Merry E. Wiesner-Hanks, eds., *The Cambridge World History*, vol. 6, *The Construction of a Global World, 1400–1800 CE* (Cambridge: Cambridge University Press, 2015).

4. There is now an extensive literature on the history of Earth's climate and a rapidly growing literature on the relationship between climate change and human history. For a synthesis of both, see John L. Brooke, *Climate Change and the Course of Global History: A Rough Journey* (New York: Cambridge University Press, 2014). For a detailed examination of the complex interactions between climate change and human societies, see Geoffrey Parker, *Global Crisis: War, Climate Change and Catastrophe in the Seventeenth Century* (New Haven, CT: Yale University Press, 2013).

5. Until recently, research on the effect of climate change on harvests was limited to marginal areas such as Scandinavia. My own work on south China has shown that

climate changes can in fact affect harvests in even semitropical areas. However, that climatic conditions affected human population dynamics does not imply a kind of geographical determinism, that is, that human societies are determined by the nature of the climate and geography in which they find themselves. Rather, people are amazingly adaptable and can create social institutions to compensate for the vagaries of climate or geography. Eighteenth-century China, for instance, had both government granaries, which dispensed grain in times of need, and markets, which moved grain from areas of surplus to those of deficit, both of which began to detach China's population dynamics from any simple response to climatic variations, but that began to happen only in the late 1700s. See Robert B. Marks, *Tigers, Rice, Silk, and Silt: Environment and Economy in Late Imperial South China* (Cambridge: Cambridge University Press, 1998), chaps. 6–8.

6. Braudel, *Civilization and Capitalism*, vol. 1, 56–57. Braudel does not include the Aztecs and Incas in his list of civilizations because they did not have iron, the wheel, and plows or large draft animals. I include them because despite lacking these, they did create empires with cities, social classes, and, in the case of the Aztecs, writing, all of which I think are emblematic of civilization. See also Jared Diamond, *Guns, Germs, and Steel* (New York: W. W. Norton, 1998), for additional discussion of why the Old World had domesticated draft animals and the New World did not.

7. J. R. McNeill, "Global Environmental History: The First 150,000 Years," in *A Companion to Global Environmental History*, ed. J. R. McNeill and Erin Stewart Mauldin (Oxford: Wiley-Blackwell, 2012), 3–17. See also Steven Mithen, *After the Ice: A Global Human History, 20,000–5,000 BC* (Cambridge, MA: Harvard University Press, 2006); David Christian, *Maps of Time: An Introduction to Big History* (Berkeley: University of California Press, 2004), chap. 4; and Diamond, *Guns, Germs, and Steel*, esp. chaps. 4–10.

8. For an excellent discussion, see Clive Ponting, *A New Green History of the World: The Environment and the Collapse of Great Civilizations* (New York: Penguin Books, 2007), chap. 4. Ponting prefers the term "transition."

9. Estimating city size in 1400 is no more precise than estimating the total population. Nonetheless, Tertius Chandler has compiled lists of the largest cities in the world in his compendium, *Four Thousand Years of Urban Growth: An Historical Census*, 2nd ed. (Lewiston, ME: Edwin Mellen Press, 1987). Although one might take issue with his figures, what interests us more at this point is the relative ranking and geographic distribution of these cities.

10. John Bellamy Foster, "Marx's Theory of Metabolic Rift: Classical Foundations for Environmental Sociology," *American Journal of Sociology* 105, no. 2 (September 1999): 366–405. Foster attributes the rift to specifically modern capitalist development, a stance which flies in the face of evidence from earlier times and other places. For an example, see Robert B. Marks, *China: An Environmental History* (Lanham, MD: Rowman & Littlefield, 2015), 177–83. Nevertheless, I do find the concept of metabolic rift to be useful if not ascribed solely to modern capitalism.

11. For the nomadic pastoralists of the Eurasian steppe, see Thomas J. Barfield, *The Nomadic Alternative* (Upper Saddle River, NJ: Prentice-Hall, 1993). Following G. W.

Hewes, Braudel lists twenty-seven identifiable groups of hunter-gatherers, seventeen nomadic peoples, and an additional eighteen "primitive agriculturists" (*Civilization and Capitalism*, vol. 1, 56–60).

12. The fixedness of farming specific plots of land gives the appearance that farming was settled and that hunting-and-gathering peoples were nomadic wanderers. But Hugh Brody suggests that the opposite was true: "A look at how ways of life take shape across many generations reveals that it is the agriculturalists, with their commitment to specific farms and large numbers of children, who are forced to keep moving, resettling, colonizing new lands. Hunter-gatherers, with their reliance on a single area, are profoundly settled. As a system, over time, it is farming, not hunting, that generates 'nomadism.' . . . In the history of . . . agricultural cultures, the combination of settlement, large families, and movement has resulted in a more or less relentless colonial frontier. An agricultural people can never rest—as farming families, as a lineage—in one place." Hugh Brody, *The Other Side of Eden: Hunters, Farmers, and the Shaping of the World* (New York: North Point Press, 2000), 86.

13. For a fascinating discussion of the "cooked" and the "raw" in the context of Chinese expansion into a frontier area, see John Shepherd, *Statecraft and Political Economy on the Taiwan Frontier, 1600–1800* (Stanford, CA: Stanford University Press, 1993).

14. Cited in Braudel, *Civilization and Capitalism*, vol. 1, 66–67.

15. See Marks, *Tigers, Rice, Silk, and Silt*, chap. 10.

16. Gregory H. Maddox, *Sub-Saharan Africa: An Environmental History* (Santa Barbara, CA: ABC-CLIO, 2006).

17. For an overview, see Christian, *Maps of Time*, 199–202.

18. For a discussion of the evidence for population sizes and distributions in the pre-Columbian Americas, see Charles Mann, *1491: New Revelations about the Americas before Columbus* (New York: Vintage Books, 2005), 35–154.

19. William Cronon, *Changes in the Land: Indians, Colonists, and the Ecology of New England* (New York: Hill and Wang, 1983).

20. This German term was used by the Nazis after World War I to express their desire, fanned by a sense that the German population had expanded beyond the ability of the German territory to sustain it, to expand at their neighbors' expense. It seems an apt term to describe what humans in general have felt about expanding their territory at the expense of the natural world.

21. There is much scholarly debate on the size of China's population and its rate of growth from 1400 to 1850. The baseline was established by Ping-ti Ho in 1953 in *Studies on the Population of China* (Chicago: University of Chicago Press), followed by Dwight Perkins, *Agricultural Development in China* (Chicago: Aldine, 1968). Where G. William Skinner thinks the generally accepted figures for 1850 of about 420 to 450 million have to be reduced to about 380 million ("Sichuan's Population in the Nineteenth Century: Lessons from Disaggregated Data," *Late Imperial China* 8, no. 1 [1987]: 1–80), F. W. Mote thinks the population in 1600–1650 and later was much larger than previously believed.

See his *Imperial China 900–1800* (Cambridge, MA: Harvard University Press, 1999), 743–47, 903–7.

22. The question of whether and how peasant farming families in Europe and elsewhere decided to limit their size is an important one that will be discussed more when we discuss the Industrial Revolution in chapter 4.

23. See Kenneth Pomeranz, *The Great Divergence: China, Europe, and the Making of the Modern World Economy* (Princeton, NJ: Princeton University Press, 2000), 36–40.

24. In much of Europe, the Church "tithed" the peasants too, expecting one-tenth of their produce. Monasteries could be large landowners as well.

25. This circumstance coincided with the very origins of civilization and persisted for many years into the twentieth century. For a brief and readable history, see Ponting, *New Green History of the World*, esp. chap. 6.

26. For a full development of this argument, see Amartya Sen, *Poverty and Famines: An Essay on Entitlement and Deprivation* (Oxford: Clarendon Press, 1981). See also David Arnold, *Famine: Social Crisis and Historical Change* (New York: Basil Blackwell, 1988).

27. On the agency of peasants in the making of their own world, see James C. Scott, *Domination and the Arts of Resistance: Hidden Transcripts* (New Haven, CT: Yale University Press, 1990). A similarly interesting case was made about black slaves in North America by Eugene Genovese, *Roll, Jordan, Roll: The World the Slaves Made* (New York: Pantheon Books, 1974).

28. Vaclav Smil, *Energy in World History* (Boulder, CO: Westview Press, 1994), esp. the section "Limits of Traditional Farming," 73–91.

29. Vaclav Smil, *Energy Transitions: History, Requirements, Prospects* (Santa Barbara, CA: ABC-CLIO, 2010), 48–50.

30. J. R. McNeill, *Something New under the Sun: An Environmental History of the Twentieth Century* (New York: W. W. Norton, 2000), 12–13.

31. Hugh S. Gorman, *The Story of N: A Social History of the Nitrogen Cycle and the Challenge of Sustainability* (New Brunswick, NJ: Rutgers University Press, 2013).

32. Michael Williams, *Deforesting the Earth: From Prehistory to Global Crisis* (Chicago: University of Chicago Press, 2003).

33. Marks, "Exhausting the Earth."

34. The idea of macro- and microparasites is developed in William McNeill, *Plagues and Peoples* (New York: Anchor Books, 1976).

35. For the time being, this formulation excludes the Americas, southern Africa, and much of Oceania.

36. This description is based on Janet Abu-Lughod, *Before European Hegemony: The World System A.D. 1250–1350* (New York: Oxford University Press, 1989). A summary is available from the American Historical Association as a pamphlet, *The World System in the Thirteenth Century: Dead-End or Precursor?* (Washington, DC: American Historical Association, 1994).

37. Immanuel Wallerstein, *The Modern World-System*, 3 vols. (New York: Academic Press, 1974–89).

38. Abu-Lughod and Wallerstein see the post-1500 world system as being something new, created by Europeans, and not related to the previous one.

39. The example of the internet, though, should sensitize us even more to the possibility that huge, complex organizations can develop without any central control. To create a webpage, for example, one need not seek the permission of anyone, other than registering a domain name.

40. Immanuel Wallerstein describes the capitalist "world-system," with a hyphen, in *The Modern World-System*, vol. 1, *Capitalist Agriculture and the Origins of the European World-Economy in the Sixteenth Century* (New York: Academic Press, 1974), 15. His use of the term "world-system" means specifically the world-system that he argues emerged first in Europe and then was spread by Europeans across the globe from 1492 on. Others use the term "world system" without a hyphen to indicate something similar yet different, such as the "polycentric" world system I have been describing (i.e., one that was a "world" but not created, diffused, or necessarily controlled by Europeans).

41. For an overview of this literature and its connection to constructing narratives of globalization, see Lynn Hunt, *Writing History in the Global Era* (New York: W. W. Norton, 2014), 61–72.

42. Kenneth Pomeranz and Steven Topik, *The World That Trade Created: Society, Culture, and the World Economy, 1400 to the Present*, 3rd ed. (New York: Routledge, 2015).

43. Monica H. Green, "Editor's Introduction to 'Pandemic Disease in the Medieval World: Rethinking the Black Death,'" *Medieval Globe* 1 (2014): 9. In this introduction Green provides an overview of what is, and what is not, known about the Black Death, including the areas that recent microbiological research has resolved, and areas that are still open to further research.

44. See the analysis and synthesis of the available evidence in Robert Hymes, "Epilogue: A Hypothesis on the East Asian Beginnings of the *Yersinia pestis* Polytomy," *Medieval Globe* 1 (2014): 285–308. Hymes bases his article on path-breaking but little-known research by Chinese microbiologist Yujun Cui and historian Cao Shuji.

45. Paul D. Buell, "Qubilai and the Rats," *Sudhoffs Archiv: Zeitschrift für Wissenschaftesgeschichte* 96, no. 2 (2012), argues that the plague could not have been transmitted from China to Europe via the Mongols, contradicting the major analysis provided by McNeill, *Plagues and Peoples*, chap. 4. I think a connection of the spread of the plague to Europe via China remains possible, if not probable. The southwestern region now known as Yunnan was later understood to be a plague reservoir and from the eighth century on was the center of its own trading world—the "Southern Silk Road"—linking it to the Indian Ocean and to Central Asia via Tibet. See Bin Yang, "Horses, Silver, and Cowries: Yunnan in Global Perspective," *Journal of World History* 15, no. 3 (2004): 281–98. Robert Hymes also makes a very strong case for plague originating in the Qinghai-Tibetan plateau, spreading to China by conquering Mongol armies, and then spreading form China to Europe (Hymes, "Hypothesis"). Monica Green also acknowledges all of the unknowns in figuring out how the plague passed from China to Europe, but she says that "microbiology makes it clear that it did move . . . the common practices of long-distance trade or animal

husbandry that facilitated the spread of Y. *pestis* to lands far distant from the Tibetan-Qinghai Plateau are yet to be discovered. But spread it did, and it is certain that human activities, unwitting though they may have been, were responsible" (Green, "Editor's Introduction," 12, 15).

46. Stuart Borsch, "Plague Depopulation and Irrigation Decay in Medieval Egypt," *Medieval Globe* 1 (2014): 125–56.

47. Michael Dols, *The Black Death in the Middle East* (Princeton, NJ: Princeton University Press, 1977). For the most current scholarship, see the articles published at the end of 2014 in the special first issue of *The Medieval Globe* under the general title "Pandemic Disease in the Medieval World: Rethinking the Black Death."

48. The term is used both by Braudel, *Civilization and Capitalism*, vol. 1, 70–72, and Ponting, *New Green History of the World*, chap. 12.

49. For examples, see Ponting, *New Green History of the World*, chaps. 1, 5, and 17.

50. E. A. Wrigley, *Continuity, Change, and Chance* (Cambridge: Cambridge University Press, 1990).

Chapter Two: Starting with China

1. Gerardus Mercator, "The Ancient World," from the *Atlas sive Cosmographicae Meditationes de Fabrica Mundi et Fabricati Figura* (Duisburg, 1595), https://www.artres.com /CS.aspx?VP3 = ViewBox_VPage&VBID = 2UN365BJKJRVQ&IT = ZoomImageTem plate01_VForm&IID = 2UNTWA531ZOS&PN.

2. Philippe Beaujard, "The Indian Ocean in Eurasian and African World-Systems before the Sixteenth Century," *Journal of World History* 16, no. 4 (December 2005): 411–65.

3. This section is based on Louise Levathes, *When China Ruled the Seas: The Treasure Fleet of the Dragon Throne, 1405–1433* (New York: Simon and Schuster, 1994), and Frederick W. Mote and Denis Twitchett, eds., *The Cambridge History of China*, vol. 7, *The Ming Dynasty, 1368–1644, Part 1* (Cambridge: Cambridge University Press, 1988), and vol. 8, *The Ming Dynasty, 1368–1644, Part 2* (Cambridge: Cambridge University Press, 1998). See also Robert Finlay, "The Treasure Ships of Zheng He: Chinese Maritime Imperialism in the Age of Discovery," *Terrae Incognitae* 23 (1991): 1–12. Contemporary interest in the voyages of Zheng He was stimulated by the 600-year anniversary in 2005 of his first voyage; the 2008 Beijing Olympics, which featured Zheng He as part of the opening ceremony extravaganza; and more recently China's determination to assert claims to the South China Sea based on the records of Admiral Zheng's voyages. For images, re-creations, and a scholarly discussion, YouTube videos are useful, especially "The Great Voyages of Zheng He," Penn Museum, October 10, 2013, a forty-eight-minute scholarly lecture/presentation by Dr. Adam Smith (http://www.youtube.com/watch?v = le7r93 whykg); and "Zheng He: The Great Voyager, 1405–1433 AD," June 9, 2012, a five-minute overview with images (http://www.youtube.com/watch?v = UPxUZOUUMLI).

4. Confucius was a minor government official and teacher who lived in the sixth century BCE. His ideas, which posited the importance of the family and the role of good government, were developed by later philosophers and became the ideological basis of the Chinese state for 2,000 years.

5. Richard von Glahn, *Fountain of Fortune: Money and Monetary Policy in China, 1000–1700* (Berkeley: University of California Press, 1996). For a discussion of the impact of a money economy on Ming-era Chinese society, see Timothy Brook, *The Confusions of Pleasure: Commerce and Culture in Ming China* (Berkeley: University of California Press, 1998).

6. Ma Huan wrote an account of this and later voyages, translated by J. V. G. Mills as *The Overall Survey of the Ocean's Shores* (Cambridge: Cambridge University Press, 1970).

7. Levathes, *When China Ruled the Seas*, is the best readable source.

8. In our own time, an analogy might be the U.S. decision both to send manned missions to the moon and to end them when the costs became too great to bear.

9. This periodization and much of the material in this section is based upon K. N. Chaudhuri, *Trade and Civilization in the Indian Ocean: An Economic History from the Rise of Islam to 1750* (Cambridge: Cambridge University Press, 1985).

10. For a discussion of Melaka and trading cities like it, see M. N. Pearson, "Merchants and States," in *The Political Economy of Merchant Empires: State Power and World Trade 1350–1750*, ed. James D. Tracy (Cambridge: Cambridge University Press, 1991).

11. For a detailed description of European trading in the Indian Ocean, see R. J. Barendse, *The Arabian Seas, 1640–1700* (Leiden: Leiden University Press, 1998), and the North American edition of his book, *The Arabian Seas, 1640–1700: The Western Indian Ocean of the Seventeenth Century* (New York: M. E. Sharpe, 2001). Barendse's point of view—assessing the role of European trading companies—is quite different from that of Chaudhuri, and so the picture he paints of the impact of Europeans is different too. An accessible summary of his argument can be found in "Trade and State in the Arabian Seas: A Survey from the Fifteenth to the Eighteenth Century," *Journal of World History* 11, no. 2 (Fall 2000): 173–226.

12. Mote and Twitchett, *Cambridge History of China*, vol. 8, 378.

13. For a detailed description and analysis of the Indian cotton industry and its trade, see Prasannan Parthasarathi, *Why Europe Grew Rich and Asia Did Not: Global Economic Divergence, 1600–1800* (New York: Cambridge University Press, 2011), esp. chaps. 2 and 4.

14. See Ross E. Dunn, *The Adventures of Ibn Battuta: A Muslim Trader of the 14th Century* (Berkeley: University of California Press, 1986).

15. See Herbert S. Klein, *The Atlantic Slave Trade* (Cambridge: Cambridge University Press, 1999), esp. chaps. 1, 3, and 5.

16. R. A. Austen, *Africa in Economic History* (London: James Currey/Heinemann, 1987), 36.

17. John Thornton, *Africa and Africans in the Making of the Atlantic World, 1400–1800*, 2nd ed. (Cambridge: Cambridge University Press, 1998), 105.

18. Thornton, *Africa and Africans in the Making of the Atlantic World*, chap. 4.

19. R. A. Austen, "The Trans-Saharan Slave Trade: A Tentative Census," in *The Uncommon Market: Essays in the Economic History of the Atlantic Slave Trade*, eds. H. A. Gemery and J. S. Hogendorn (New York: Academic Press, 1979).

20. Gregory H. Maddox, *Sub-Saharan Africa: An Environmental History* (Santa Barbara, CA: ABC-CLIO, 2006).

21. For a critique of these seemingly geographically determined definitions, see Martin W. Lewis and Karen Wigen, *The Myth of Continents: A Critique of Metageography* (Berkeley: University of California Press, 1997).

22. This section is based on Joseph Needham, "The Epic of Gunpowder and Firearms, Developing from Alchemy," in *Science in Traditional China: A Comparative Perspective* (Cambridge, MA: Harvard University Press, 1981), chap. 2.

23. Geoffrey Parker, *The Military Revolution: Military Innovation and the Rise of the West, 1500–1800*, 2nd ed. (Cambridge: Cambridge University Press, 1996), chaps. 1–2.

24. For a discussion, see Parker, *Military Revolution*, chap. 1.

25. For the details, see Janet Abu-Lughod, *Before European Hegemony: The World System A.D. 1250–1350* (New York: Oxford University Press, 1989), chap. 4.

26. Dias gave it the name "Cape of Storms," but his sovereign thought that would deter sailors and so renamed it the "Cape of Good Hope." Whatever its name, the Cape of Good Hope actually is not the southernmost tip of Africa—that is Cape Agulhas.

27. Quoted in Chaudhuri, *Trade and Civilization*, 65.

28. Chaudhuri, *Trade and Civilization*, 63.

29. Although spices continued to seep into Europe via the Red Sea route, the establishment of a direct sea route connecting Asia and Europe all but doomed Venice as an economic power in Europe.

30. These are derived from Chaudhuri, *Trade and Civilization*, 17.

31. Andre Gunder Frank, *ReOrient: Global Economy in the Asian Age* (Berkeley: University of California Press, 1998).

Chapter Three: Empires, States, and the New World, 1500–1775

1. Dennis O. Flynn and Arturo Giraldez argue that 1571 thus marks the true beginning of the first globalization since only then did contact among all regions of the world become routine. "Born with a Silver Spoon: The Origin of World Trade in 1571," *Journal of World History* 6, no. 2 (Fall 1995): 201–21.

2. See Geoffrey Parker, *Global Crisis: War, Climate Change and Catastrophe in the Seventeenth Century* (New Haven, CT: Yale University Press, 2013), xxiii, and John L. Brooke, *Climate Change and the Course of Global History: A Rough Guide* (New York: Cambridge University Press, 2014), 438–66.

3. For a scholarly comparison of these two very different political economies, see R. Bin Wong, *China Transformed: Historical Change and the Limits of European Experience* (Ithaca, NY: Cornell University Press, 1997), part 2.

4. For a description of the "fatal synergy" of the colder climate and the wars of conquest in China, see Parker, *Global Crisis*, chap. 5.

5. See Takeshi Hamashita, "The Intra-Regional System in East Asia in Modern Times," in *Network Power: Japan and Asia*, ed. Peter J. Katzenstein and Takashi Shiraishi (Ithaca, NY: Cornell University Press, 1997), chap. 3.

6. Parker, *Global Crisis*; see also Geoffrey Parker and Lesley M. Smith, eds., *The General Crisis of the Seventeenth Century*, 2nd ed. (London: Routledge, 1997).

7. For some exceptions, see C. A. Bayly, *Imperial Meridian: The British Empire and the World, 1780–1830* (London: Longman, 1993).

8. For a discussion of the size and distribution of the human population of the Americas before 1492, as well as the ways these peoples had "humanized" the American landscape, see Charles C. Mann, *1491: New Revelations of the Americas before Columbus* (New York: Alfred A. Knopf, 2005), chaps. 3–4, 8.

9. Humans may have migrated to the Americas as early as 35,000 years ago, but the consensus among scholars is about 15,000 BCE. See Richard E. W. Adams and Murdo J. MacLeod, eds., *The Cambridge History of the Native Peoples of the Americas*, vol. 2, part 1 (New York: Cambridge University Press, 2000), 28. See also Mann, *1491*, 105–9, 150–51.

10. Pronounced "Me-shee-ka." Nineteenth-century historians began calling these people Aztecs, after the name of the place from which they supposedly originated, Aztlan.

11. War prisoners played an important role in Mexican religious practice. The Mexica believed—or at least their priests told them—that their gods had set the universe into motion by their individual sacrifices, and that to keep the world going, in particular to ensure that the sun came up every morning, it was imperative to honor the gods through ritual sacrifice of human beings. Bloodletting on the central altar in the city was thus a daily ritual. Additionally, the Mexica developed an especial fondness for the god of war, Huitzilopochtli, who demanded extra sacrifices. When the temple to this god was completed in 1487, reportedly 80,000 people were sacrificed to the god.

12. For additional insights, see Jared Diamond, *Guns, Germs, and Steel* (New York: W. W. Norton, 1998), chap. 3.

13. See Alfred W. Crosby, *The Columbian Exchange: The Biological and Cultural Consequences of 1492* (Westport, CT: Praeger, 2003). Crosby's thesis has been tested, confirmed, and elaborated upon; a Google search of "Columbian Exchange" returns about 1.5 million results.

14. Bruce G. Trigger and Wilcomb E. Washburn, eds., *The Cambridge History of the Native Peoples of the Americas*, vol. 1, *North America* (Cambridge: Cambridge University Press, 1996), part 1, 361–69.

15. Leslie Bethell, ed., *The Cambridge History of Latin America*, vol. 2 (Cambridge: Cambridge University Press, 1984), chap. 1.

16. For an engaging discussion of scholarly reconstructions of the human population of the pre-1492 Americas, see Charles C. Mann, *1491: New Revelations of the Americas Before Columbus*, 2nd ed. (New York: Vintage Books, 2011), 35–151.

17. Walter F. Ruddiman, *Plows, Plagues, and Petroleum: How Humans Took Control of Climate* (Princeton, NJ: Princeton University Press, 2010), chap. 12. See also Charles C. Mann, *1493: Uncovering the New World Columbus Created* (New York: Alfred A. Knopf, 2011), 31–34.

18. For a brief summary, see Thomas A. Brady Jr., "The Rise of Merchant Empires, 1400–1700: A European Counterpoint," in *The Political Economy of Merchant Empires: State Power and World Trade 1350–1750*, ed. James D. Tracy (Cambridge: Cambridge University Press, 1991), 117–60.

19. Dennis O. Flynn and Arturo Giraldez, "Spanish Profitability in the Pacific: The Philippines in the Sixteenth and Seventeenth Centuries," in *Pacific Centuries: Pacific and Pacific Rim History since the Sixteenth History*, ed. Dennis O. Flynn, Lionel Frost, and A. J. H. Latham (London: Routledge, 1999), 23.

20. Andre Gunder Frank, *ReOrient: Global Economy in the Asian Age* (Berkeley: University of California Press, 1998), 131.

21. See Frank, *ReOrient*, chap. 4, for the data cited in these paragraphs.

22. William Atwell, "Ming China and the Emerging World Economy, c. 1470–1650," in *The Cambridge History of China*, vol. 8, *The Ming Dynasty, 1368–1644, Part 2*, ed. Denis Twitchett and Frederick W. Mote (Cambridge: Cambridge University Press, 1998), 400–402.

23. Quoted in Fernand Braudel, *Civilization and Capitalism, 15th–18th Century*, vol. 2, *The Wheels of Commerce* (New York: Harper and Row, 1981), 178.

24. The story of sugar and slavery can be found in Sidney W. Mintz, *Sweetness and Power: The Place of Sugar in Modern History* (New York: Viking Press, 1985), and in Bethell, *Cambridge History of Latin America*, vols. 1–2.

25. See Alfred Crosby, *Ecological Imperialism: The Biological Expansion of Europe, 900–1900* (Cambridge: Cambridge University Press, 1986), chap. 4.

26. Richard Grove, *Green Imperialism: Colonial Expansion, Tropical Island Edens and the Origins of Environmentalism, 1600–1800* (Cambridge: Cambridge University Press, 1995), chap. 6.

27. J. R. McNeill, *Mosquito Empires: Ecology and War in the Great Caribbean, 1620–1914* (New York: Cambridge University Press, 2010).

28. John Thornton, *Africa and Africans in the Making of the Atlantic World, 1400–1800*, 2nd ed. (Cambridge: Cambridge University Press, 1992), 14.

29. See Herbert S. Klein, *The Atlantic Slave Trade* (Cambridge: Cambridge University Press, 1999); Thornton, *Africa and Africans in the Making of the Atlantic World*.

30. As described in an exhibit at Britain's National Maritime Museum: "The slave trade was part of a global trading system. British products and Indian goods were shipped to West Africa and exchanged for slaves. The slaves were taken to the Americas in return

for sugar, tobacco, and other tropical produce. These were then sold in Britain for processing into consumer goods, and possible re-export."

31. Jan de Vries, "The Limits of Globalization in the Early Modern World," *The Economic History Review* 63 (New Series), no. 3 (2010): 710–33, https://www.jstor.org/stable /40929823.

32. For maps on the migrations discussed in this section, see Russell King et al., *The Atlas of Human Migration: Global Patterns of People on the Move* (Oxon, UK: Earthscan, an imprint of Taylor & Francis, 2010), esp. pp. 18–27.

33. Patrick Manning with Tiffany Trimmer, *Migration in World History*, 2nd ed. (New York: Routledge, 2013), 12.

34. For an interesting example from pre-Columbian North America, see Larry Benson, Kenneth Petersen, and John Stein, "Anasazi (Pre-Columbian Native-American) Migrations during the Middle-12th and Late-13th Centuries—Were They Drought Induced?," *Climate Change* 83, nos. 1/2 (2007): 187–213.

35. That is the argument made by Eliot Dickinson, *Globalization and Migration: A World in Motion* (Lanham, MD: Rowman & Littlefield, 2017).

36. John C. Chasteen, *Born in Blood and Fire: A Concise Chronicle of Latin America*, 4th ed. (New York: W. W. Norton, 2016), 68–75. I thank Daniela Vega for bringing this source to my attention. Chasteen also provides numerous telling examples of the lived experiences of native, enslaved, and Spanish women during conquest and colonization.

37. For fascinating stories of these communities, see John E. Wills, Jr., *1688: A Global History* (New York: W. W. Norton, 2001).

38. Eugene D. Genovese, *Roll, Jordon, Roll: The World the Slaves Made* (New York: Random House, 1972).

39. Olaudah Equiano, *The Interesting Narrative of the Life of Olaudah Equiano, Or Gustavus Vassa, the African*, various editions.

40. Solomon Northup, *12 Years a Slave* (New York: Penguin Books, 2012).

41. For China's northern border, see Jonathan Schlesinger, *A World Trimmed in Fur: Wild Things, Pristine Places, and the Natural Fringes of Qing* (Stanford, CA: Stanford University Press, 2017), chap. 4.

42. For a historiographical overview, see Parker, *Global Crisis*, xv–xx, xxi–xxix, 710–13.

43. Parker, *Global Crisis*, chap. 13.

44. Parker, *Global Crisis*, chaps. 5–12.

45. Charles Tilly, *Coercion, Capital, and European States, A.D. 990–1990* (Oxford: Basil Blackwell, 1990), 176–77.

46. Tilly, *Coercion, Capital, and European States*, 38–43. Tilly says twenty-five to twenty-eight states in 1990, numbers preceding the 1991 breakup of the Soviet Union and its former client states.

47. For an instructive history of the development of the idea of popular sovereignty in England and its American colonies, see Edmund S. Morgan, *Inventing the People: The Rise of Popular Sovereignty in England and America* (New York: W. W. Norton, 1988).

48. Tilly, Coercion, Capital, and European States, 47–54. The proximity to these cities, according to Tilly, led to the formation of three different kinds of European states. Wealthy cities could afford to hire their own mercenary armies (the "capital-intensive" path to state formation); rulers far away from cities and their capitals had to rely on force mobilized from a rural nobility (the "coercion-intensive" path) to build states; and those with a combination of cities and their dependent countryside used a combination. Tilly argues that the latter, exemplified by England and France, proved to be the most successful kind in the competitive European state system.

49. On the Navigation Acts, see John J. McCusker and Russell R. Menard, The Economy of British America, 1607–1789 (Chapel Hill: University of North Carolina Press, 1985), 46–50.

50. Prasannan Parthasarathi, Why Europe Grew Rich and Asia Did Not: Global Economic Divergence, 1600–1850 (New York: Cambridge University Press, 2011), chap. 5. For more on the particularities of the English case, see Brooke, Climate Change and the Course of Global History, 451–66.

51. Quoted in Geoffrey Parker, "The Emergence of Modern Finance in Europe, 1500–1730," in The Fontana Economic History of Europe, vol. 2, ed. Carlo M. Cipolla (Glasgow: William Collins Sons, 1974), 530.

52. "Much of what Philip [II of Spain] needed for his armies was not available within peninsular Spain. His repeated efforts to establish factories producing cannon and other needed commodities always failed to flourish. Perversely, from a Spanish point of view, it was exactly in places where the king's will was not sovereign that economic activity and arms production concentrated. . . . Thus, for example, the bishopric of Liege, adjacent to the Spanish Netherlands but not under Spanish rule, became the major seat of armaments production for the Dutch wars, supplying a large proportion of the material needed by both the Spanish and the Dutch armies." William McNeill, The Pursuit of Power: Technology, Armed Force, and Society since A.D. 1000 (Chicago: University of Chicago Press, 1982), 113.

53. Werner Sombart, quoted in Braudel, Civilization and Capitalism, vol. 2, 545.

54. See Fred Anderson, Crucible of War (New York: Alfred A. Knopf, 2000), for an engaging narrative of these events and of George Washington's role.

55. According to E. J. Hobsbawm, "The result of this century [the eighteenth] of intermittent warfare was the greatest triumph ever achieved by any state [Britain]: the virtual monopoly among European powers of overseas colonies, and the virtual monopoly of world-wide naval power." Quoted in Andre Gunder Frank, World Accumulation, 1492–1789 (New York: Monthly Review Press, 1978), 237.

Chapter Four: The Industrial Revolution and Its Consequences, 1750–1850

1. The Chinese used coal for fuel as early as the Han dynasty 2,000 years ago, and for similar reasons, both the Chinese 1,000 years ago during the Song dynasty and the

English in London beginning in the sixteenth century used coal because of the exhaustion of wood supplies. For China, see Robert B. Marks, *China: An Environmental History* (Lanham, MD: Rowman & Littlefield, 2017), 158–62. For England, see John L. Brooke, *Climate Change and the Course of Global History: A Rough Journey* (New York: Cambridge University Press, 2014), 459–66. See also Jack A. Goldstone, "Efflorescences and Economic Growth in World History: Rethinking the 'Rise of the West' and the Industrial Revolution," *Journal of World History* 13, no. 2 (2002): 323–89.

2. As with the term "agricultural revolution," some have objected to the use of the term "revolution" to describe this process. Because I think the effects were indeed revolutionary, and because of long-standing usage, I will continue to use the term here. For a discussion of the issues surrounding the use of the term, see E. A. Wrigley, *Continuity, Chance, and Change: The Character of the Industrial Revolution in England* (Cambridge: Cambridge University Press, 1988), chap. 1.

3. For a detailed and clear analysis, see Prasannan Parthasarathi, *Why Europe Grew Rich and Asia Did Not: Global Economic Divergence, 1600–1850* (New York: Cambridge University Press, 2011), esp. chaps. 4–5.

4. Quoted in Prasannan Parthasarathi, "Rethinking Wages and Competitiveness in the Eighteenth Century: Britain and South India," *Past and Present* 158 (February 1998): 79.

5. Parthasarathi, "Rethinking Wages and Competitiveness."

6. For the particulars of how consumer tastes created demand for imports, see Carole Shammas, *The Pre-Industrial Consumer in England and America* (Oxford: Oxford University Press, 1990).

7. Parthasarathi, "Rethinking Wages and Competitiveness," 79.

8. "And behind these protected walls, British cotton masters experimented with an imported raw material [cotton] and sought to imitate and surpass Indian goods. State intervention of this sort was to be a staple of British policy making well into the nineteenth century." Parthasarathi, *Why Europe Grew Rich*, 145.

9. Geoffrey Parker, "Europe and the Wider World, 1500–1750: The Military Balance," in *The Political Economy of Merchant Empires: State Power and World Trade 1350–1750*, ed. James D. Tracy (Cambridge: Cambridge University Press, 1991), 179–80.

10. Parker, "Europe and the Wider World," 180.

11. The argument that slavery was integral to the rise of global capitalism was forcefully made first by Eric Williams, *Capitalism and Slavery* (Chapel Hill: University of North Carolina Press, 1994 [1944]). For a recent statement of that argument focusing on the United States, see Edward E. Baptist, *The Half That Has Never Been Told: Slavery and the Making of American Capitalism* (New York: Basic Books, 2014).

12. John J. McCusker and Russell R. Menard, *The Economy of British America, 1607–1789* (Chapel Hill: University of North Carolina Press, 1985), 46–49, 77, 161.

13. Parthasarathi, *Why Europe Grew Rich*, 90.

14. McCusker and Menard, *The Economy of British America*, 121.

15. In the 1830s, the Lancashire region was processing 400 million pounds of raw cotton into yarn. "This was achieved without a profound transformation in sources of energy for the process of production, however" (Parthasarathi, *Why Europe Grew Rich*, 153–54).

16. Jan DeVries, "The Industrial Revolution and the Industrious Revolution," *Journal of Economic History* 54 (1994): 249–70.

17. See Kenneth Pomeranz, *The Great Divergence: China, Europe, and the Making of the Modern World Economy* (Princeton, NJ: Princeton University Press, 2000), 40–41, for a discussion and critique.

18. Culture too is often added to this explanation, in particular Max Weber's "protestant ethic" argument. Briefly, Weber argued that a particular form of Protestantism—Calvinism—instilled in its adherents a set of beliefs that led to honesty, hard work, thriftiness, rational calculation, and productivity. These cultural attributes that arose only among some men in northwestern Europe—Weber's "protestant ethic"—led them to become the first capitalists and captains of industry. Part of his "proof" was to examine religion in China and in India (in two books, *The Religion of China: Confucianism and Taoism*, and *The Religion of India: The Sociology of Hinduism and Buddhism*) to show that neither of those sets of beliefs contained anything like what he calls *The Protestant Ethic and the Spirit of Capitalism* and hence that capitalism did not develop there. While these books by Max Weber are interesting explorations in comparative religious history, I think there are better explanations for the Industrial Revolution, as argued throughout this chapter. For a counterargument in favor of Weber's thesis, see David S. Landes, *The Wealth and Poverty of Nations: Why Some Are So Rich and Some So Poor* (New York: W. W. Norton, 1998), esp. 174–79.

19. Quoted in Robert B. Marks, *Tigers, Rice, Silk, and Silt: Environment and Economy in Late Imperial South China* (Cambridge: Cambridge University Press, 1998), 284–85.

20. James Z. Lee and Wang Feng, *One Quarter of Humanity: Malthusian Mythology and Chinese Realities* (Cambridge, MA: Harvard University Press, 1999), 105.

21. James L. Brooke argues that by the mid-nineteenth century, China was in the throes of a Malthusian overpopulation crisis. See *Climate Change and the Course of Global History*, 472–75. The idea that China experienced an eighteenth-century "population explosion" has been questioned in F. W. Mote, *Imperial China 900–1800* (Cambridge, MA: Harvard University Press, 1999), 743–49, 903–7.

22. See Marks, *Tigers, Rice, Silk, and Silt*; Peter Perdue, *Exhausting the Earth: State and Peasant in Hunan, 1500–1850* (Cambridge, MA: Harvard University Press, 1987); Anne Osborne, "The Local Politics of Land Reclamation in the Lower Yangzi Highlands," *Late Imperial China* 15, no. 1 (June 1994): 1–46.

23. For an overview of the ecologies of Chinese agriculture, see Marks, *China*, esp. chap. 6, "Environmental Degradation in Modern China, 1800–1949."

24. Carol Shiue and Wolfgang Heller, "Markets in China and Europe on the Eve of the Industrial Revolution," *American Economic Review* 97, no. 4 (September 2007): 1189–1216.

25. Pierre-Etienne Will and R. Bin Wong, *Nourish the People: The State Civilian Granary System in China, 1650–1850* (Ann Arbor: University of Michigan Press, 1992).

26. See Marks, *Tigers, Rice, Silk, and Silt*, chap. 8.

27. Pomeranz, *Great Divergence*, chap. 2.

28. For an overview, see Marks, *China*, 195, 231–32.

29. The historical and intellectual problem of why what we call the "industrial revolution" happened first in a part of England has been the subject of extensive scholarly investigation and debate. For a thoughtful discussion of a new way to think about "why England, and why not China?," see Jack A. Goldstone, "Efflorescences and Economic Growth in World History: Rethinking the 'Rise of the West' and the Industrial Revolution," *Journal of World History* 13, no. 2 (2002): 323–89.

30. Pomeranz, *Great Divergence*, 242–43.

31. Francesca Bray, *Technology and Gender: Fabrics of Power in Late Imperial China* (Berkeley: University of California Press, 1997); Jack Goldstone, "Gender, Work, and Culture: Why the Industrial Revolution Came Early to England but Late to China," *Sociological Perspectives* 39, no. 1 (1996): 1–21; Pomeranz, *Great Divergence*, 249–50.

32. The title for this subheading comes from Perdue, *Exhausting the Earth*. See also Robert B. Marks, " 'Exhausting the Earth': Environment and History in the Early Modern World," in *The Cambridge World History*, ed. Jerry H. Bentley, Sanjay Subrahmanyam, and Merry E. Wiesner-Hanks (Cambridge: Cambridge University Press, 2015).

33. John F. Richards, *The Unending Earth: An Environmental History of the Early Modern World* (Berkeley: University of California Press, 2003).

34. According to James L. Brooke, "agriculture and land clearance have played a major warming role. Land that is cleared of forest, often through burning, emits huge amounts of CO_2, as does the annual plowing and harrowing of soil. But agriculture also contributes huge amounts of methane to the atmosphere, either from cattle digestive systems or emissions from rice paddies, essentially artificial wetlands, which are also a source of natural methane emissions" (*Climate Change and the Course of World History*, 477).

35. Tamara L. Whited et al., *Northern Europe: An Environmental History* (Santa Barbara, CA: ABC-CLIO, 2005), 80.

36. Anne Osborne, "Highlands and Lowlands: Economic and Ecological Interactions in the Lower Yangzi Region under the Qing," in *Sediments of Time: Environment and Society in Chinese History*, ed. Mark Elvin and Ts'ui-jung Liu (New York: Cambridge University Press, 1998), 203–34.

37. Conrad Totman, *The Green Archipelago: Forestry in Preindustrial Japan* (Berkeley: University of California Press, 1989).

38. Parthasarathi, *Why Europe Grew Rich*, 181–82.

39. Robert B. Marks, "Explanations of Species Extinction in Europe and China," in Alan Karras and Laura Mitchell, eds., *Encounters Old and New in World History: Essays Celebrating and Inspired by Jerry Bentley* (Honolulu: University of Hawaii Press, 2017), 121–35.

40. Parthasarathi, *Why Europe Grew Rich*, 161.

41. E. J. Hobsbawm, *The Age of Revolution, 1789–1848* (New York: New American Library, 1964), 51.

42. Parthasarathi, *Why Europe Grew Rich*, 151. The causes are a subject of intense debate: Did the British cause it, or were there other reasons? For a brief summary of the debate, see Pomeranz, *Great Divergence*, 294.

43. Brooke, *Climate Change and the Course of Global History*, 464–65.

44. Pomeranz, *Great Divergence*, chap. 6.

45. Parthasarathi, *Why Europe Grew Rich*, 155.

46. In addition to Brooke and Parthasarathi, see the earlier analysis by E. J. Hobsbawm, *Industry and Empire* (New York: Penguin, 1968), chap. 2.

47. James L. Brooke sees this as part of "The Seventeenth-Century English Energy Revolution" (*Climate Change and the Course of Global History*, 459–66).

48. Parthasarathi, *Why Europe Grew Rich*, 157–62. For an early and fascinating account of why a burgeoning iron and coal industry in China during the Northern Song dynasty (960–1126) looked like it might turn into the first industrial revolution centuries before the English experience, see Robert Hartwell, "A Revolution in the Chinese Iron and Coal Industries during the Northern Sung [Song], 960–1126 A.D.," *Journal of Asian Studies* 21, no. 2 (1962): 153–62.

49. Hobsbawm, *Age of Revolution*, 63–65.

50. See Andre Gunder Frank, *ReOrient: Global Economy in the Asian Age* (Berkeley: University of California Press, 1998), 297–317.

51. E. A. Wrigley, *Continuity, Chance, and Change: The Character of the Industrial Revolution in England* (Cambridge: Cambridge University Press, 1988), 54–55; Pomeranz, *Great Divergence*, 59–60.

52. Pomeranz, *Great Divergence*, 274–76.

53. Parthasarathi, *Why Europe Grew Rich*, 164–70.

54. Parthasarathi, *Why Europe Grew Rich*, 170–75. See also R. Bin Wong, *China Transformed: Historical Change and the Limits of European Historical Experience* (Ithaca, NY: Cornell University Press, 1999).

55. David Landes developed this point in *The Unbound Prometheus: Technological Change and Industrial Development in Western Europe from 1750 to the Present* (Cambridge: Cambridge University Press, 1969), esp. 61, 104.

56. Lissa Roberts and Simon Schaffer, as discussed in Parthasarathi, *Why Europe Grew Rich*, 219–22.

57. For good discussions of these issues, see Frank, *ReOrient*, 185–95, and Pomeranz, *Great Divergence*, 43–68. John M. Hobson goes much further, arguing that virtually all of modern science and technology, among other cultural creations, came from Asia and spread from there to Europe. See *The Eastern Origins of Western Civilization* (Cambridge: Cambridge University Press, 2004).

58. A different way of looking at the flows of silver to China has been proposed by Dennis O. Flynn and Arturo Giraldez in "Cycles of Silver: Global Economic Unity

through the Mid-18th Century," *Journal of World History* 13, no. 2 (Fall 2002): 391–427. Rather than seeing demand for tea as causing Britons to pay for it with silver, Flynn and Giraldez argue that China's demand for silver created a higher value for it there, compared with gold, than in Europe. China's problem was how to "buy" silver from the British, finding tea the best commodity available. From this perspective, the Chinese in effect "hooked" the British on tea, stimulated a demand for the mild stimulant there, and then reaped the benefit of silver flowing into China's economy.

59. Sidney W. Mintz, *Sweetness and Power: The Place of Sugar in Modern History* (New York: Viking Press, 1985), 112–13.

60. Frederick Wakeman Jr., *The Fall of Imperial China* (New York: Free Press, 1975), 123.

61. The entire letter can be found in Harley Farnsworth MacNair, *Modern Chinese History: Selected Readings* (Shanghai: Commercial Press, 1923), 2–9.

62. There was actually a very complicated triangular trading system involving not just EIC merchants, but private Indian and Scottish merchants as well, by which raw cotton was taken to China, tea purchased in China, and then sold in London. See Wakeman, *Fall of Imperial China*, 123–25. Moreover, the innovations of the EIC in creating convertible paper notes to enable the stockholders to realize profits back in London probably had begun to lessen the importance of actually moving silver around the world to settle accounts. Nonetheless, the British government apparently continued to act as though that was happening and that it was a problem.

63. W. D. Bernhard, *Narrative of the Voyages and Services of the Nemesis, from 1840 to 1843; and of the Combined Naval and Military Operations in China*, vol. 1 (London: Henry Colburn, 1844), 4.

64. See Daniel Headrick, *The Tools of Empire: Technology and European Imperialism in the Nineteenth Century* (New York: Oxford University Press, 1981).

65. William H. Roberts, *Civil War Ironclads: The U.S. Navy and Industrial Mobilization* (Baltimore, MD: Johns Hopkins University Press, 2007), 9–12. I thank Astra Yatroussis for this insight and source.

66. Louis Dermigny, quoted in Parker, "Europe and the Wider World," 184.

67. The term "Anthropocene" was first put forward in 2002 by Paul J. Crutzen, a Dutch atmospheric chemist (who in 1995 shared the Nobel Prize in Chemistry with F. Sherwood Rowland and Mario J. Molina for work they had done in discovering the "ozone hole"). Geologists have developed a chronology of Earth's evolving history (eons, eras, and periods) and the geologic criteria for distinguishing among them, including, for example, the Jurassic period (150–200 million years ago). The last part (epoch) of the geologic period the Earth now is in, the Quaternary, is known as the Holocene ("The Recent Epoch") and began about 15,000 years ago with the end of the last ice age. The history of what may be thought of as human "civilization" following the emergence of agriculture ten to four thousand years ago has unfolded in the relatively supportive climatic conditions of the Holocene. Crutzen's idea was that the emissions of carbon dioxide and methane arising from the Industrial Revolution beginning two centuries ago around

1800 ushered in a new geological period created by the actions of humans ("anthropo-genic," meaning caused by humans), not nature; he called this new period the "Anthro-pocene," the era of humans on Earth. Since then, others have accepted Crutzen's idea but have debated the timing of the beginning of the Anthropocene. William Ruddiman argues it began some 6,000 years ago with settled agriculture and the carbon dioxide and methane released by farming, while others such as J. R. McNeill think that it really only began around 1950 with the post–World War II era. For the arguments and evidence on when to date the onset of the Anthropocene, see Will Steffen, Paul T. Crutzen, and John R. McNeill, "The Anthropocene: Are Humans Now Overwhelming the Great Forces of Nature?," *Ambio* 36, no. 8 (December 2007): 614–21, and Will Steffen, Jacques Grine-vald, Paul Crutzen, and John McNeill, "The Anthropocene: Conceptual and Historical Perspectives," *Philosophical Transactions of the Royal Society* A 369 (2011): 842–67.

68. China's Song-era (960–1279) "medieval industrial revolution" certainly is one example. Additionally, Jack A. Goldstone uses the concept of "efflorescences" to describe those times and places where what looked like conditions similar to those that ushered in the Industrial Revolution prevailed but did not lead to the industrial breakthrough that England experienced. He examines specifically the cases of seventeenth-century Holland, northwestern Europe in the twelfth to thirteenth centuries, and eighteenth-century Qing China and concludes that the crucial difference with England in the late eighteenth and early nineteenth centuries was the development of the steam engine. Jack A. Goldstone, "Efflorescences and Economic Growth in World History: Rethinking 'the Rise of the West' and the Industrial Revolution," *Journal of World History* 13, no. 2 (Fall 2002): 323–89.

69. For the argument and supporting evidence leading to this conclusion, see Pomer-anz, *Great Divergence*. For an abbreviated version, see Kenneth Pomeranz, "Two Worlds of Trade, Two Worlds of Empire: European State-Making and Industrialization in a Chinese Mirror," in *States and Sovereignty in the Global Economy*, ed. David A. Smith, Dorothy J. Solinger, and Steven C. Topik (London: Routledge, 1999), 74–98. For a critique of this thesis, see P. H. H. Vries, "Are Coal and Colonies Really Crucial? Kenneth Pomeranz and the Great Divergence," *Journal of World History* 12 (Fall 2001): 407–46. In *Why Europe Grew Rich and Asia Did Not*, Prasannan Parthasarathi adds the global competitive perspec-tive, varying ecological circumstances, and the differential role of the state to the under-standing that Pomeranz provides.

Chapter Five: The Gap

1. GDP is the total value of all goods and services produced in an economy, usually delimited by national boundaries.

2. Fernand Braudel, *Civilization and Capitalism, 15th–18th Century*, vol. 2, *The Wheels of Commerce*, trans. Sian Reynolds (New York: Harper and Row, 1982), 134.

3. Braudel, *Civilization and Capitalism*, vol. 2, 134.

4. The term "third world" came about after World War II in the context of the Cold War between the United States (and its European allies) and the Soviet Union, the first and second worlds, respectively. To chart a path with some independence from both the Americans and the Russians, "developing" but poor nations like India, Egypt, and Indonesia came to be known as the third world. By the 1970s, even poorer parts of the world, Africa in particular, began to be seen as the fourth world. All of these terms reflect the divisions of wealth and power that have come to define the modern world.

5. For the story of how opium growing in the inland province of Yunnan got connected to a late-nineteenth-century bubonic plague outbreak, see Carol Benedict, *Bubonic Plague in Nineteenth-Century China* (Stanford, CA: Stanford University Press, 1996).

6. Carl A. Trocki, *Opium, Empire, and the Global Political Economy: A Study of the Asian Opium Trade, 1750–1950* (London: Routledge, 1999), 126.

7. See Edward R. Slack Jr., *Opium, State, and Society: China's Narco-Economy and the Guomindang, 1924–1937* (Honolulu: University of Hawaii Press, 2001).

8. For a recent example, see David Clinginsmith and Jeffrey G. Williamson, "India's Deindustrialization in the 18th and 19th Centuries," August 2005, http://www.tcd.ie/Eco nomics/staff/orourkek/Istanbul/JGWGEHNIndianDeind.pdf.

9. For the story of the rise and decline of India's cotton textile industry, at least in Bengal, see Debendra Bijoy Mitra, *The Cotton Weavers of Bengal, 1757–1833* (Kolcata: Temple Press, 1978), 98.

10. S. Ambirajan, *Classical Political Economy and British Policy in India* (Cambridge: Cambridge University Press, 1987), 54–55.

11. Trocki, *Opium, Empire, and the Global Political Economy*, xiii, 8–9.

12. Jack A. Goldstone, "Efflorescences and Economic Growth in World History: Rethinking 'the Rise of the West' and the Industrial Revolution," *Journal of World History* 13, no. 2 (Fall 2002): 336.

13. David Harvey, *Paris, Capital of Modernity* (New York: Taylor & Francis, 2006). I thank Alicia Pennypacker for both the insight and the source.

14. Brian DeLay, *War of a Thousand Deserts: Indian Raids and the U.S.-Mexican War* (New Haven, CT: Yale University Press, 2008).

15. Benjamin Madley, *An American Genocide: The United States and the California Indian Catastrophe* (New Haven, CT: Yale University Press, 2017). For a fascinating interpretation of the Mexican-American War that puts it in environmental context, see J. R. McNeill, *Mosquito Empires: Ecology and War in the Greater Caribbean, 1620–1914* (New York: Cambridge University Press, 2010), 287–95.

16. Sergei Witte, "An Economic Policy for the Empire," in *Readings in Russian Civilization*, 2nd ed., vol. 2, ed. Thomas Riha (Chicago: University of Chicago Press, 1969), 419. Had it not been for Russia's defeat by Germany in World War I and the successful Bolshevik (Communist) Revolution of 1917, Witte's plans may well have transformed Russia in ways he had envisioned. As it was, the capitalist countries of western Europe and the United States cut off the new Soviet Union from loans and other forms of direct foreign investment, which Witte's plan had depended on for industrializing Russia.

Instead, the Soviet Union had to pioneer a new path, epitomized from the late 1920s on as a succession of "Five-Year Plans," where the funds for investment in industry were squeezed from a newly collectivized agriculture. Despite the expropriation of private property in both cities and the countryside, the abolition of free markets, and hence the creation of a "planned economy" run by communist bureaucrats, the Soviet Union did achieve remarkable levels of industrial growth, especially of heavy industry, all the way to the beginning of their involvement in World War II.

17. A. J. H. Latham, *The International Economy and the Underdeveloped World, 1865–1914* (London: Routledge, 1978), 175: "China's large trade deficit [caused by opium] in these years was an important feature of the international economy."

18. The quotes and the material in this paragraph and the next two are based on Anthony N. Penna, *The Human Footprint: A Global Environmental History* (Malden, MA: Wiley-Blackwell, 2010), 181–87, 193–95. Hundreds of examples could be provided from all around the world, from the early nineteenth century to the present day, for the most polluted places on Earth today are those undergoing the most rapid industrialization, in particular China and India.

19. Gregory T. Cushman, *Guano and the Opening of the Pacific World: A Global Ecological History* (New York: Cambridge University Press, 2013).

20. For China, see the section "The Built Environment: Cities and Waste" in Robert B. Marks, *China: An Environmental History* (Lanham, MD: Rowman & Littlefield, 2017), 177–83. A description of Japan's system is in "Fecal Matters: A Prolegomenon to Shit in Japan," an as-yet-unpublished article kindly supplied to me by David L. Howell of the history department of Harvard University.

21. For an excellent comparative analysis of the use of night soil in China, Japan, India, and western Europe that also addresses the larger historical issues taken up in this book, see Dean T. Ferguson, "Nightsoil and the 'Great Divergence': Human Waste, the Urban Economy, and Economic Productivity, 1500–1900," *Journal of Global History* 9 (2014): 379–402.

22. Hugh S. Gorman, *The Story of N: A Social History of the Nitrogen Cycle and the Challenge of Sustainability* (New Brunswick, NJ: Rutgers University Press, 2013), 64–69.

23. John L. Brooke, *Climate Change and the Course of Global History* (New York: Cambridge University Press, 2014), 479, 488.

24. Adam Hochschild, *King Leopold's Ghost: A Story of Greed, Terror, and Heroism in Colonial Africa* (Boston: Houghton Mifflin Harcourt, 1998).

25. For Japan, see Mikiso Hane, *Peasants, Rebels, Women, and Outcastes: The Underside of Modern Japan* (Lanham, MD: Rowman & Littlefield, 2003).

26. For the United States, see Jeremy Brecher, *Strike* (San Francisco: Straight Arrow Books, 1972).

27. Karl Marx and Friedrich Engels, *The Communist Manifesto* (New York: Washington Square Press, 1964), 57–59, 78–79.

28. For maps on the migrations discussed in this section, see Russell King et al., *The Atlas of Human Migration: Global Patterns of People on the Move* (Oxon, UK: Earthscan, an imprint of Taylor & Francis, 2010), esp. pp. 26–37.

29. For additional stories of European migration to the Americas, see Eliot Dickinson, *Globalization and Migration: A World in Motion* (Lanham, MD: Rowman & Littlefield, 2017), 30–38.

30. Dickinson, *Globalization and Migration*, 39.

31. This section is largely based on Adam McKeown, "Global Migration, 1846–1940," *Journal of World History* 15, no. 2 (June 2004): 155–89; specific quotes are from pp. 166, 171, 173, and 175, successively.

32. Trevor R. Getz and Liz Clarke, *Abina and the Important Men: A Graphic History* (New York: Oxford University Press, 2012). This graphic story is based on transcripts from an 1876 trial and shows how one woman became enslaved (despite it having been outlawed) to supply palm oil for export to Europe for use in industrial processes there. I would like to thank Kelsey Sherman for bringing this source to my attention.

33. This definition is based on E. J. Hobsbawm, *Nations and Nationalism since 1780*, 2nd ed. (Cambridge: Cambridge University Press, 1992), 80.

34. Ernest Gellner, *Nations and Nationalism* (Ithaca, NY: Cornell University Press, 1983), esp. chaps. 1 and 7.

35. For a brief discussion, see Lynn Hunt, *Writing History in the Global Era* (New York: W. W. Norton, 2014), 1–11.

36. See Joyce Appleby, Lynn Hunt, and Margaret Jacob, *Telling the Truth about History* (New York: W. W. Norton, 1994), chaps. 2 and 3.

37. Hobsbawm, *Nations and Nationalism*, 88.

38. Madley, *An American Genocide*.

39. See, for example, Brian Bond, ed., *Victorian Military Campaigns* (New York: Frederick A. Praeger, 1967).

40. The fascinating story is told in Hochschild, *King Leopold's Ghost*.

41. Quoted in Daniel Headrick, *The Tools of Empire: Technology and European Imperialism in the Nineteenth Century* (New York: Oxford University Press, 1981), 118.

42. That ditty may have captured the balance of power at that moment between Africans and Europeans, but overall the balance between Europeans and others, especially those who used guerrilla tactics against European armies, was rapidly narrowing and would disappear altogether in the twentieth century. Where British armies at the end of the eighteenth century could defeat Indian armies six or seven times as large, by the early nineteenth century they could defeat Indian armies only twice as large. Finally, by the 1840s, the British had to use armies equally as large and with superior firepower to defeat Indian armies. Clearly, future third-worlders could quickly acquire use of the most advanced European arms to eliminate the European technological advantage. By the 1950s and 1960s, as both the French and then the United States were to learn in Vietnam, an occupied people determined to gain independence could effectively employ guerrilla tactics to stymie even the most advanced armies. To defeat that kind of mobilized population would have required five to six times as many troops as the guerrilla army, and by the late 1960s it was clear that the American public would not allow an escalation of

troop strength from 500,000 to several million. Given those military and political realities, the American defeat in Vietnam was a foregone conclusion. On the declining arms advantage of European armies in Africa and Asia, see Philip D. Curtin, *The World and the West: The European Challenge and the Overseas Response in the Age of Empire* (Cambridge: Cambridge University Press, 2000), chap. 2.

43. The West African state founded by returned American slaves, Liberia, was also independent, as was a small part of Morocco.

44. C. A. Bayly, *Indian Society and the Making of the British Empire* (Cambridge: Cambridge University Press, 1988), 138–39.

45. Warren Dean, *With Broadax and Firebrand: The Destruction of the Brazilian Atlantic Forest* (Berkeley: University of California Press, 1995), 181.

46. Richard H. Grove, *Green Imperialism: Colonial Expansion, Tropical Island Edens and the Origins of Environmentalism, 1600–1860* (Cambridge: Cambridge University Press, 1995), chaps. 5 and 6.

47. For the story of global deforestation, see Michael Williams, *Deforesting the Earth: From Prehistory to Global Crisis* (Chicago: University of Chicago Press, 2003).

48. Brooke, *Climate Change and the Course of Global History*, 498.

49. Mike Davis, *Late Victorian Holocausts: El Niño Famines and the Making of the Third World* (London: Verso Press, 2001).

50. See especially Michael Adas, *Machines as the Measure of Men: Science, Technology, and Ideologies of Western Dominance* (Ithaca, NY: Cornell University Press, 1989).

51. Quoted in Eugen Weber, *A Modern History of Europe: Men, Cultures, and Societies from the Renaissance to the Present* (New York: W. W. Norton, 1971), 1001.

52. For a discussion of the role of racism in motivating Europeans to conquer foreign land, see John M. Hobson, *The Eastern Origins of Western Civilization* (Cambridge: Cambridge University Press, 2004), chap. 10.

Chapter Six: The Great Departure

1. This argument is developed in John M. Hobson, *The Eastern Origins of Western Civilization* (Cambridge: Cambridge University Press, 2004), chap 10.

2. Vaclav Smil calls this period "the Age of Synergy." See *Creating the Twentieth Century: Technical Innovations of 1867–1914 and Their Lasting Impact* (Oxford: Oxford University Press, 2005).

3. Eric Hobsbawm, *The Age of Extremes: A History of the World, 1914–1991* (New York: Pantheon, 1996), 12.

4. In Eliot Dickinson's formulation, the Global North includes the wealthy industrialized countries of Europe and North America, while the Global South is the poorer countries in Africa, Asia, Latin America, and the Middle East. Eliot Dickinson, *Globalization and Migration* (Lanham, MD: Rowman & Littlefield, 2017), 17.

5. Unless otherwise noted, this extraordinary story of the importance of nitrogen and its synthesis as ammonia is based upon Vaclav Smil, *Enriching the Earth: Fritz Haber,*

Carl Bosch, and the Transformation of World Food Production (Cambridge, MA: MIT Press, 2001). For an elaboration and extension, see Hugh S. Gorman, *The Story of N: A Social History of the Nitrogen Cycle and the Challenge of Sustainability* (New Brunswick, NJ: Rutgers University Press, 2013).

6. In 1995, Timothy McVeigh blew up the Murrah Federal Office Building in Oklahoma City with a bomb composed of nitrogen fertilizer and kerosene.

7. For a look at this relationship from the perspective of the production of chemicals used in both agriculture and the military, see Edmund Russell, *War and Nature: Fighting Humans and Insects with Chemicals from World War I to Silent Spring* (New York: Cambridge University Press, 2001).

8. Gregory T. Cushman, *Guano and the Opening of the Pacific World: A Global Ecological History* (New York: Cambridge University Press, 2013).

9. For a discussion, see Hannah Ritchie, "How Many People Does Synthetic Fertilizer Feed?," *Our World in Data*, November 7, 2017, https://ourworldindata.org/how-many -people-does-synthetic-fertilizer-feed.

10. Vaclav Smil, *Enriching the Earth: Fritz Haber, Carl Bosch, and the Transformation of World Food Production* (Cambridge, MA: The MIT Press, 2004).

11. If, as demographers predict, the world's population will peak at about nine billion around the year 2050, the twentieth century will have seen the largest human population increase ever, making it unique in world history. See William McNeill, "Demography and Urbanization," in *The Oxford History of the Twentieth Century*, ed. Michael Howard and Wm. Roger Louis, 10–21 (New York: Oxford University Press, 1998). The reason demographers expect that population will stabilize is that as societies urbanize and industrialize, their populations experience a "demographic transition" where families become smaller, with children at about the number (2.1) needed to replace their parents.

12. For the first three years, World War I "was fought predominantly with agrarian resources," not industrial ones. C. A. Bayly, *The Birth of the Modern World, 1780–1914* (Oxford: Blackwell, 2004), 455.

13. Hobsbawm, *Age of Extremes*, 97–98.

14. Thomas Piketty, *Capital in the Twenty-First Century* (Cambridge, MA: Belknap Press, 2014), 146–49.

15. Daniel Immerwahr, *How to Hide an Empire: A History of the Greater United States* (New York: Farrar, Straus and Giroux, 2019), 10–11, 17.

16. Immerwahr, *How to Hide an Empire*, 262–77.

17. Immerwahr, *How to Hide an Empire*, 14. For the full details of the sometimes bloody struggles against U.S. rule, including in the Philippines, and the complexities of determining state policy toward its territories, see part II: "The Pointillist Empire," chaps. 13–22.

18. Japan's "Greater East Asia Co-Prosperity Sphere" would have driven Europe and America from Asia and replaced them with Japan as the industrialized core of a system that still had the rest of Asia providing food and raw materials to Japan.

19. At the time of partition in 1947, Pakistan was divided into two parts, east and west. In 1971, following decades of neglect by west Pakistan, where the government was located, rebellion in the east resulted in the creation of the new country of Bangladesh.

20. The phrase is from Eric Hobsbawm, *The Age of Empire, 1875–1914* (New York: Pantheon, 1987).

21. Japan fostered industrial development in its colonies in Korea and Manchuria, in part because of the ready accessibility of coal, iron ore, and petroleum there, and in part because those colonies were physically close and relatively easier to administer directly. Taiwan, though, taken from China in 1895, was designed to be a rice- and sugar-producing agricultural colony.

22. The concept of the "nuclear winter" and human extinction is explored in Jonathan Schell, *The Fate of the Earth* (New York: Alfred A. Knopf, 1982).

23. As Paul Kennedy makes clear in *The Rise and Fall of the Great Powers: Economic Change and Military Conflict from 1500 to 2000* (New York: Random House, 1987), that relationship between economic productivity and military power has been true for the past five hundred years.

24. For the environmental history of the Soviet Union, see Paul Josephson et al., *The Environmental History of Russia* (New York: Cambridge University Press, 2013), and the path-breaking studies by Douglas Weiner, *Models of Nature* (Pittsburgh, PA: University of Pittsburgh Press, 2000), and *A Little Corner of Freedom* (Berkeley: University of California Press, 2002).

25. The term is from Judith Shapiro, *Mao's War on Nature: Politics and the Environment in Revolutionary China* (New York: Cambridge University Press, 2001).

26. The literature on China's environmental problems is large. For overviews, see chapter 7 of Robert B. Marks, *China: An Environmental History* (Lanham, MD: Rowman & Littlefield, 2017), and Judith Shapiro, *China's Environmental Challenges* (Malden, MA: Polity Press, 2012).

27. Much of the following is based on David Reynolds, *One World Divisible: A Global History since 1945* (New York: W. W. Norton, 2000), chap. 5.

28. Vince Beiser, "Concrete Is the Stuff Civilization Is Made of. But for All Its Blessings, There Are Huge Environmental Costs," *Los Angeles Times*, June 17, 2018.

29. See Smil, *Creating the Twentieth Century*, chap. 2, "The Age of Electricity."

30. Herbert Marcuse, *One-Dimensional Man* (Boston: Beacon, 1964).

31. The terms are from J. R. McNeill, *Something New under the Sun* (New York: W. W. Norton, 2000), 296–97.

32. For an extended discussion of autos, oil, and the environment, see McNeill, *Something New under the Sun*, esp. chap. 7.

33. See Hobson, *Eastern Origins of Western Civilization*, chap. 11.

34. The late-twentieth-century "rise of East Asia" is as much a regional phenomenon involving China and Japan as specific to any one of those states. See Giovanni Arrighi, Mark Selden, and Takeshi Hamashita, eds., *The Resurgence of East Asia: 500, 150 and 50 Year Perspectives* (New York: Routledge, 2003), esp. the introduction and chap. 7.

35. For maps on the migrations discussed in this section, see Russell King et al., *The Atlas of Human Migration: Global Patterns of People on the Move* (Oxon, UK: Earthscan, an imprint of Taylor & Francis, 2010), especially those in part two, "A World in Flux: Contemporary Global Migration Patterns," and part three, "The Age of Migration: Hybrid Identities of Human Mobility."

36. Dickinson, *Globalization and Migration*, 116–17. For a discussion of the division of the world into the Global North and the Global South, see pp. 17–18, and chaps 3–4.

37. Two main sources for these estimates are Zbigniew Brzezinski, *Out of Control: Global Turmoil on the Eve of the Twenty-First Century* (New York: Touchstone, 1993); and Matthew White, *Historical Atlas of the Twentieth Century* [electronic resource], https://trove.nla.gov.au/work/29888341. See also "Necrometrics: Estimated Totals for the Entire 20th Century," http://necrometrics.com/all20c.htm.

38. Adam McKeown, "Global Migration, 1846–1940," *Journal of World History* 15, no. 2 (2004): 184.

39. For a discussion of this and other issues related to migration, see Joyce P. Kaufman, *Introduction to International Relations*, 2nd ed. (Lanham, MD: Rowman & Littlefield, 2018), 238–49.

40. Shapiro, *China's Environmental Challenges*, 44–45.

41. Peter Jay, *The Wealth of Man* (New York: PublicAffairs, 2000), 246–47.

42. Hobsbawm, *Age of Extremes*, 363.

43. In 2001 in much of sub-Saharan Africa, 50 percent or more of children did not get a primary school education, 100 or more infants per 1,000 died, and half of the population subsisted on less than one dollar per day. These statistics mark life for millions in India, Pakistan, Southeast Asia, and China as well. What that means for daily life is illustrated by a story from rural China where hundreds of millions lack health insurance or access to government-supported clinics. Unable to pay the twenty-five to sixty cents to a rural clinic for care, people suffer at home and die: "Every year hundreds of millions of rural Chinese . . . face the clash between health and poverty, knowing that if they treat their illnesses they will lack the money needed for marriage, education and, sometimes, food." For the story, see "Wealth Grows, but Health Care Withers in China," *New York Times*, January 14, 2006, A1, A7.

44. See World Bank, "Heavily Indebted Poor Countries," http://web.worldbank.org /WBSITE/EXTERNAL/TOPICS/EXTDEBTDEPT/0,,contentMDK:20260049~menuPK :64166739~pagePK:64166689~piPK:64166646~theSitePK:469043,00.html.

45. In 2001, the international community adopted the "Millennium Development Goals," one of which was to halve the number of extremely poor people (defined as those making less than one U.S. dollar per day) by 2015; see http://www.un.org/millennium goals.

46. Dana Cordell, Jan-Olof Drangert, and Stuart White, "The Story of Phosphorus: Global Food Security and Food for Thought," *Global Environmental Change* 19, no. 2 (2009): 294.

47. See "Promises, Promises," editorial, *New York Times*, August 22, 2005, A16.

48. See "U.S.-Africa Leaders Summit," White House, http://www.whitehouse.gov/us
-africa-leaders-summit.

49. This section is based on Thomas Piketty, *Capital in the Twenty-First Century*,
Arthur Goldhammer trans. (Cambridge, MA: Harvard University Press, 2014), esp. part
3, "The Structure of Inequality," 237–467.

50. See the discussion of the significance of Piketty's work in Jo Guldi and David
Armitage, *The History Manifesto* (Cambridge, UK: Cambridge University Press, 2014),
79–81.

51. S&P Capital IQ, Global Credit Portal, Economic Research, "How Increasing
Income Inequality Is Dampening U.S. Economic Growth, and Possible Ways to Change
the Tide," August 5, 2014, https://www.globalcreditportal.com/ratingsdirect/renderArti
cle.do?articleId=1351366&SctArtId.

52. Hobsbawm, *Age of Extremes*.

53. Francis Fukuyama, *The End of History and the Last Man* (New York: Free Press,
1992).

54. Samuel Huntington, *The Clash of Civilizations and the Remaking of the Twentieth-
Century World Order* (New York: W. W. Norton, 2000).

55. But as Jamal Nassar warns, the label "terrorist" is very slippery: it is applied by
states to those who attack them, while to the dispossessed seeking their own sovereignty
they may well be seen as freedom fighters. Nassar examines the questions of how and
why the latest round in the "war on terror" has become intertwined with the processes of
globalization and radicalized Islam in *Globalization and Terrorism: The Migration of Dreams
and Nightmares* (Lanham, MD: Rowman & Littlefield, 2005).

56. This point about the modern world system was first made most powerfully and
elegantly by Immanuel Wallerstein in his groundbreaking work, *The Modern World-
System: Capitalist Agriculture and the Origins of the European World-Economy in the Sixteenth
Century* (New York: Academic Press, 1974).

57. See Herman E. Daly, "The Perils of Free Trade," *Scientific American* (November
1993): 50–57.

58. Michael Hardt and Antonio Negri, *Empire* (Cambridge, MA: Harvard University
Press, 2000).

59. Most recently on December 26, 2018, during a visit to U.S. troops stationed in
Iraq: "US Won't Be World's 'Policeman,' Trump Says during Surprise Visit to Iraq," *Straits
Times*, December 27, 2018, https://www.straitstimes.com/world/united-states/in-a-first
-trump-makes-surprise-visit-to-us-troops-in-iraq.

60. For a discussion of those various energy regimes and transitions, see Vaclav Smil,
Energy Transitions: History, Requirements, Prospects (Santa Barbara, CA: Praeger, 2010).

61. The concept of deterritorialization was first developed in the late 1970s in French
social theory and philosophy and has been used in various disciplines and contexts to
illuminate various social, political, and cultural phenomena. Mostly deterritorialization is
discussed in terms of globalization and the cross-border movements of capital that call
into question the ability of the territorial nation-state to regulate. Some theorists go on

to argue that deterritorialization is then followed by reterritorialization, where the people in states that have been deterritorialized get incorporated into a larger or different territory that is not their nation-state but something else vaguely and threateningly global. Here, I use the commonsense definition of deterritorialization put forward by historian Lynn Hunt later in this section. For an earlier discussion and use of the concept, see Gearóid Ó Tuathail and Timothy W. Luke, "Present at the (Dis)integration: Deterritorialization and Reterritorialization in the New Wor(l)d Order," *Annals of the Association of American Geographers* 84, no. 3 (1994): 381–98.

62. For discussions from different points of time and perspectives, see Joseph E. Stiglitz, *Globalization and Its Discontents Revisited: Anti-Globalization in the Era of Trump* (New York: W. W. Norton, 2018), and J. Ann Tickner, *Gendering World Politics: Issues and Approaches in the Post–Cold War Era* (New York: Columbia University Press, 2001).

63. David Harvey, *A Brief History of Neoliberalism* (Oxford: Oxford University Press, 2005).

64. G8 Delegations and Documents 2001, Genoa, Italy, http://www.g8.utoronto.ca /summit/2001genoa. The original G7 countries are Canada, France, Germany, Italy, Japan, the United Kingdom, and the United States. Russia was invited to join the G7 in 1998, so now it is sometimes called the "G8," or the "G7 plus Russia."

65. Lynn Hunt, *Writing History in the Global Era* (New York: W. W. Norton, 2014), 54–55. For her discussion of deterritorialization, Hunt cites Jan Aart Scholte, *Globalization: A Critical Introduction* (Hampshire, UK: Palgrave Macmillan, 2000).

66. European Union, "The History of the European Union," https://europa.eu/euro pean-union/about-eu/history_en.

67. Quoted in Dickinson, *Globalization and Migration*, 109.

68. Quoted in Eleanor Busby, "Merkel Appears to Take Aim at Trump with Vow to Take on More Responsibility in World," *Independent*, January 1, 2018, https://www.inde pendent.co.uk/news/world/europe/angela-merkel-trump-germany-chancellor-new-year -speech-us-president-rebuke-a8706416.html.

69. Mitchell Learner, "The Trump Presidency Marks the End of the American Century," *Washington Post*, September 3, 2018; Kori Schake, "The Trump Doctrine Is Winning and the World Is Losing," *The New York Times Sunday Review*, June 17, 2018.

70. The experience of Ecuador suggests that the gambit may not work out so well for China, or for the countries to which it has loaned billions of dollars for infrastructure projects. See Nicholas Casey and Clifford Krauss, "It Doesn't Matter If Ecuador Can Afford This Dam. China Still Gets Paid," *New York Times*, December 24, 2018.

71. James Dobbins, "The Global Order Will Outlast U.S. Leadership," *Wall Street Journal*, July 24, 2018.

72. Michael Pillsbury, *The Hundred-Year Marathon: China's Secret Strategy to Replace America as the Global Superpower* (New York: St. Martin's Press, 2016).

73. The phrase "The Great Departure" follows in the tradition of Karl Polanyi's *Great Transformation: The Political and Economic Origins of Our Time* (Boston: Beacon Press,

1957), and Kenneth Pomeranz's *The Great Divergence: China, Europe, and the Making of the Modern World Economy* (Princeton, NJ: Princeton University Press, 2000).

74. Most of this section is based on McNeill, *Something New under the Sun.*

75. Daly, "Perils of Free Trade," 56.

76. For a more optimistic prognosis of the implications of the Anthropocene than presented here, see Diane Ackerman, *The Human Age: The World Shaped by Us* (New York: W. W. Norton, 2014).

77. J. R. McNeill and Peter Engelke, *The Great Acceleration: An Environmental History of the Anthropocene since 1945* (Cambridge, MA: Harvard University Press, 2014). See also Will Stefan et al., "The Trajectory of the Anthropocene: The Great Acceleration," *Anthropocene Review* 2, no. 1 (2015): 81–98.

78. Millennium Ecosystem Assessment, Ecosystems and Human Well-Being: Synthesis (Washington, DC: Island Press, 2005), 1.

79. J. D. Edixhoven, J. Gupta, and H. H. G. Savenije, "Recent Revisions of Phosphate Rock Reserves and Resources: A Critique," *Earth System Dynamics* 5, no. 2 (2014): 491–507.

80. James Elser and Elena Bennett, "A Broken Biogeochemical Cycle," *Nature* 478 (October 2011): 29–31.

81. Gorman, *Story of N*, 102–7, 111, 125, 132–47. On postwar environmental mitigation efforts more broadly, see Brooks, *Climate Change and the Course of Global History: A Rough Journey* (Cambridge: Cambridge University Press, 2014), 543–46.

82. Johan Rockström et al., "A Safe Operating Space for Humanity," *Nature* 461 (September 2009): 472–75; Stockholm Resilience Center, "The Nine Planetary Boundaries," https://www.stockholmresilience.org/research/planetary-boundaries/planetary-boundaries/about-the-research/the-nine-planetary-boundaries.html.

83. Cordell et al., "The Story of Phosphorus," 300.

84. Smil, *Enriching the Earth*, chap. 7.

85. William Ruddiman argues that methane from agriculture began affecting global climate as early as 5000 BCE and may have stopped the natural climate cycle from tipping the Earth into another ice age. See *Plows, Plagues, and Petroleum: How Humans Took Control of Climate* (Princeton, NJ: Princeton University Press, 2010), esp. part 3 and "Afterword to the Princeton Science Library Edition," 195–214.

86. Brooke, *Climate Change and the Course of Global History*, 547–48. Brooke also explains (548–52) why the cause-and-effect connection between the increase in greenhouse gases and global temperatures is more complex than a simple one-to-one relationship.

87. For a brief discussion, see Marks, *China: An Environmental History*, 360–62.

88. UNFCCC (United Nations Framework Convention on Climate Change), "Katowice Climate Change Conference, 2–14 December 2018," https://unfccc.int. "COP24" stands for Conference of the Parties 24.

89. The Center for Biological Diversity, "The Extinction Crisis," https://www.biologicaldiversity.org/programs/biodiversity/elements_of_biodiversity/extinction_crisis. See also

Elizabeth Kolbert, *The Sixth Extinction: An Unnatural History* (New York: Henry Holt, 2014).

90. WWF (World Wildlife Fund), M. Grooten and R. E. A. Almonds, eds., *Living Planet Report 2018: Aiming Higher* (Gland, Switzerland: WWF, 2018).

91. Peter Wohlleben, *The Hidden Life of Trees: What They Feel, How They Communicate*, trans. Jane Billinghurst (Vancouver, BC: David Suzuki Institute, 2016).

92. As demonstrated by the recent novel by Richard Powers, *The Overstory* (New York: W. W. Norton, 2018).

93. Michael Williams, *Deforesting the Earth: From Prehistory to Global Crisis* (Chicago: University of Chicago Press, 2003), 420.

94. Ruddiman, *Plows, Plagues, and Petroleum*, 149.

95. Brooke, *Climate Change and the Course of Global History*, 529–30.

96. R. McLellan, L. Iyengar, B. Jeffries, and N. Oerlemans, eds., *Living Planet Report 2014: Species and Spaces, People and Places* (Gland, Switzerland: World Wide Fund for Nature [WWF], 2014).

97. For an overview, see Elizabeth Kolbert, *The Sixth Extinction: An Unnatural History* (New York: Henry Holt, 2014).

98. The Easter Island warning is cited in Clive Ponting, *A Green History of the World: The Environment and the Collapse of Great Civilizations* (New York: Penguin, 1993), and David Christian, *The Maps of Time: An Introduction to Big History* (Berkeley: University of California Press, 2004). Jared Diamond explores the fate of civilizations in *Collapse: How Societies Choose to Fail or Succeed* (New York: Viking, 2005).

99. These are very complicated questions, and the only thing we know for sure about the future is that it cannot be predicted. Nonetheless, social and natural scientists have modeled four different scenarios to try to examine likely stresses and outcomes. For a discussion, see Bert de Vries and Johan Goudsblom, eds., *Mappae Mundi: Humans and Their Habitats in a Long-Term Socio-Ecological Perspective; Myths, Maps, and Models*, 2nd ed. (Amsterdam: Amsterdam University Press, 2003), chap. 8. See also Ruddiman, *Plows, Plagues, and Petroleum*, chap. 19, "Consuming Earth's Gifts," 190–94.

100. For a sharply worded argument that develops this point in detail, see Naomi Klein, *This Changes Everything: Capitalism vs. the Climate* (New York: Simon & Schuster, 2014).

101. See Klein, *This Changes Everything*; an earlier formulation can be found in Herman E. Daly and John B. Cobb Jr., *For the Common Good: Redirecting the Economy toward Community, the Environment, and a Sustainable Future*, 2nd ed. (Boston: Beacon, 1994), esp. chap. 11.

102. This argument is made by Hobsbawm in *Age of Extremes*.

103. In an illuminating essay on the relative strategic power of China and the United States, Bruce Cumings casts doubt on the narrative of "the rise of China" supplanting the global role of the United States. See Bruce Cumings, "The 'Rise of China'?," in *Radicalism, Revolution, and Reform in Modern China: Essays in Honor of Maurice Meisner*, ed. Catherine Lynch, Robert B. Marks, and Paul G. Pickowicz, 185–207 (Lanham, MD: Lexington Books, 2011).

104. Francis Fukuyama, "Exporting the Chinese Model," Project Syndicate, https://www.project-syndicate.org/onpoint/china-one-belt-one-road-strategy-by-francis-fukuyama-2016–01. See also Pillsbury, *The Hundred-Year Marathon.*

105. This phrase was first used by Peter Perdue with respect to late imperial China; see *Exhausting the Earth: State and Peasant in Hunan, 1500–1850* (Cambridge, MA: Harvard University Press, 1987).

Conclusion: Changes, Continuities, and the Shape of the Future

1. Paul Kennedy, *The Rise and Fall of the Great Powers: Economic Change and Military Conflict from 1500 to 2000* (New York: Random House, 1987).

2. Graham Allison, "The Thucydides Trap: Are the U.S. and China Headed for War?" *Atlantic,* September 24, 2015, https://www.theatlantic.com/international/archive/2015/09/united-states-china-war-thucydides-trap/406756. For his full argument and evidence, see Graham Allison, *Destined for War: Can America and China Escape Thucydides's Trap?* (Boston: Houghton Mifflin Harcourt, 2017).

3. At ceremonies commemorating the one-hundredth anniversary of the end of World War I, French president Emmanuel Macron warned of the dangers of nationalism to world peace and stability to an audience of sixty world leaders, including U.S. president Trump, Russian president Vladimir Putin, and others who have been stoking the fires of nationalism within their countries. Press reports described Macron's speech as a "rebuke" to these leaders. David Nalamura, Seung Min Kim, and James McAuley, "Macron Denounces Nationalism as a 'Betrayal of Patriotism' in Rebuke to Trump at WWI Remembrance," *Washington Post,* November 12, 2018. See also Noah Bierman, "Trump Walks Alone as Macron Rips into Nationalism," *Los Angeles Times,* November 12, 2018.

4. In the 1950s, China's communist leader Mao Zedong issued the slogan "People Will Control Nature!" (*Ren ding sheng tian*). See Robert B. Marks, *China: An Environmental History* (Lanham, MD: Rowman & Littlefield, 2017), 313–15.

5. For a 1970s-era statement of this idea, see the Keep America Beautiful public service announcement "Crying Indian," run on TV on the second Earth Day, April 22, 1971, https://www.youtube.com/watch?v=j7OHG7tHrNM.

6. Crispin Tickell, "Societal Responses to the Anthropocene," *Philosophical Transactions of the Royal Society A* 369 (2011): 926–32.

7. See two articles by Dennis O. Flynn and Arturo Giraldez, "Path Dependence, Time Lags, and the Birth of Globalization: A Critique of O'Rourke and Williamson," *European Review of Economic History* 8 (2004): 83; and "Born Again: Globalization's Sixteenth-Century Origins (Asian/Global versus European Dynamics)," *Pacific Economic Review* 13 (2008): 359–87. While I have used their definition of globalization, the concept is contested. Others argue that this approach privileges global economic processes. They highlight instead case studies that focus on the ways in which consumer tastes created commodities out of substances such as coffee, chocolate, or sugar, for example; and

those that highlight the cross-cultural border crossings of transnational networks of merchants. Lynn Hunt calls the former "top-down" approaches to the study of globalization, and the latter "bottom-up" approaches. She doesn't argue that one is better than the other, but that over time the results of both approaches might result in a more all-encompassing understanding, or what she calls an "alternative paradigm," of globalization. For a discussion, see Lynn Hunt, *Writing History in the Global Age* (New York: W. W. Norton, 2014), 44–77. As readers will have noticed, I have paid attention to the ways people have lived through, channeled, and changed globalizing forces.

8. See especially Michael Pillsbury, *The Hundred-Year Marathon: China's Secret Strategy to Replace America as the Global Superpower* (New York: St. Martin's Press, 2015). Based on his reading of Chinese military documents and interviews with Chinese officials, Pillsbury argues that China has been planning its rise to global hegemony for some time and now has a strategic plan to realize that vision.

9. Quoted in Jo Guldi and David Armitage, *The History Manifesto* (Cambridge, UK: Cambridge University Press, 2014), 14.

Index

Page numbers in *italics* indicate illustrations, figures, or their captions.

About the Author

Robert B. Marks is professor of history and environmental studies at Whittier College and the author of *China: An Environmental History* (Rowman & Littlefield, 2017) and *Tigers, Rice, Silk, and Silt: Environment and Economy in Late Imperial China* (Cambridge University Press, 1998). In 1996 he received the Aldo Leopold Award for the best article in the journal *Environmental History* and has published numerous other articles on China's environmental history. Holding his position at a college that focuses on undergraduate education, Marks regularly teaches a course for entering college students on the origins of the modern world and in 2000 received Whittier College's Harry W. Nerhood Teaching Excellence Award.

WORLD SOCIAL CHANGE
Series Editor: Mark Selden